THE NATIONAL TRUST BOOK OF

Wild Flower
Gardening

THE NATIONAL TRUST BOOK OF

Wild Flower Gardening

JOHN STEVENS

Photography by Geoff Dann

The Globe Pequot Press

Chester, Connecticut

To Louise, Nikki and Charlie

Project Editor Jane Birdsell
Editor Heather Dewhurst

Art Editor Jane Warring

Editorial Director Jackie Douglas
Art Director Roger Bristow

Colour illustrations Vanessa Luff

First American edition published Fall 1988 by
The Globe Pequot Press

First published in Great Britain in 1987
by Dorling Kindersley Publishers Limited,
9 Henrietta Street, London WC2E 8PS
in association with The National Trust

Library of Congress catalog card number: 88-80498

ISBN 0-87106-886-9

Manufactured in Italy

CONTENTS

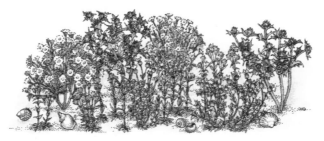

Wildflower Gardening in National Trust Gardens

Within its role of managing many of the great gardens of Britain the National Trust accepts the responsibility for conserving many forms of plant life threatened by extinction. Wildflower gardening is part of this role and provides an opportunity to create attractive areas within gardens for the conservation of native and naturalized flowers. This is often continued as part of a long-established tradition at a property and has been increased over the past decade in areas of other gardens where it enhances the overall design.

John Sales

John Sales
Chief Gardens Adviser

Woodland glade *(above) A drift of martagon and Pyrenean lilies at Benthall Hall.*

Seaside flower reserve *(right) The National Trust owns over 400 miles of coastline.*

A shady stairway *(far right) at Scotney Castle shelters wild ferns.*

An early-summer meadow *(left) at Scotney.*

Introduction

Ten years ago the idea of creating a wildflower garden would have been thought ridiculous by most people; fifty years ago, when wild flowers grew in abundance in the countryside, it would have had no meaning at all. I know that many gardeners still regard wild flowers as weeds, and the idea of all those dandelion clocks flying around in the breeze is a nightmare to many. But ideas are changing fast, and a quiet revolution is taking place in our gardens.

Wild areas of the countryside are disappearing so fast that many gardeners feel a need to bring vanishing wild flowers into their gardens. They have found it possible to create in a few square yards a flowering meadow that, amazingly, within a few years looks not unlike a traditional hay meadow; or a drift of bluebells and red campion in a shady spot to recapture the image of a flowering woodland in spring. Not only do many wild flowers make colourful garden plants; they also attract a marvellous array of wildlife.

The vanishing countryside

It is a sad reflection on the way the landscape has been managed over the last forty years that growing wild flowers in gardens is playing an increasingly important part in conserving wildlife.

It is many thousands of years since the primeval forest cover was cleared; from neolithic times our countryside has been a farmed landscape. Originally the pattern

The natural look (above), with drifts of flowers forming their own patterns by self-seeding.

An ancient hay meadow (right) will include a rich variety of flowers.

Nature's colour combinations (left) Here bluebells, greater stitchwort and red campion mix.

Traditional field boundaries such as this mixed hedgerow are valuable refuges for both plants and animals.

Clifftop flowers (above) on undeveloped coastline.

A field boundary (below) missed by the sprayer.

was one of shifting agriculture, with marginal lands coming into cultivation and then gradually reverting back to scrub and woodland, but for many centuries now lowland Britain, at least, has been dominated by agriculture. Since the Second World War, however, there has been a dramatic increase in the intensity of this agricultural use. With the advent of mechanization – deep ploughing, deep drainage, increasingly larger fields on which to operate the larger machines – and reliance on great quantities of inorganic fertilizers to ever-increase yields, the old meadows, copses and downlands have disappeared at an alarming rate. Forty per cent of broadleaved woodland, 80% of heaths, 95% of unimproved meadows and 125,000 miles of hedgerow have disappeared from our countryside since 1945. With them, we have lost the habitats of many of our wild plants and animals.

The remaining countryside must be cherished now for future generations. The National Trust and many other conservation organizations are doing all they can to save unspoilt areas of countryside, both in nature reserves and elsewhere. But conservation can begin at home, in our own parishes and in our own gardens.

Growing rare flowers (left) If you are lucky, less common flowers such as this moorland spotted orchid will seed themselves in your garden. Be suspicious of rare plants offered for sale: they may have been illegally collected or imported at the expense of threatened natural colonies.

Cornfield flowers (left) have been eradicated in the countryside by modern intensive farming. Growing them in gardens or special reserves is our only chance of preserving such beautiful flowers as the vivid pink corncockle in the background.

Using gardens to conserve plants

Growing wild flowers in your garden that were once plentiful in the surrounding countryside but have now become scarce or even extinct is an important contribution to the local ecology, in particular the wildlife associated with those plants. Deliberately trying to grow rare plants in gardens is not quite such a straightforward matter, however.

Many people ask me if I have rare plants in my collection and whether I sell the seed of them. My answer to this is that rare plants are normally best left to survive in their own specialized habitats. If rare plants are to be grown in gardens, seed has to be collected at least initially from a wild population. Creating a demand for rare seed seems to me to be rather counterproductive, and it might well give rise to

Growing wild flowers in a border Gardeners have been growing native plants for centuries. Here columbine and lady's-mantle, both now uncommon in the wild, make a romantic combination with sweet cicely and white dame's-violet in front of a low wall.

Flowers for butterflies *(left)* It is important to grow a wide range of wild flowers to include many of the essential food plants. Here a green-veined white feeds on purple tufted vetch.

The importance of ponds *(far left)* Even the smallest town garden can include a pond to attract wildlife.

Bees *(left) will flock to your wildflower garden, filling the air with their contented buzzing.*

Pond-watching *is addictive. As you adjust your eyes for reflections you will see airborne insects darting above as well as swimmers scurrying beneath the surface. Here a couple of camouflaged frogs climb out of the water.*

Leaf-eaters *such as this splendid garden tiger moth caterpillar are an integral part of the wildlife garden.*

the sort of plant snobbery that exists in conventional gardening. I personally am quite happy to grow the easy and more common wild flowers: they are certainly no less beautiful.

Wildflower gardens for wildlife

I think that many gardeners are beginning to realize just how much wildlife can be attracted to a garden. When the countryside was teeming with wildlife and every parish had at least a few flowering meadows, copses, thickets, hedges, a wood, ponds and maybe other havens for flowers, birds, insects and mammals, we were quite happy to enjoy the wildlife in the countryside. Now the garden has become a haven and the wildflower garden can be a genuine nature reserve.

Native plants are by far the best for supporting insects and animals, and the wider the range of plants, the better.

A wildflower garden should be in harmony with nature. Wild plants don't need fertilizers and will flourish in poor soil. Lush growth will only encourage pests which are not normally a problem with wild plants. If you encourage enough wildlife into your garden, natural predators will keep any pests under control.

Planting a wildflower border The original scheme here was purple/blue/lilac, with the flowers planted in bold drifts, and backed by a row of giant mulleins. Contrasting textures and shapes – the spear-like anise hyssop and the filigree larkspur – enliven the grouping, as do the scarlet poppies that have seeded themselves indiscriminately, breaking up any formality in the design.

Growing wild flowers

There is no need to go to the extreme of creating a botanically accurate habitat for each plant: most wild flowers, even if they occur naturally in specialized habitats, are amazingly adaptable, and there is no need to worry just because thousands of years of evolution have confined them to specialized areas. Wild plants are used to surviving the competition of other flowers and grasses and can therefore be grown in quite a different way to garden flowers. (They may of course be grown like garden flowers without competition, in which case they will often grow larger than they would in the wild.)

Wild flowers, after all, are native plants adapted often to hard conditions, unlike so many garden plants which may be thousands of miles from their natural habitats and require rather more care and attention to give of their best. If you want

Introducing wild flowers (above) In this garden a species rose has been underplanted with foxgloves.

Wild groupings (right) Nature is the best guide. The rich colour and texture of heather combines unexpectedly with honeysuckle and gorse.

to create a natural-looking wildflower garden, the best soil for the plants may be poor, dry or waterlogged!

The approach to wildflower gardening
To create and enjoy a wildflower garden requires a different approach to gardening and will perhaps be difficult for those very tidy gardeners who must always keep the upper hand. After the initial planting you should allow things to develop in their own way. Self-seeding will create informal and natural-looking associations that you could never achieve by planning. Your aim should be to guide things in the right direction and let nature do the rest.

Surprises will abound: scarlet poppies will spring up in unexpected places; mulleins will appear towering above the surrounding vegetation; and as if by magic the butterflies and birds will arrive.

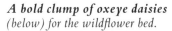

Flowering paths (above) Allow wild plants to decorate your walks.

From formal to wild (left) In this corner of my garden a small conifer and a stone pond are now surrounded by an informal flowering lawn.

A bold clump of oxeye daisies (below) for the wildflower bed.

A hidden corner
In this woodland garden a patch of cyclamen behind an old tree is lit by a shaft of sunlight. Wildflower gardens will become full of surprises as the plants and the wildlife they attract adapt themselves to the site and make it their own.

New directions

I am quite sure that growing wild flowers in the garden makes us more appreciative of them in the countryside. It is a tremendous thrill to come upon a flower unexpectedly and be able to name it and to understand why it is growing there.

A wildflower garden is a constant delight. There is always scope for experiment: why not try growing some seaside plants inland, for instance, or sowing seed at odd times in containers for flowers out of season either indoors or out. If you're really short of space, you could even try growing a miniature wildflower garden. Believe it or not, it is quite possible to create a miniature meadow in a large tray, to be cut with scissors! I must say I would stop short of the bonsai woodland, but there is no accounting for taste!

Splashes of colour *(left)*
Vivid sheets of blue cornflowers, scarlet poppies and mayweed light up this cornfield patch at the height of its season. Even a windowbox or pot planted with these annuals will brighten a dull corner.

A wild tapestry *(left)* *This tangle of water plants, including water mint and spearwort, shows how exquisite the detail of a wildflower garden can be. There is no need to have vast acres of woodland or meadow to enjoy growing wild plants.*

Creating
Wildflower
Gardens

WILD FLOWERS FOR
Sunny Gardens

Most flowers that thrive in sunny sites are dependent on man for survival. They evolved gradually as farmers cleared the primeval forest in order to grow food and graze livestock. It is these areas that have been affected most by the radical changes in land use that have taken place over the past forty years as a result of more intensive farming and the great increase in the development of towns and roads. Many habitats have been lost altogether and the wild flowers that competed with or (in the case of corncockle) contaminated the main crop have been eradicated from the remaining agricultural land. The once common sight of cornfields bright with the colour of poppies, cornflowers, corncockle and corn marigolds has largely disappeared. Vast areas of grazing pastures have been ploughed or 'improved'. The exquisitely rich flora of chalk downlands has been enormously reduced by ploughing and aerial spraying. Traditional, flower-rich hay meadows have been almost totally eradicated in many areas of the country and now only remain as nature reserves. Many areas rich in flowers have been brought into cultivation with the use of powerful machinery, herbicides and drainage techniques not available years ago. Even the field boundaries once so rich in wild flowers have been ploughed to the edge.

The effect of these changes is that when we walk in the countryside, especially country that is intensively farmed, the only wild flowers we see are relegated to the road verges and small areas of waste ground. Many of the beautiful flowers of the meadows and cornfields have not been able to establish in these other habitats and now can only be enjoyed in nature reserves. Others keep a precarious hold, often on road verges that desperately need protection. These road-verge communities are often a last remnant of a local meadow flora lost for ever.

A sunny garden can therefore become a vital conservation area, as well as being colourful and enjoyable, humming with bees and graced by exquisite butterflies. A beautiful range of meadow flowers can be grown in the garden, either as a colourful blend in a flowerbed, or mixed with grasses in a mini-meadow area. The annual cornfield flowers will make a blaze of colour in only a few months after planting. Whatever the size of your garden, the sunniest areas are where you will probably spend most of your time outside: sitting, sunning, listening to the birds, watching the butterflies and lulled by the hum and buzz of insects. This is where you can enjoy the fruits of your labours and relax and dream a little.

The lost countryside (left) *A cornfield flower reserve just coming into flower shows the richness and colour that has been obliterated by modern intensive farming methods.*

Meadow garden in early summer

Few of our beautiful old flowering hay meadows remain –
modern farming methods have 'improved' grassland and
eradicated most of the colourful flowers. You can create your
own meadow patch in quite a small area.

The plants on this page were all grown in gardens; wild flowers should not be taken from the countryside.

Black medick
*(above) is found
in the lowest layer
of the meadow.*

**Common
mouse-ear** *(left)
has tiny, starlike
flowers in June.*

Lady's bedstraw
and **selfheal** *(left)
flower in late summer.
Lady's bedstraw
(ferny leaves) has
yellow flowers and
selfheal purple.*

Quaking-grass *(below
left) is one of the
prettiest grasses. Its
heads quiver in the
slightest breeze.*

**Perforate St
John's-wort** *(below).
Later in the summer this
will have golden-yellow
flowers.*

Ribwort plantain
*(right) has a deep root
system that resists
drought.*

Oxeye daisy
*(right) often
dominates a new
meadow for the
first year or two.
It attracts bees and
butterflies.*

Red campion *(left) is
often seen on the
woodland edge. Pink
forms are common.*

**Meadow
crane's-bill**
*(right) spreads
easily once
established.*

Hoary plantain
*(below) is an unusual
plant that looks prettiest
in a drift.*

**Creeping
buttercup** *(left) is
the most invasive
of the buttercups.*

Smooth tare (right) is a lovely foliage plant with a most delicate appearance.

Common vetch (above) climbs above the other foliage to show off its bright flowers.

Common bird's-foot trefoil (above) prefers poor, well-drained soil.

Cowslip (left). This plant has gone to seed, having flowered before the grasses grew up.

Bush vetch (right) is the first vetch to flower. It also grows in shady lanes and hedges.

Meadow vetchling (below) is another scrambling vetch with bright flowers.

Kidney vetch (right) is a real show-stopper and good for bees and butterflies.

Red clover (below right) adds a marvellous flush of colour to any meadow and the bees love it.

Salad burnet (below) is a foliage plant with a taste of cucumber.

Yellow rattle (left) is a semi-parasitic annual that will only grow with grasses. It seeds itself from year to year.

White clover (below) makes good ground cover and is a favourite with the bees.

Mouse-ear hawkweed (below) is a lovely miniature plant that makes good ground cover in dry, sunny situations. It seeds freely.

Cat's-ear (right) is very colourful and produces dandelion-like clocks of seed.

Meadow garden in high summer

The flowering meadow in high summer is predominantly
coloured with the warm pinks and purples of field scabious,
greater knapweed and musk mallow, whilst lady's bedstraw and
cat's-ear provide cheerful splashes of yellow.

The plants on this page were all grown in gardens; wild flowers should not be taken from the countryside.

Cat's-ear
*(below) is a
survivor. Its long
roots make it
drought-resistant.*

**Greater
knapweed** *(left)
grows best on light
or chalky soils.*

Meadow crane's-bill
*(left) in a fertile soil
grows into a bushy plant
covered in flowers. It is
less bold, but just as
pretty, in meadows.*

**Clustered
bellflower**
*(below) will only
establish well on
light, chalky
grassland.*

Musk mallow *(below)
can also have white
flowers. The foliage is
musk-scented.*

Spear thistle *(right)
will become invasive if
allowed to seed in
cultivated soil. It is very
attractive to bees and
butterflies.*

Wild basil
*(right) was once
used as a strewing
herb. It prefers
chalky soil.*

**Common
centaury** *(left)
grows in dry
grassland and
open woods.*

Field scabious *(below) attracts butterflies, and is the largest-flowered scabious.*

Lady's bedstraw *(below) is a low, spreading plant for light soils that will make a sheet of golden yellow.*

Pepper-saxifrage *(below), or sulphurwort, has a strong odour.*

Selfheal *(below) is a spreading plant that can be cut short for a flowering lawn.*

Spiny restharrow *(below left) is a colourful food plant of the common blue butterfly.*

Broad-leaved dock *(left) Cut the pretty red seed-heads to prevent an invasion.*

Yarrow *(below) is a spreading plant with many medicinal properties.*

Harebell *(below) prefers poor grassland.*

Marjoram *(below) is a herb that is attractive to bees and butterflies.*

Hoary plantain *(below) has a delicate scent and is very attractive to bees.*

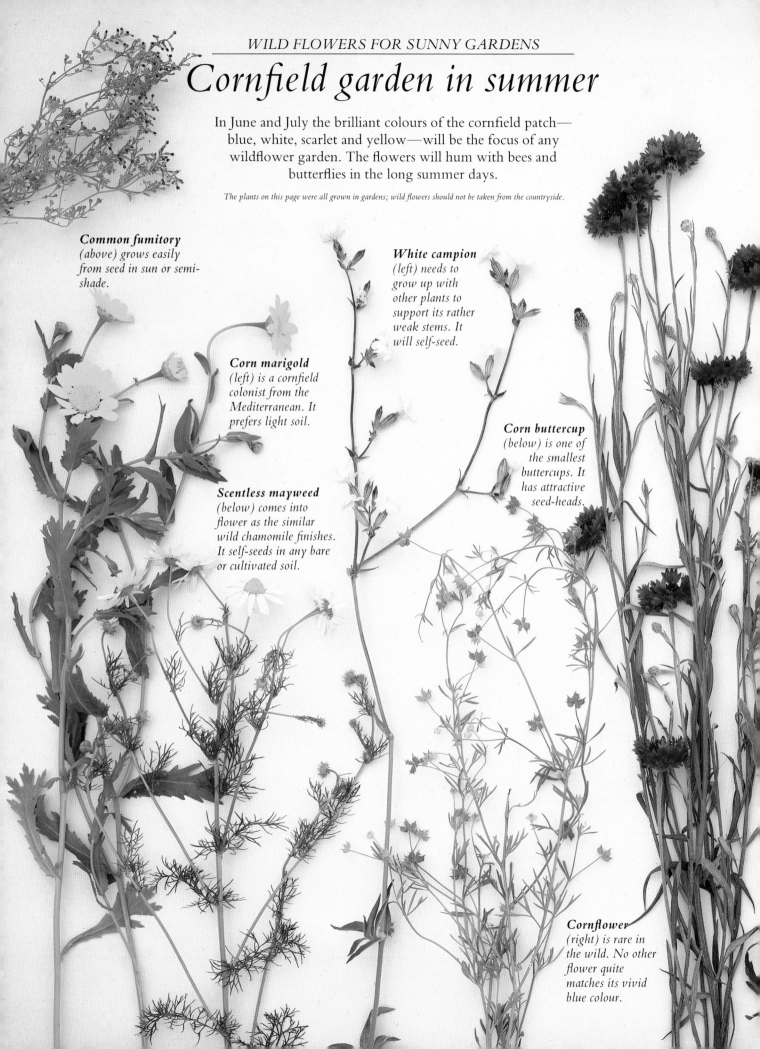

Cornfield garden in summer

In June and July the brilliant colours of the cornfield patch—
blue, white, scarlet and yellow—will be the focus of any
wildflower garden. The flowers will hum with bees and
butterflies in the long summer days.

The plants on this page were all grown in gardens; wild flowers should not be taken from the countryside.

Common fumitory
*(above) grows easily
from seed in sun or semi-
shade.*

White campion
*(left) needs to
grow up with
other plants to
support its rather
weak stems. It
will self-seed.*

Corn marigold
*(left) is a cornfield
colonist from the
Mediterranean. It
prefers light soil.*

Corn buttercup
*(below) is one of
the smallest
buttercups. It
has attractive
seed-heads.*

Scentless mayweed
*(below) comes into
flower as the similar
wild chamomile finishes.
It self-seeds in any bare
or cultivated soil.*

Cornflower
*(right) is rare in
the wild. No other
flower quite
matches its vivid
blue colour.*

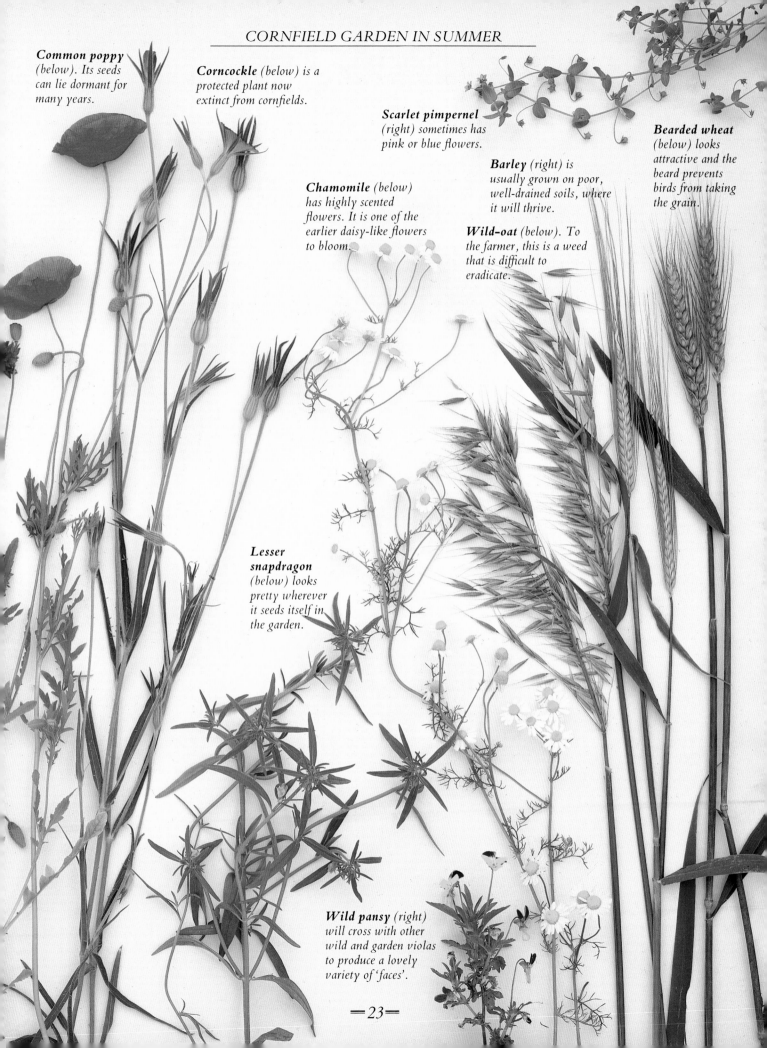

Common poppy *(below). Its seeds can lie dormant for many years.*

Corncockle *(below) is a protected plant now extinct from cornfields.*

Scarlet pimpernel *(right) sometimes has pink or blue flowers.*

Chamomile *(below) has highly scented flowers. It is one of the earlier daisy-like flowers to bloom.*

Barley *(right) is usually grown on poor, well-drained soils, where it will thrive.*

Wild-oat *(below). To the farmer, this is a weed that is difficult to eradicate.*

Bearded wheat *(below) looks attractive and the beard prevents birds from taking the grain.*

Lesser snapdragon *(below) looks pretty wherever it seeds itself in the garden.*

Wild pansy *(right) will cross with other wild and garden violas to produce a lovely variety of 'faces'.*

Sunny wildflower gardens

Sunny gardens: the options

You can grow a huge range of wild flowers in a sunny garden. Not every garden has the space for a flowering hay meadow but it is surprising how little space you need for wild flowers. A friend of mine lodged in a small suburban house with a tiny front garden of only a few square metres. He sowed this with a cornfield flower mixture and it was a blaze of colour in the summer. The attention that little patch attracted was amazing!

Even if you have a paved backyard, every gap in the paving or brickwork is a potential home for a wild plant. Yarrow, wild carrot, lady's bedstraw, harebell, and even tall, stately mullein, can grow from a tiny crack in the paving. In fact, it is not absolutely necessary to have a garden at all. You can grow a lovely range of flowers in a window-box, wooden tub or even a terracotta pot—most are worth trying indoors too, though they may be short-lived. Many wild flowers grow in inhospitable environments and poor soil, so they will adjust happily to the confined space of a container.

You may be surprised, however, at the flowering times—pot-grown primroses can flower in autumn. This is the experimental end of wildflower gardening and anything is worth a try—even daisies at Christmas.

In a town garden wild flowers will not only remind you of peaceful weekends in the country but will attract wildlife in profusion. If you want to keep your garden simple with a nicely cut lawn, then why not have a narrow border of mixed wild flowers, just a metre wide, and as they gradually seed into the grass nearest them let that strip grow up into a strip of 'meadow'.

The wildflower bed

Here you can really go to town and grow all your favourite wild flowers together. For season-long interest start with the early spring bulbs like snowdrops and wild daffodils and continue through the season with bright butterfly flowers like honesty and dame's-violet, with the delicate white-flowered meadow saxifrage for the front of the border. For early summer, plant blue and white Jacob's-ladder, perhaps growing with the herb caraway and the jewel-like wild pansy, which will continue through the season. For high summer there is nothing more beautiful than a combination of musk mallow (pink and white forms), mauve small scabious and purple greater knapweed. Although wild flowers of all colours seem to go well together a simple scheme such as this last can be very beautiful and effective.

Wild flowers often have a shorter flowering season and smaller flowers than garden flowers, so they should be planted in groups for real impact. Most will, of course, seed if allowed to do so, and then the real excitement of wildflower gardening begins with what I call 'creative weeding'. This is not as silly as it may sound. It is the chance combination of flowers and foliage in the wildflower garden that is invariably the most successful. So

A blue/purple scheme Vivid larkspur backed by anise hyssop, with yellow mullein and scarlet poppies for variety.

Wild marjoram

Wild pansy

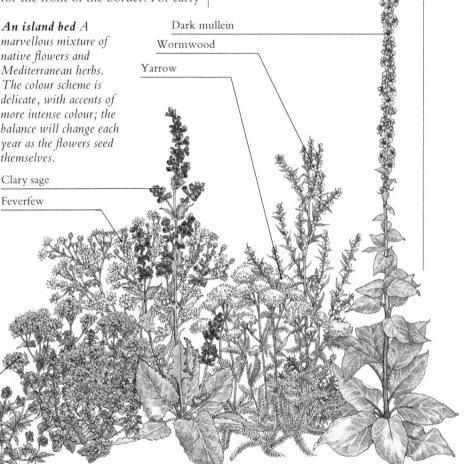

An island bed A marvellous mixture of native flowers and Mediterranean herbs. The colour scheme is delicate, with accents of more intense colour; the balance will change each year as the flowers seed themselves.

Clary sage

Feverfew

Dark mullein

Wormwood

Yarrow

A colourful border in high summer
The herb borage mixed with field scabious and spires of purple loosestrife with a carpet of golden corn marigold in the background.

Foliage is very important in a wildflower border as it must provide a backdrop to the often short-lived flowers. Ferns, sweet cicely, wild carrot, burnet-saxifrage and lady's-mantle all have attractive foliage.

Mixing wild flowers with garden plants

Wild flowers can be mixed very successfully with other flowers. If you confine your additions to herbs and the old-fashioned cottage garden flowers you can't go far wrong. The reason why these mixtures almost always work is that herbs are all wild plants from somewhere (mostly the Mediterranean) and have been very little 'improved' by gardeners, and the old cottage favourites are also mostly single flowers not too far removed from their wild origins. It is the overbred modern varieties of flowers or exotic introductions that will look too brash and well-groomed in a wildflower garden.

when all the many seedlings appear in the autumn and the spring, try to identify them and decide to leave a clump of this and the odd plant of that. Add to these all those you missed or never had time to weed and your border will be totally different every year. You feel you are gardening dangerously! Not quite in control, but far more exhilarating for that. For some people the unpredictability is unbearable, but for the true wildflower gardener this is where the art and the pleasure lie.

Don't take too much notice of the traditional rules of garden design either. If a giant mullein seeds itself at the front of the bed it will look stunning. We all know of course that tall plants should remain at the back and small plants at the front, but wild flowers just won't conform!

Against a sunny wall *Viper's-bugloss is surrounded by oxeye daisy and pink common vetch.*

Containers for sunny positions

For the spring, cowslips make a spectacular show in a container. Sow some bright and colourful annuals in the same pot and they will take over once the cowslips have died back. Scarlet pimpernel, forget-me-not, wild pansy, common poppy and cornflower all look good as gap-fillers or in an arrangement on their own, and vetches of all sorts look wonderful trailing over the side of a container. For maximum impact group one species only in some pots—corn marigold or hare-bell are good choices.

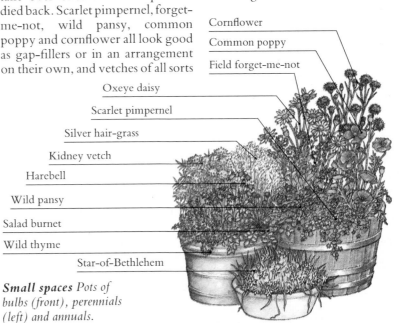

Cornflower
Common poppy
Field forget-me-not
Oxeye daisy
Scarlet pimpernel
Silver hair-grass
Kidney vetch
Harebell
Wild pansy
Salad burnet
Wild thyme
Star-of-Bethlehem

Small spaces *Pots of bulbs (front), perennials (left) and annuals.*

Some particularly colourful herbs to use are clary sage, borage, pot marigold, hyssop, all the thymes, sage, caraway, bergamot, anise hyssop, chamomile, bronze fennel, feverfew, oregano and mountain-mint. Many of these herbs are aromatic, and so they are particularly valuable for growing beneath windows.

The modern cottage garden, containing a wide variety of colourful flowers, owes very little to times past and had its origins in Victorian England. Modern cottage gardens are created usually by those who have time and money to make a colourful romantic garden that would have been quite impossible for the cottagers of old. Before the Industrial Revolution cottagers were farm labourers and craftsmen who had little time for gardening and would not normally have had access to many cultivated flowers. They grew plants for practical reasons, and the variety would have been quite small. Apart from vegetables, they would have grown culinary and medicinal herbs, dye plants and a few simple flowers of early introduction. In fact many of the flowers of early gardens were wild flowers which had medicinal use or were used as dye plants.

From lists of garden plants of the fifteenth century we know that borage, chamomile, horehound, lavender, sage, southernwood and thyme were widely grown plus many wild flowers. From Thomas Tusser in

A colourful tangle This early summer mixture of flowers and grasses is designed to attract bees and butterflies: it includes pink and white dame's-violet, campion, nettles and the ubiquitous poppy.

A cottage garden mixture Round leek-heads mix here with sages and dark mullein. Opium poppies have gone to seed in the background.

the sixteenth century we have far more detailed lists that include roses (especially sweet briar and the Gallica roses), most of the Mediterranean herbs, clove pink, columbine, cornflower, dame's-violet, feverfew, French and pot marigold, hollyhock, larkspur, love-in-a-mist, snapdragon, stock, sweet william and wallflower. In the seventeenth century double-flowered forms of common flowers such as feverfew, chamomile and daisies were being selected.

What one mixes with wild flowers is really a matter of taste. I grow several attractive North American herbs such as anise hyssop and mountain-mint, both of which are good bee plants and mix well with our native flowers.

The important thing is to grow any cultivated plants you include in the wildflower garden in a natural way. Treat them just the same as the wild flowers, allowing them to self-seed and grow 'wild' amongst the native plants. Weeding should be very restrained as you are trying to achieve a dense planting and some of those marvellous natural combinations of flowers which usually only happen quite by chance.

Lawns

Lawns have always been an essential ingredient of the English garden. A flowering or herb lawn looks most appropriate in the informal setting of a wildflower garden. Unless your lawn has been regularly treated with fertilizer or weedkiller (which will have boosted the growth of grasses and killed the flowering plants), or has only recently been laid, it will have the potential to make a flowering sward. If you get down on your hands and knees and have a good look at the lawn, you will see that a high proportion of it is not grass at all but consists of a great variety of plants which you will probably not recognize if they are not in flower. Most lawns contain plantains, speedwell, yarrow, dandelion, buttercup, daisy, selfheal, clover, trefoils, black medick and maybe violets. Other plants worth introducing are the pretty mouse-ear hawkweed which flowers first in May and spreads itself by runners as well as seed; cat's-ear, a dandelion-like flower that can grow to 60 cm (2 ft) tall but when in a lawn will flower at 15 cm (6 in) or so; and wild thyme, although this will only survive on a poor soil.

A spring-flowering lawn by a yew hedge. The flowers include dandelions, lesser celandines, slender speedwell, primroses and daisies.

Let the lawn grow in the spring (or part of it) and you will be amazed at the flowers in it. If you have a new, high-quality lawn then you will have to decide whether to introduce a few flowers into it deliberately.

Think of the lawn as a spring meadow which, apart from a single cut in March, you leave to grow until well into June or even July and then keep cut for the rest of the year. For the March mowing the blades should be set at their highest – you will only top the flowers and they will all flower again later.

Don't confuse the lawn with the meadow proper. In order for the rosette-forming and very low-growing lawn species to survive the lawn must be cut short for most of the season. If it is allowed to grow tall like a meadow the daisies and other small plants will disappear.

Single species lawns

A few herbs and wild flowers can be grown on their own to make a dense, often fragrant ground-cover. A small area planted in this way makes an attractive contrast to grass.

Since Tudor times the apple-scented chamomile lawn has been an essential part of any fragrant garden. Wild chamomile (*Chamaemelum nobile*) makes a fine lawn but requires regular mowing, as left to themselves the plants will grow to 45 cm (1½ ft).

The alternative is a non-flowering clone called 'Treneague', said to have originated from the Buckingham Palace lawn. This needs no cutting and because it produces no flowers cannot be grown from seed, but plants or small plantlets are readily available from wildflower and herb nurseries. Both chamomiles require a fertile but well-drained, rather light soil to do their best. They will also need weeding, so don't be too ambitious. A square metre is much more appropriate than a full-size lawn.

Some of the carpeting thymes make lovely lawns and our native wild thyme is ideal for this. It is best to start with small plants that will spread and can be divided up and increased. Don't be too ambitious to start with. A mixture of thymes with different leaf colour and texture can be attractive. Thymes don't mind being walked on, but remember when you

are walking barefoot over a flowering lawn the bees will be foraging and they don't appreciate being stepped on! Thymes will do best on a well-drained, gritty soil.

Yarrow, if kept cut, makes a decorative ground-cover and spreads vigorously. If it is occasionally allowed to grow a few inches high the plants will often flower.

Flowering banks

There are few more marvellous sights than a bank tumbling with wild flowers. If you have an existing grassy bank, this can be planted up with lots of lovely wild flowers. Most banks are well drained and the soil is usually rather poor so that the grasses in your basic seed mixture will not grow too vigorously, and will probably only need cutting once a year, in the autumn. You can grow any of the meadow flowers that like a well-drained soil and especially some of the chalk flowers. Common bird's-foot-trefoil loves light, poor soil and lady's bedstraw will spread like mad, with showers of tiny, bright yellow flowers. Bladder campion looks lovely on a bank and if part of the bank is in shade, foxgloves will do well. Perhaps the loveliest flower of all for a bank is the harebell – once established, it will self-seed readily on a site where it is not overtaken by grass.

If the bank has a clay base and stays fairly green all summer, meadow flowers from the heavier soils will do well. Start the season with cowslip,

A chalk bank in full flower The short, fine grasses typical of such poor growing conditions allow the flowers to be displayed to their best advantage.

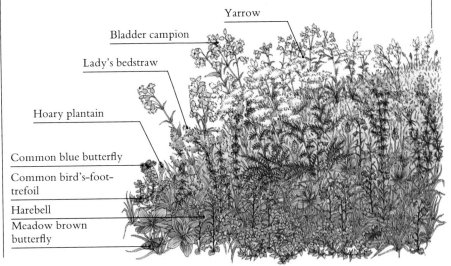

Yarrow

Bladder campion

Lady's bedstraw

Hoary plantain

Common blue butterfly

Common bird's-foot-trefoil

Harebell

Meadow brown butterfly

which will seed itself all down the bank if the soil suits. Oxeye daisy, knapweeds, scabious (field and devil's-bit), kidney and tufted vetch and the yellow meadow vetchling can follow in summer. Wild white clover makes excellent ground-cover; or black medick (yellow flowers) will give cover early in the season. Some red clover will give a touch of bright colour and spiny restharrow – as well as being an exceptionally pretty pink flower in July – will stop people sliding down the bank!

A chalk bank
Chalk downland has an immensely rich and beautiful flora consisting of low-growing and mostly colourful species. These plants thrive amongst the short grasses grazed by sheep and in a soil low in nutrients which prevents vigorous grasses and herbs taking over the smaller plants. By constructing a chalk bank or mound following the simple design pioneered by a conservation-conscious Hertfordshire school in the 1960s (see p. 136), the conditions can to some extent be re-created. No soil is required. The top few centimetres of soil should be pulverized to form a seed-bed, and it will then be possible to seed straight on to the chalk.

Grass and flower seed mixtures for chalk areas are available from wild-flower seed merchants. They should be seeded directly on to the chalk in autumn and lightly raked and firmed in. In future years many extra plants either difficult or unobtainable from seed can be introduced. Quaking-grass is a really worthwhile addition, as are clustered bellflower, common rock-rose, cowslip, dropwort,

Early summer meadows are full of sunny colours. Buttercups, oxeye daisies, red clover, sorrel and grasses are seen in silhouette against a perfect blue sky.

harebell, lady's bedstraw, marjoram, perennial flax, salad burnet, sheep's-bit, small scabious, wild carrot and wild thyme.

An area of such low fertility needs infrequent cutting. This type of bank or mound would make a decorative feature in the smallest garden, adding an interesting landscape feature to what is often a dull, flat rectangle.

Flowering meadows
The hay meadow is to me the most satisfying area of the wildflower garden. When the sun shines and the many species of flowers are bright with colour; butterflies, bees and other insects are flitting from one flower to the next; and the delicate grasses are moving in the breeze, this is the best part of the garden. You can see so dramatically here how simple it is to attract wildlife into the garden. My own small meadow, a few metres square, attracts common blue butterflies every spring and they are never seen anywhere else in the garden. There is nectar and pollen to feed on, grasses and other food plants for the caterpillars, seed for the birds, and cover for small mammals.

Hay meadows require minimum maintenance, so once the seed has been sown you can sit back and enjoy it! Seed mixtures are now available

from a number of specialist seed suppliers. Some are general-purpose mixtures that will suit most soils, but you can also obtain mixtures for particular soil types and habitats. The range of flowers in a mixture designed for a chalk soil will be very different from those commonly found (and best suited to) acid soils. In a garden situation most of the mixtures should prove quite adaptable, but for best results it is advisable to test your soil first (see p. 132). Mixtures for chalk or sandy soils, in particular, require good winter drainage and low fertility.

If you are planning to have a meadow area, you should be prepared to learn how to use a scythe. It is possible to hire a motor scythe for a large area, or you could try using a strimmer on a small meadow patch, but a hand scythe is really the best answer, and provided you take it steadily and establish a good rhythm it's really a simple tool to use.

The type of meadow you have depends not only on what seed mixture you sow, but also on when you mow it. The two basic kinds are the

A mown grass path, here bordered by rough hawkbit, harebells and feathery grasses, makes an ideal way of exploring a flowering meadow area.

late spring/early summer meadow and the late summer meadow. The spring meadow is the traditional hay meadow, where the majority of flowers will have set their seeds by July. This was normally cut in early July or even at the end of June, but to ensure all the flowers and grasses have seeded themselves the cut can be postponed until mid to late July. This type of meadow contains the maximum number of different species. I have a friend with an ancient hay meadow that contains over eighty species of flowers and grasses. If your seed mixture contains later-flowering species, and you cut in July before they flower, they will grow up again and flower in the autumn. You will notice that they flower at a much lower level, maybe 30 cm (1 ft) instead of 60 cm (2 ft) or higher.

The late summer meadow is more like a roadside verge where many flowers bloom in July and August and do not seed until autumn. This meadow would include the lovely knapweeds and scabiouses. It should be cut in September/October, by which time most of the seed-heads will be mature. If the meadow contains none of the spring flowers, it can be mowed over in the spring to hold back the grasses if they are growing away vigorously. This will in no way hurt the later flowers: their growth

will be encouraged by keeping the grass shorter early in the season.

Of course, your mowing pattern can be varied from year to year. It is all marvellously experimental and you will discover that the programme you adopt will cause a noticeable variation in the flowers that bloom. See p. 130 for how to sow a meadow area, and pp. 144–5 for full details of maintenance techniques.

A cornfield patch

The flowering cornfield is a sight that has almost disappeared from our agricultural land – drifts of scarlet poppies, carpets of golden corn marigolds, brilliant blue sheets of cornflowers and purply-pink corncockles. Efficient seed cleaning and selective herbicides ensure that little else except the crop emerges nowadays. Occasionally, where the spray has missed an area, it will still turn scarlet in summer with poppies whose seed has been in the soil for twenty, or even fifty years. Golden corn marigold is occasionally seen on light, sandy soils, often in a sugar-beet field where the spraying programme

A cornfield mixture in high summer is thick with flowers. Yellow corn marigolds, blue cornflowers, pink corncockles and red poppies are mixed together in a swirl of primary colours.

Single-colour annual beds A more restrained sowing has resulted in a preponderance of poppies, relieved by a hint of white campion and yellow rattle.

has been less intense. Cornflowers and corncockles, however, have gone from the fields for ever.

The survival of many of these lovely flowers is really now in the hands of gardeners and the creators of special reserves in country parks, farms, and on road verges.

There are therefore many good reasons for keeping a patch of cornfield flowers, but the main reason must be that it is a wonderful, fast-growing colourful patch that can be maintained year after year. The requirements are simple: a patch of cultivated ground as small as 6 sq m/yd is sufficient, and a suitable seed mixture, available from wildflower seedsmen. Seeding is best done in September. The reason for this is that a lot of the seedlings will grow several inches before the winter while others, especially poppies, germinate much better after a winter in the soil. With an autumn start you don't need to worry about dry conditions, and of course you have the pleasure of flowers a month earlier than if you sow in spring. The area will flower from early June until well into August from an autumn sowing in the south of England (a little later in the north). If you cannot seed in autumn then sow in spring: the flowering season will simply be a month later but the poppies will be thinner as they germinate best after the winter cold.

A cornfield patch will self-seed successfully year after year, although you may have to clear the ground and start again every so often if weeds become too invasive. See p. 130 for full instructions on creating and maintaining a cornfield area.

Feature plants for sunny sites

These are some of the favourite flowers of meadows and hedgerows: meadow buttercup, oxeye daisy, common poppy, cowslip and musk mallow. Use them to make vivid splashes of colour, or as jewel-like highlights in a more subdued scheme.

Yarrow
Achillea millefolium

Yarrow is one of nature's survivors, and is distinctive at every stage of growth. The foliage is feathery and delicate and the flat white flower-heads are made up of many tiny flowers, sometimes with a lovely touch of carmine. The dried flower-heads are very attractive. Yarrow grows along road verges, in meadows and in garden lawns; its creeping rootstock and ability to seed ensure its survival in most soils. Providing yarrow is kept in the meadow area and not allowed to ramp away in the cultivated garden, it is to my mind an essential decorative plant for any wild garden. A lawn may be created from yarrow, if it is kept mown most of the time and only allowed to grow up and flower late in the season, which it will do at a much lower height than if it was growing naturally.

Season: June–September   **Height:** 8–40 cm (3–16 in)
Cultivation: Yarrow is a perennial that does best in a well-drained soil, but it is very adaptable. Plant 20–30 cm (8–12 in) apart, remembering that it will spread. Sow seed in prepared soil any time from early spring until September. If you want to introduce yarrow into an existing area of grass, grow the seed in trays and plant out the seedlings in spring or autumn. If the grass is thin with bare soil showing, then the area can be raked and seed sprinkled on and firmed or pressed into the soil.
Other sites: Seaside garden.

Corncockle
Agrostemma githago

Corncockle, or corn campion, is now extinct in our cornfields and is in fact so rare in the wild that it is a protected species. Few people know the flower now except older farmers who remember well how the poisonous seed contaminated their grain. We can now only recreate the marvellous site of a mass of jewel-like corncockle in the garden or cornfield flower reserve.

Because the plant is so tall it needs to be grown either up against a wall or fence or through other sturdy plants. A small cornfield-flower reserve will look stunning. Mix corncockle with cornflowers, chamomile, mayweed, red poppies and maybe corn marigold. To be really authentic, add some wheat or barley to the mixture: it will be the most colourful area in the garden!

There is no need to worry that you will contaminate any nearby fields by growing corncockle in the garden because the large, black seeds it produces are not eaten by birds and are too heavy to be carried in the wind, so they will fall and germinate near the parent plant.

Season: June–August
Height: 30–120 cm (1–4 ft)
Cultivation: Corncockle is an annual. Sow the seed in any garden soil where it is to flower and cover with soil. Sow in August–September for flowers the following June, or in early spring for flowers in July–August.
Other sites: None.

Quaking-grass
Briza media

Most gardeners think of grass as something to be mowed or scythed down. But quaking- or totter-grass is one of our loveliest grasses and deserves a place in any garden. It is not a grass most people have seen as it grows in old established grassland that has not been heavily fertilized. It would find no place in a modern, high-yielding sward. For those lucky enough to have seen the quivering, shimmering heads of a drift of quaking-grass in an old flowering hay meadow or upland hillside, it is an unforgettable sight. The whole field seems alive with its movement in the slightest breeze.

As the grass will grow in most soils and even in shade this is a grass to add to any flowering meadow mixture. It will grow well on chalk, clay and in a semi-woodland situation. Grow a good clump of it in the flower border and it will attract more interest than many of the flowers. The heads when dried are superb for flower decorations.

Season: June–August **Height:** 20–80 cm (8 in – 2½ ft)
Cultivation: Quaking-grass is a perennial plant that will flower one or two years after sowing. It is adaptable to most soils and situations. Sow the seed in spring or late summer in a well-prepared soil, to provide a good seed bed. If you want to add quaking-grass to an existing grassy area, sow the seed in trays and plant out in early spring or autumn, spacing the young plants at least 30 cm (1 ft) apart.
Other sites: Semi-shade.

Clustered bellflower
Campanula glomerata

Clustered bellflower is one of the many colourful chalk-land plants. The flowers have a richness and intensity of colour that is difficult to beat. When grown in the garden without the competition of grasses and other plants, clustered bellflower looks spectacular and is worthy of any flower border. In the wild garden it is without doubt a chalk or light-land plant and will never compete with the lush vegetation in rich and heavy soils or survive in cold, wet, heavy soils in winter. To grow this plant in grass it would be necessary to create a chalk mound or at least an area of rather poor, well-drained soil where grasses would grow thinly; the lovely clustered bellflower would then grow to half the height it would in the garden but look more beautiful for that. It looks superb as a special feature plant in a rock garden.

Season: June–August **Height:** 10–30 cm (4–12 in)
Cultivation: Clustered bellflower is a perennial plant. Sow the tiny seed in seed trays, not in open ground, as the seed can take a long time to emerge. Do not cover the seed but place a sheet of glass on top of the tray to keep in moisture then leave in a shady spot outdoors. Sow during the autumn and seed will germinate in early spring, or before. Prick out into pots when large enough and plant out the following autumn or spring.
Other sites: None: clustered bell-flower needs full sun.

Harebell
Campanula rotundifolia

Harebells are surprisingly adaptable plants that flourish in the wild, both in damp, peaty areas and in dry, chalky soils. They grow in profusion on the heather moors and roadsides of Scotland, where they are known as the bluebells of Scotland. In the north of England too, roadsides are often turned blue with a mass of harebells, their dainty flower-heads nodding on slender stems, and often growing with the lovely wetland plant, meadow-sweet. Further south, harebells are associated more with well-grazed chalk downland, where they grow with wild thyme and bird's-foot-trefoil, although this combination also flourishes on acid heaths.

Harebells are lovely delicate flowers for the garden and fit into the smallest area. Grow them in the rock garden, or on a grassy bank mixed with bladder campion and bird's-foot-trefoil or on a chalk bank with wild thyme. They also do well in window-boxes or tubs.

Harebells seed themselves profusely and, if you plant a few in a small patch of soil, the area will be filled with self-sown seedlings in no time. Sometimes a white form of harebell will appear, which is worth preserving as it will not come true from seed.

Season: July–September   **Height:** 15–40 cm (6–16 in)
Cultivation: Harebells are perennial plants that grow easily from seed, which should be sown in spring. Scatter the dust-like seed on the surface of the soil or compost of a seed tray and firm or lightly water in. Plants may be planted into short grass during autumn or spring.
Other sites: Semi-shade; rock garden; seaside garden.

Cuckooflower
Cardamine pratensis

Cuckooflower, or lady's smock, is a flower of early spring. Many country names of wild flowers refer to the time of year that they bloom, and cuckooflower is a good example, flowering in April and May and coinciding with the evocative call of the cuckoo. In the wild, cuckoo-flowers usually form great sheets covering a damp meadow. The individual flowers vary in colour: most are so pale they look white but in fact they are usually a pale lilac or pink, veined with darker lilac.

Cuckooflowers are reasonably plentiful all over the country but are most common in the north and west where there are more undrained meadows. They are easy to naturalize in moist grassland and, once established, they will spread vigorously.

Cuckooflower is closely related to bittercress and watercress and is itself edible; it used to be eaten in salads and may still be by the adventurous! It is also an important food plant of the orange-tip butterfly.

In the garden, cuckooflowers should be planted in a patch of moist grass or in a damp area near the pond. They enjoy a little shade so they would do well in the partial shade of trees, walls or fences. Plant them with ragged-robin for some early spring colour.

Season: April–June   **Height:** 15–40 cm (6–16 in)
Cultivation: Cuckooflower is a perennial plant that grows easily from seed. Sow seed in early summer or autumn in moist, fertile soil and firm or water it into the ground. Plants self-seed profusely and can also be propagated by placing a single leaf, taken from the base of the stem, on the surface of a seed tray of compost and keeping it moist; it will quickly form roots.
Other sites: Semi-shade; water garden.

Cornflower
Centaurea cyanus

Cornflowers, or corn bluebottles, are simple flowers of great beauty with intense blue flower-heads waving on tall, slender stems. I think John Clare sums up our feelings over these lovely cornfield flowers when he says "the blue cornbottles crowding their splendid colours in large sheets over the land and troubling the cornfields with destroying beauty". Nowadays, we have to re-create this brilliant landscape on a more modest scale in the garden, country park or on the farm nature reserve. However, our countryside is far from colourless with acres of brilliant yellow oil seed rape and the odd field of blue borage presenting a lovely sight to passers-by.

Cornflowers have of course been cultivated in the garden for centuries. Purple, white and pink forms sometimes occur naturally, and were much used by gardeners. A double flower was developed which is still very popular in the cut-flower trade.

Cornflowers can be grown anywhere in the sunny garden but their slender stems will flop around if not supported by other plants. Grow them with a mixture of red poppies and chamomile for the necessary support and to produce a spectacular display: red, white and blue is always a stunning combination.

Season: June–August   **Height:** 20 cm-1 m (8 in-3 ft)

Cultivation: The cornflower is an annual plant of cultivated soil. Scatter the seed thinly in early autumn or spring and rake it in or cover it lightly with soil. If seed is sown in spring, the plants will flower rather late, so an autumn sowing is best. This also applies when sowing a cornfield mixture. If cornflowers are grown in bare soil they will self-seed readily.

Other sites: None.

Greater knapweed
Centaurea scabiosa

Greater knapweed is closely related to the cornflower but is a perennial plant, usually growing in grassland on light soil. It is without doubt one of the most attractive wild flowers for the garden, being smothered with beautiful, large, purple-crimson blooms in July and August. It is in fact very similar in appearance to black knapweed, or hardheads, but is much more showy. The flower-head is made up of many overlapping bracts like tiles; when the flower is over and the seed gone, a lovely creamy-silver fringed cup is left, providing splendid winter decoration.

Greater knapweed really does attract the insects to your garden. Butterflies enjoy it and bees are drawn to the plant as if it was a magnet. In my large patch, one sunny day in early August, it looked as if there was a bee on every bloom. As some flowers are opening, others are fading, and as they begin to fade the goldfinches descend to plunder the seeds.

Greater knapweed was once taken medicinally as a tonic and it was also a useful wound herb.

Season: July–August   **Height:** 30–80 cm (1–1½ ft)

Cultivation: Greater knapweed is a perennial plant that is easily grown from seed. Sow seed in a seed tray in spring and cover lightly with soil. Plant out in grass from autumn to spring and in cultivated soil at any time. Or sow seed where it is to flower in autumn or spring and cover lightly with soil. Thin seedlings to 60 cm (2 ft) apart.

Other sites: Semi-shade.

Corn marigold
Chrysanthemum segetum

Chicory
Cichorium intybus

On the light, gravelly and rather acid soils of east Suffolk, large fields of golden yellow flowers can still be seen in summer. These are corn marigolds and they look beautiful on this scale. The plant certainly thrives on light soil, although in the garden it seems to be very accommodating. Like most of our cornfield flowers it is not truly native but probably came in with seed corn from southern Europe a long time ago, possibly in neolithic times. Corn marigold really does make a beautiful garden plant with dozens of large, golden flower-heads above bushy foliage. Mixed with other cornfield flowers such as mayweed and red poppy it looks spectacular.

It is an interesting fact that farmers have been trying to banish this colourful flower from their fields for centuries. In the reign of Henry VI of England in the fifteenth century severe penalties were handed out to any of his tenants who did not eradicate this weed! In Denmark it was banished by law. Conservation organizations are now establishing special reserves for these 'arable weeds'. Don't be tempted to liven up your neighbouring cornfield by scattering seed of corn marigold or other colourful flowers, as you will bring wildflower conservation into disrepute.

Season: June–September   **Height:** 20–50 cm (8–20 in)
Cultivation: Sow the seed where it is to flower in spring, or in autumn if it is part of a cornfield mixture. Scatter the seed thinly and rake in or cover lightly with soil. Corn marigold plants will self-seed readily.
Other sites: None.

I cannot remember how often I have been asked what that beautiful bright blue flower is! Chicory, or wild succory, is the flower and it has delightful clear blue, star-like flowers as large as a dandelion. It is quite rare in the wild but a closely related form is becoming more and more popular in vegetable gardens and this will produce the same blue flowers if it is allowed to do so. Its natural habitat is on chalk and sandy soils on roadsides and cultivated ground all over Europe.

Chicory is a valuable fodder crop and is still sown on grassland for grazing. The roots used to be cooked like parsnip, roasted or boiled, and eaten as a vegetable, probably since biblical times.

Chicory grows in any soil and will thrive in very light soil where many other plants do not grow. It is quite a tall plant so grow it at the back of the bed or up against a fence or wall for the best effect. It also needs to be in a position that receives the morning sun as the flowers open at sunrise and close about midday.

Season: July–October
Height: 30 cm–1 m (1–3 ft)
Cultivation: Chicory is a hardy perennial plant which grows easily from seed. Sow the seed thinly where the plants are to flower in spring or late summer. Cover lightly with soil. Thin seedlings to a minimum of 30 cm (1 ft) apart.
Other sites: None.

Wild carrot
Daucus carota

Wild carrot is one of our most common wild flowers found growing on waysides, chalk grassland, light and sandy soils, in old meadows, and near the sea. It is distinctive in appearance; its flat, white flower-heads are beautiful and its foliage is decoratively divided, like the cultivated varieties of carrot. In good garden soil, the plant will grow very tall with as many as a dozen stems and looks extremely attractive. It can also be included in a meadow mixture as it establishes well and flowers over the whole summer. When the flowers fade, decorative seed-heads, like birds' nests, are formed, which add interest to a bare winter garden.

Wild carrot has had many uses through the ages. In the seventeenth century its leaves were used to decorate ladies' head-dresses. The seeds were used medicinally to treat coughs, colic and hiccups as well as kidney disease and infections of the bladder, while carrot tea was considered good for relieving flatulence. Wild carrot also yields a strong green dye.

Season: June–August/September
Height: 45–60 cm (1½–2 ft)
Cultivation: Wild carrot is a biennial or short-lived perennial which
will grow in most soils but seems to
persist longer in chalk or light, sandy
soils, if it is grown with grasses. Sow
seed in early autumn or spring and
cover it very lightly with soil. Wild
carrot self-seeds readily.
Other sites: Rock garden; seaside
garden.

Teasel
Dipsacus fullonum

Teasel is a stately architectural plant growing to a height of 2 m (6 ft) or over. Being a biennial plant, all that can be seen for the first year is a giant rosette of bristly leaves hugging the ground. The following spring up and up goes the thick spiny stem, leaves clasped round it like cups. The long, spiny flower-heads with mauve flowers attract bees and later seed-eating birds who delight in pulling out the seeds. Once the seeds have gone, the dried heads can be cut to provide attractive winter flower decorations.

A variety of this teasel has a seed-head with hooks on the spines that has long been grown for the cloth indus-try. In fact it is still grown because no synthetic substitute has been inven-ted. The seed-heads are used for rais-ing a nap on cloth (teasing).

Plant teasel where it will be sil-houetted against the skyline for its full dramatic effect.
Season: July–August (flowers);
autumn—winter for heads.
Height: to 2 m (6 ft)
Cultivation: Teasel is a biennial plant, so seed sown one year will normally flower the next and then the plant is over. Therefore sow seed in two consecutive years and allow the plants to self-seed. You will have teasels for evermore. Seed is best sown where it is to flower, preferably in a clay soil or one that does not dry out in summer.
Other sites: Semi-shade.

Viper's-bugloss
Echium vulgare

Viper's-bugloss sounds a rather daunting plant, the sort of plant to keep at bay! It is however marvellously colourful and grows normally on the breckland of Norfolk, on sandy and chalk soils and near the sea. But in spite of being essentially a lightland plant, it is completely adaptable to all soils. When grown in the garden it will compete with the showiest garden flowers, so brilliant is the colour and so profuse the blooms. If you look closely, you can see that the flowers are beautifully marked. They are loved by bees – in fact, there is a constant hum from the flowers for several weeks in the summer!

The strange name of the plant comes from its use for the treatment of the bite of the spotted viper. The flowers, like those of borage, to which it is closely related, were used to mix into cordials and were also candied.

Season: June–September   **Height:** 80 cm (2½ ft)

Cultivation: Viper's-bugloss is a biennial plant that is easily grown from seed sown in late summer where it is to flower. Thin the seedlings to 45 cm (18 in) apart. The plants will self-seed profusely. With its long tap root, the plant will survive any drought, but cannot easily be transplanted unless it is very young. It will also tolerate slightly acid soil conditions.

Other sites: None.

Bell heather
Erica cinerea

Bell heather is one of our three common heathers. The other two are the common heather or ling (see p. 165) and the cross-leaved heath. All are familiar in upland Britain, and in the few remaining areas of lowland heath in the south, but except for common heather they are rarer in the rest of northern Europe. All these heathers are good garden plants, but they like different conditions. Common heather is the most adaptable of the three; cross-leaved heather is a wetland plant; and bell heather is a plant of dry heaths and does not tolerate any lime.

Bell heather with its lovely drooping red-purple bells is the most beautiful of the three heathers. It is most often seen in association with common heather, forming the typical heather landscape that we all love. This plant, like all heathers and heaths, is a marvellous garden plant that makes excellent ground-cover. Bees love the flowers and heather honey is justly famous. It also had many uses, from making thatch and rope to dyeing wood.

In order to give heathers the acid conditions they like, it is best to construct a peat garden (see p. 132).

Season: July–September   **Height:** 30 cm (1 ft)

Cultivation: Bell heather is a woody perennial under-shrub. Take cuttings in August by pulling (not cutting!) a non-flowering shoot off the plant. Plant the cutting in a small pot containing seed or cutting compost. Dipping the stem in a suitable hormone rooting powder will help. You can buy plants from specialist nurseries.

Other sites: Semi-shade.

Dropwort
Filipendula vulgaris

Dropwort is closely related to meadowsweet and to my mind is an even more attractive flower. It is really the lightland meadowsweet, growing on gravelly and chalky soils. In the garden, however, it also grows well in heavy clay and my plants have survived very wet conditions in winter. The flowerbuds are of a deep rose colour and it is this combination of buds and large, white open flowers – clustered together in fluffy balls at their height – that makes the flower-heads particularly attractive.

Dropwort is a stunning feature plant for the garden, not only for its flowers but also for its decorative fern-like foliage, and looks good in any border or mixed bed. It will also establish well in grassland, although to do well the soil should be rather light or chalky. If you have room in your garden for several plants together, then this will create a most beautiful effect. Or you could perhaps grow it with a mixture of grasses and no other plants.

Season: June–August

Height: 10–50 cm (4–20 in)

Cultivation: Dropwort is a perennial plant and is easy to grow from seed. Sow either where it is to flower or in trays in spring or early autumn, covering very lightly with soil. It is best not to sow seed direct into grass: put in small plants instead.

Other sites: None.

Fritillary
Fritillaria meleagris

Fritillaries are unusual and beautiful flowers bearing distinctive chequered markings on their petals. These markings gave the plant its common names of snake's head fritillary and guinea-hen flower because of its likeness to snake's scales and guinea fowl feathers. Fritillaries were favourite garden plants in the fifteenth and sixteenth centuries, and it is possible that the wild form is an escape. It is without doubt a native flower of France and Yugoslavia. Most of the old fritillary meadows have been ploughed up this century and these plants are now rare, found mainly on sites which are nature reserves.

Fritillaries grow naturally in moist meadows, including those that are flooded in winter. On a good loam soil they will naturalize readily and spread from seed. It is best to start with a few bulbs in a group and let them spread naturally to form a drift.

The flowers are enjoyed by bees and, unfortunately, by rabbits, who will readily demolish the plants.

Season: March–May   **Height:** 20–40 cm (8–16 in)

Cultivation: Fritillaries are perennial plants that grow from bulbs. Offsets can be removed in autumn and planted into a pot of compost; or sow the seeds thinly in a small pot of compost and cover lightly. Leave the pot outside over winter, covered with glass. Plants will take up to five years to flower from seed and should not be planted out until they have done so. Plant fritillaries out in moist grassland.

Other sites: Water garden.

Meadow crane's-bill
Geranium pratense

This is a most handsome plant – the largest of the crane's-bills – bearing rich, purple-blue blooms in summer. In cultivated soil meadow crane's-bill produces many stems and a profusion of flowers, growing much larger than in the wild. Plants can also be found with white flowers.

Meadow crane's-bill is not common in the wild, being one of the species that has suffered as a result of agricultural intensification. Where it does occur, however, it grows in great profusion, especially on road verges, where it is a wonderful sight. Although the plant is choosy where it grows in the wild, it is certainly not difficult to establish, and naturalizes readily in the meadow garden, especially if the soil is slightly chalky.

Meadow crane's-bill is worth inspecting closely at seeding time. When the round seeds are fully ripe and brown, they are catapulted several feet away from the parent plant. By this means a single plant will spread every year in all directions.

Season: June–August　**Height:** 30–80 cm (1–2½ ft)
Cultivation: Meadow crane's-bill is a perennial plant easily grown from seed. Rub the seed between two sheets of sandpaper to speed germination, and then sow in open ground in late spring or summer. Space the seeds 6–15 cm (3–6 in) apart, and cover lightly with soil. If sowing in a seed tray, the seeds should be closer, spaced 1–2 cm (¼–1 in) apart and covered lightly with soil.
Other sites: Semi-shade.

Rough hawkbit
Leontodon hispidus

Rough hawkbit is closely related to dandelion and is similar in both its properties and appearance. The yellow dandelion-like flowers used to be a common and colourful sight in old meadows, especially on chalky land. But now that so many of these old grasslands have been ploughed, the plant is no longer so plentiful.

The bright golden flowers of rough hawkbit are an essential ingredient of a flowering meadow area, and will thrive in a fairly dry, alkaline soil with medium fertility and full sun. It is a fast and easy plant to establish and will often flower the first season from an autumn sowing. It spreads rapidly and will give a blaze of colour for weeks.

Rough hawkbit has a beautiful dandelion-clock seed-head, which has a browny tinge to it, unlike the pure silvery-white clock of the dandelion. The seeds can be collected much more easily than dandelion seeds, as they do not fly away so readily, and will stay on the plant for a day or two after opening. Like the dandelion, the leaves of rough hawkbit are edible. The whole plant has also been used medicinally as a treatment for jaundice and for treating kidney complaints. There is an ancient belief that hawks ate the leaves to sharpen their sight, hence the common name.

Season: June–September　**Height:** 10–40 cm (4–16 in)
Cultivation: Rough hawkbit is perennial and seed may be sown where it is to flower in early autumn or spring. To produce plants for planting into grassland, sow seed thinly in a seed tray from early spring to autumn. Press it firmly into the soil and do not cover. Keep the tray in a cold frame until germination takes place.
Other sites: None.

Oxeye daisy
Leucanthemum vulgare

The oxeye daisy, moon daisy or marguerite is normally one of the first plants to establish when a wild meadow mixture is sown. For the first couple of years it will probably dominate the meadow and then gradually as other, slower plants establish, the sheet of waving white heads will be mixed more evenly with other flowers.

Oxeye daisies flower in early summer and look most striking mixed with grasses only—try red fescue, crested dog's-tail, meadow foxtail, smooth meadow-grass and yellow oat-grass; to extend the meadow's season of interest, knapweed, scabious and yarrow will follow the daisies to give you colour into August.

Oxeye daisy is traditionally associated with stormy weather, and in Germany bunches of flowers used to be hung over barn doors to ward off lightning. The roots and leaves were used as a flavouring for soups and stews, but I must say I haven't tried them. The leaves were recommended as a salad vegetable, but I think I would class this as emergency food only!

Season: May–Sept **Height:** 20–80 cm (8 in–2½ ft)

Cultivation: Oxeye daisy is a perennial plant that grows easily from seed. Sow the seed where it is to grow in early autumn or in spring and cover very lightly with soil. Germination will take only 2–3 weeks. To sow into established grassland, cut the grass short in early autumn and broadcast the seed.

Other sites: Semi-shade.

Common toadflax
Linaria vulgaris

The brilliant yellow flowers of toadflax brighten roadsides and dry banks from July until early autumn. It is a vigorous, sprawling plant which is so full of bloom in its season that the small, flax-like leaves are hardly noticed at all. The flowers look like tiny snapdragons, and are perfectly designed to attract bees, which have tongues long enough to reach the nectar.

Each plant produces tens of thousands of round, flat, black seeds, and also spreads by underground runners, especially in a loose or dry soil. It will be obvious therefore that it is somewhat invasive. Don't on any account introduce it into cultivated soil unless you want an exclusive show of it! Reserve it instead for wilder, grassy areas where competition will keep it under control.

The flowers yield, according to the type of mordant used in the process, a yellow, orange, green or brown dye. An interesting idea from Sweden is to infuse the plant in milk which creates a powerful fly poison. The flies should settle in the milk and succumb to the poison liquor. This might be worth a try!

Season: July–October **Height:** 30–80 cm (1–2½ ft)

Cultivation: WARNING: *This plant is best grown in grass; it is very difficult to control in cultivated soil.* Common toadflax is a perennial creeping plant that grows readily from seed. Sow the seed in spring or early autumn either where it is to flower or in trays and cover very lightly with soil. Mature plants may also be divided in spring or autumn and planted out 60 cm (2 ft) apart. You can limit its spread by cutting off the flower-heads as soon as it has finished flowering.

Other sites: None.

Common bird's-foot-trefoil
Lotus corniculatus

This is a low-growing, carpeting plant, with bright yellow flowers that are at their best in May and June. The fact that it is so common in no way diminishes its delicate beauty; the flowers which at first sight appear to be egg-yolk yellow are, in fact, often beautifully tinted with orange and brown, and the young buds have an almost crimson tinge to them. The whole effect is very colourful.

Common bird's-foot-trefoil is a very adaptable plant, found growing wild in many different habitats. It thrives on chalk pastures where turf is fine and short, and is also common on dry heaths where it can be seen growing with tormentil, harebell, ribwort and wild thyme. It also grows on the poor, sandy and shingly soils of the seaside with lady's bedstraw, mouse-ear hawkweed, biting stonecrop and common centaury; and on the sea cliffs where it grows with such colourful flowers as thrift and sea campion.

All these combinations of flowers would be well worth growing in the garden, in any area of poor or sandy soil. When working out planting schemes it is always best to look at these simple but beautiful wild plant communities for ideas, as they can rarely be bettered.

Common bird's-foot-trefoil is an important food plant of the common blue butterfly, and is also one of the best nectar plants for bees.

Season: May–August **Height:** 10–40 cm (4–16 in)
Cultivation: Common bird's-foot-trefoil is a perennial plant. Rub the seed between sheets of sandpaper to speed germination, then sow thinly where it is to flower in late summer or spring, pressing it into the soil. Alternatively, sow seed 2 cm ($\frac{1}{2}$ in) apart in a seed tray of compost. This plant enjoys the addition of gritty sand to a moist or fertile soil.
Other sites: Rock garden; seaside garden.

Ragged-robin
Lychnis flos-cuculi

A mass of ragged-robin in full flower makes a lovely colourful sight in the garden. The deeply divided rose-red petals give the flowers an attractive ragged appearance. Ragged-robin is now declining in the wild as so many of our wetlands have been drained and cultivated, but where it is found, it often grows with marsh-marigold, square-stalked St John's-wort and meadowsweet.

Ragged-robin is readily naturalized in any moist or moisture-retentive soil. It looks best growing in grass and there is no better place to grow a drift of this colourful flower than in the marshy area by a pond. It flowers in late spring and early summer and for this reason it is also called the cuckoo flower – a name that is used for many other spring wild flowers.

Ragged-robin produces an abundance of tiny, dark seeds which rattle around in the small brown capsules until they are ripe. Once the capsules open, the seed is spread around by the stems waving in the wind. The plant belongs to the same family as pinks and campions and has the same type of seed capsule.

Season: May–August
Height: 30–50 cm (12–20 in)
Cultivation: Ragged-robin is a perennial plant. Sow seed in the soil in spring or late summer; or sow seed in trays of compost at any time from spring until early autumn. Press the seed into the soil or compost.
Other sites: Semi-shade; water garden.

Musk mallow

Malva moschata

Musk mallow is one of our prettiest wild flowers and has been grown as a garden plant for many years. It is a bushy plant with large, clear pink flowers produced in great profusion, and when it's not in flower, the bright green, divided leaves provide splendid decoration.

In the wildflower border it mixes well with annuals such as common poppy, larkspur and chamomile. It also looks marvellous growing in a meadow with oxeye daisy, vetches, scabious and knapweed. The plant prefers well-drained, fertile soil and will establish well on gravel where the underlying soil provides some moisture and fertility.

The plant gives off a delicate musky perfume in warm weather or when the leaves are handled. Bees are frequent visitors to the flowers for nectar and pollen.

Season: July–September **Height:** 30–75 cm (1–2½ ft)
Cultivation: Musk mallow is a perennial plant that grows easily from seed. Sow seed in late summer, early autumn or in spring where it is to flower and press it into the soil; or sow seed in a seed tray of compost spaced 2 cm (1 in) apart at any time from spring to autumn, and cover lightly with compost.

Other sites: Semi-shade.

Common restharrow

Ononis repens

Common restharrow is a colourful, low shrub that will look attractive growing in a wildflower border with many of the lightland and seaside plants such as common bird's-foot-trefoil, lady's bedstraw and sea campion. Its trailing stems spread quickly along the ground, rooting at intervals. The fine, hairy leaves of the plant have a resinous scent but the rose-pink flowers are scentless.

Common restharrow is a plant of rather poor, dry alkaline soil. In the wild, it is commonly found growing on sandy grasslands and cliff tops near the sea, and inland on light, chalky soils.

Its common name was derived from the effect its tough and fibrous roots had on the harrow and plough. The roots literally used to stop – rest – the harrow in its tracks. It was also of annoyance to farmers because, if cattle grazed on the plants, the milk, and then the butter and cheese, became tainted. Although farmers disliked the plant, however, the young shoots were eaten, either boiled or raw in salads, and were sometimes even pickled.

Season: June–September **Height:** to 30 cm (1 ft)
Cultivation: Common restharrow is a perennial plant. The seed is hard coated and should be scarified – rubbed between sheets of sandpaper – to hasten germination before sowing. Sow the seed in late summer or spring, spacing it at least 2 cm (1 in) apart. Cover only very lightly with soil. Transplant before the plants have developed an extensive root system.

Other sites: Seaside garden.

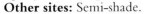

Cotton thistle
Onopordum acanthium

Cotton thistle, or Scotch thistle, is a magnificent giant plant growing up to 3 m (9 ft) tall. It is a marvellous architectural plant that would make a stunning feature in any garden – in a border or against a wall. It is grown more for its large and beautiful, silvery-green leaves than for its flowers. The leaves are viciously spined and covered with a white cottony down, which comes off if rubbed. The stout, well-branched stem has attractive wing-like appendages growing from it; the flowers are a beautiful light purple colour and very attractive to bees.

Cotton thistle is occasionally found naturalized on waste ground and roadsides, especially on sandy and chalky soil. It seeds itself readily.

There are certain culinary advantages to growing cotton thistle: the young stalks can be peeled and eaten; and the thistle heads can be cooked and eaten like globe artichokes, which are close relatives, but somehow I don't think the idea will catch on.

Pliny states that a decoction of cotton thistle applied to a bald head will restore healthy hair growth!

Season: July–September
Height: 45 cm–3 m (1½–9 ft)
Cultivation: Cotton thistle is a biennial plant so will normally flower in its second season and then die. Sow seeds in twos or threes where they are to grow and cover lightly with soil; if more than one seedling emerges, transplant the others when they are small, at least 1 m (3 ft) apart.
Other sites: None.

Marjoram
Origanum vulgare

Marjoram is well known as a culinary herb but less familiar as a native wild flower. With its lovely rose-purple flowers, it makes a most colourful hedgerow, meadow or border plant and will self-seed profusely. Marjoram establishes best in grass on light soil, but in the border it is tolerant of heavier conditions.

Many of its former habitats have now sadly been destroyed, but it is still to be found growing on chalk hills with wild thyme, and on road verges and wood margins with wild basil. One of its prettier common names – joy-of-the-mountains – describes perfectly the lovely mass of pink or white blooms that appear on the mountainsides in Greece and in other Mediterranean countries, where many different forms of marjoram grow.

Marjoram leaves have a very strong scent, which has always made it a valuable culinary herb. The leaves were once used to flavour and preserve beer, and are now used to make a most pleasant tea that has many beneficial properties. Because of its scent, marjoram used to be an important strewing herb in the sixteenth century.

Since ancient Greek times, marjoram has been used medicinally to treat a wide variety of ailments. Its leaves contain strongly antiseptic oils which were used to treat coughs, colic and indigestion. The plant is also mildly sedative and is beneficial used in the bath. It is also used as an inhalant and as a poultice.

Bees and butterflies are very attracted to marjoram. Its flowers also yield a purple dye.

Season: July–September
Height: 30–60 cm (1–2 ft)
Cultivation: Marjoram is a bushy and woody perennial herb. Sow the dust-like seed thinly where it is to flower, or on compost in a seed tray from spring to late summer. Press it into the soil or compost; do not cover.
Other sites: Semi-shade.

Common poppy
Papaver rhoeas

Poppies are one of the most colourful flowers to grow in the garden, and if they are allowed to self-seed, many exciting colour combinations will result with other flowers. Poppies are one of the basic ingredients of the cornfield patch, together with corncockle and cornflower. The big scarlet petals look very beautiful mixed with all sorts of flowers, from white and yellow mayweed, to the blue flowers of larkspur and viper's-bugloss.

Poppy seed will only grow year after year in a soil that is kept cultivated, and will not persist in grass. The seed is very long lasting and will lie dormant for many years in undisturbed ground. Every season, after the land is ploughed (providing no harmful sprays have been used), poppies appear like magic, turning the cornfields in high summer to sheets of scarlet and gold. Poppies go back to the beginnings of civilization and are seen as flowers of survival, nostalgia and remembrance.

Poppies are not so much weeds, as companions of corn, and they were often grown for an economic reason: their seed. Although not as valuable as opium poppy seed, common poppy seed was harvested for use as a flavouring to cover cakes and bread; and the oil from the seed was used as an olive oil substitute. The petals were at one time collected by children to be made into a syrup.

Season: June–August **Height:** 20–60 cm (8 in–2 ft)
Cultivation: Poppies are annual flowers that grow easily from seed, so long as the seed is sown before the winter, as it requires a period of cold to trigger germination. Sow the seed thinly in cultivated ground where it is to flower. Press it into the soil and do not cover. Poppies self-seed readily.
Other sites: None.

Cowslip
Primula veris

These beautiful nodding flowers, once so plentiful in old meadows, are now becoming established on road verges where they are safe from the plough and the sprayer. Cowslip meadows can still be found but are declining because of modern farming methods.

The flowers are a wonderful sight in a meadow garden during April and May. At this time of year the grasses and other flowers are still low, allowing the cowslip flowers to dance in the spring breezes. Cowslips are also very suitable for growing in the hedgebank in a semi-shady situation, and they even grow in open woods. The plants favour chalky soil and thrive on chalky boulder clay.

Cowslip flowers are erect when in bud and then they begin to droop as they open, to protect the nectar and pollen from the weather. At this stage they have a lovely sweet scent. Later, when fertilization has taken place, the flower-heads become erect again. The ripened seed-heads can be harvested as late as the end of July.

Season: April–May **Height:** 10–20 cm (4–9 in)
Cultivation: Cowslips are perennial plants that are easily grown from seed. Sow the seed in a nursery bed in autumn and firm it in; or sow seed on compost in trays and leave them outside in a sheltered spot over winter covered with glass. Germination will take place in spring. Slightly unripened seed will often germinate within a few weeks. Plant small plants out in grassland in the following autumn or winter. Established plants can be divided up and replanted during the autumn.
Other sites: Semi-shade.

Selfheal
Prunella vulgaris

Meadow buttercup
Ranunculus acris

Selfheal is a most attractive flower and a superb, colourful groundcover plant: it sends out runners which root and send up flower stems. The rich purple-blue is most attractive, but sometimes pink and even white forms occur. Planting selfheal in a patch of low-growing grass will make a vivid splash of colour on a lawn or grassy bank. The area should hum with insect life: selfheal is a plant much visited by bees and butterflies.

Selfheal is a familiar plant in large parts of the world. It grows over most of Europe and North America, and has also been found in the Himalayas. John Gerard in his *Herbal* rated selfheal the best of wound herbs along with bugle, and Culpeper also extols its virtues. The plant has many common names that indicate its use as a wound herb, including carpenter's herb, sticklewort, and touch-and-heal. Selfheal is still used in herbal medicine especially as a gargle for sore throats and inflammation of the mouth, and for cuts, burns and bruises.

This is an easy plant to establish as it not only spreads by runners but also produces plenty of seed. It is an important constituent of any meadow mixture, although in very tall grass it can be overlooked. Perhaps it is best in a flowering lawn; its low growth and spreading habit allow it to be cut fairly short.

Season: June–October **Height:** 10–30 cm (4–12 in)
Cultivation: Selfheal is perennial and once established may be split up in spring and planted out 15–20 cm (6–8 in) apart either in bare soil or existing grass. It also grows easily from seed sown in spring or late summer where it is to flower and covered lightly with soil. Young plants can be transplanted into short grass in spring or autumn. Selfheal will grow in most soils including those which are rather acid, but does best if the soil is fertile.
Other sites: Semi-shade.

Meadow buttercup and the very similar bulbous buttercup (which flowers a month earlier, in May) are probably the best known flowers of the countryside. Fields of yellow buttercups bring back memories of childhood rambles through early summer meadows shining golden with them, and of holding the flower up to your chin to see whether you had a liking for butter. This sheet of brilliant yellow over a meadow is a sight that is becoming less and less common. In fact, it is now a sign of an 'unimproved' meadow, as the buttercup offers no food value to livestock and is now usually replaced with grasses to make the meadow more productive. The bulbs of bulbous buttercup are loved by pigs.

There is another common buttercup, the creeping buttercup of wet, badly drained or acid soils. This spreads so vigorously it is often a terrible menace in the garden but, like the other buttercups, it does make a terrific picture in full flower.

Buttercups have many country names, including butter-and-cheese, butter-rose, gildcup and blister plant. This last name refers to the acrid juice which can cause blisters and was once used medicinally. Another common country name is kingcup, which is confusing as this is now the commonly accepted name for the marsh-marigold.

Season: June–August **Height:** 20–50 cm (8–20 in)
Cultivation: Meadow buttercups are perennials that are best sown in a mixture of flowers and grasses. If you want to grow them separately, sow seed where it is to flower in spring or autumn and cover lightly with soil. Young plants may be transplanted in spring or autumn into grass that has been cut short.
Other sites: Semi-shade.

Yellow rattle
Rhinanthus minor

Meadow saxifrage
Saxifraga granulata

Yellow rattle is a rather unusual and pretty plant that is decreasing in the wild as old pastures and hay meadows are ploughed up or improved. Where it does grow it grows in great profusion. It is a semi-parasitic plant that will only grow in association with certain other plants, mainly grasses. There is no point, therefore, in sowing seed in a flowerbed, bare soil or a seed-tray. Nor will it grow if you sow it in spring! But sow it in autumn with a mixture of meadow grasses and it will be in flower in June. I seeded a 10-acre field with a flowering hay-meadow mixture in September and by the following June, yellow rattle was the predominant flower!

The unusual name refers to the fact that when ripe the seed literally rattles in its case as the plant blows in the wind or is disturbed by someone walking through the meadow. There are many other country names that refer to the rattling seeds, for instance, baby's rattles, rattle-penny, money-grass.

Being semi-parasitic and an annual flower, yellow rattle is extremely vulnerable to the changing patterns of farming, so it is a most important flower to conserve.

Season: June–August   **Height:** 10–50 cm (4–20 in)
Cultivation: Yellow rattle is an annual. It will grow in most soils including very acid ones. Sow it in autumn with a mixture of meadow grass. Once established it will self-seed readily.
Other sites: None: yellow rattle needs full sun.

Meadow saxifrage is a lovely flower but it is not easy to find in the wild. It usually occurs in old meadows but its distribution is localized. It has few leaves except for a rosette at the base, so when in flower—and it sends up many flower stems—its largish white blooms make quite a picture. Once the flowers are over and the plant has seeded there is very little to be seen of it: the leaves tend to die off in summer.

This is a really worthwhile plant to establish in the garden. It looks good either growing with other flowers or in grass. It does seem to be fussy about soil though, preferring neutral, gravelly soils. Any disturbance of the soil will spread the cluster of tiny tubers that forms the root of the plant, and so propagate it, or you can dig the plant up in autumn and divide the root by hand.

Season: April–June   **Height:** 10–30 cm (4–12 in)
Cultivation: Meadow saxifrage is a perennial. It grows easily from seed which is dust-like but produced in some quantity. Sow in trays in spring or autumn, using gritty potting compost. Scatter the seed on the surface and do not cover. Transplant the seedlings as soon as they are large enough to handle into individual pots. Plant them into well-drained soil the following spring.
Other sites: Semi-shade; rock garden.

Small scabious

Scabiosa columbaria

Small scabious is an exceptionally pretty plant. The flowers are paler and more delicate than field scabious, but the plant is shorter, more branched and produces an amazing abundance of blooms over many weeks from July to September. It is attractive in bud as well as in bloom and when the flowers are over, the green seed-heads are most beautifully constructed, like a honeycomb.

In the garden small scabious is a lovely plant to grow in the wildflower border, where its bushy and robust habit will stop it falling about. It will also establish well in a meadow mixture on a chalky or rather light soil. It has a long tap root which enables it to penetrate far into the soil for moisture and minerals, and so it is able to withstand very dry conditions. In the wild it grows in rather dry, chalky pastures often amongst quaking-grass, kidney vetch and common rock-rose.

Being a bushy plant, small scabious needs cutting back after it has flowered or seeded. If it is cut down almost to the ground before seeding, it will shoot again and may produce more flowers late into the autumn. Small scabious is a good bee plant and all the late garden butterflies will enjoy feeding from it.

Season: July–September   **Height:** 15–70 cm (6 in–2½ ft)
Cultivation: Small scabious is a perennial plant which produces plenty of seed. Collect the seed when the seed-head begins to lose its green colour and the head breaks up easily in the hand. Either cut the stem off and hang it up to dry, or pick the heads off the plant and leave them to finish ripening in a paper bag. Birds are fond of the seeds when they start to ripen, so this will give you a good indication of when to harvest them. Sow the seed in spring or late summer; it should be pressed into the soil but not covered. If you want to move the plants, this should be done when they are young, or the long tap root might get broken. Young plants can be planted in grass during autumn and winter.
Other sites: None.

Red clover

Trifolium pratense

With its beautiful rich red flowers, red clover makes a very colourful addition to a flowering meadow mixture, where the predominant colours are normally white, yellow and blue. But make sure you plant the true wild form as agricultural varieties of red clover often prove too vigorous and can take over the garden. Red clover will grow in the garden on most soils that are free draining, and will withstand poor and moderately dry conditions.

Wild red clover is now becoming quite rare as agricultural varieties have taken over and naturalized in the countryside. The true red clover is a much smaller, less vigorous plant than the cultivated form and has flowers of a much richer red. It grows in old pastures along waysides, often on chalky soil, and is worth looking out for when walking in the country.

Red clover has always been associated with nectar and children often used to suck the sweet flowers. Some of its old country names such as 'honeysuck', 'honeystalks' and 'sugar plums' affirm this. In spite of the high nectar content, however, red clover is not a very good source of nectar for the honey bee as this bee cannot normally reach the supply. The longer-tongued bumblebees and butter-flies, however, really feast from it, so it is well worth growing for this reason alone.

The plant has long been used medicinally for cleansing the blood, soothing the nerves, promoting sleep and restoring fertility. The flowers are also most decorative added as a garnish to a green salad, together with many other flowers such as wild pansy, violet and borage.

Season: May–September   **Height:** 10–40 cm (4–16 in)
Cultivation: Red clover is a perennial plant that grows readily from seed. Rub the seed between two sheets of sandpaper to speed germination. Sow the seed on a firm surface and press it into the soil.
Other sites: None.

Dark mullein
Verbascum nigrum

Dark mullein is a most beautiful flowering plant for the garden. From a dense rosette of large, dark green leaves, the plant sends up a tall flower stem, usually with several upright branches, each spike being densely covered in yellow blooms with purple centres. Dark mullein can remain in flower for many weeks. In the mixed wild-flower border dark mullein will provide a strong vertical accent and when in flower it will become a dramatic focal point. The best way to grow it is undoubtedly in a group, as the maze of bright yellow spires of differing heights, and at different stages of flowering, look very effective.

As each of its hundreds of flowers produces many hundreds of seeds, it may well be advisable to cut off most of the seeding stems to prevent the plant self-seeding too profusely all over the garden. Any unwanted seedlings should be transplanted when young. In the wild, dark mullein is normally found growing on chalky and sandy soil. It will withstand considerable drought and in a fertile soil will grow to an impressive size. It is also tolerant of rather acid conditions.

Season: June–September
Height: 60–120 cm (2–4 ft)
Cultivation: Dark mullein is a bien-nial plant so it normally flowers the season after sowing. Sow seed on the surface of the soil in spring or early summer where the plants are to flower. If too many seedlings come up, then transplant them when they are at the four-leaf stage. Germina-tion is erratic.
Other sites: None.

Wild pansy
Viola tricolor

Pansies have always held a fascination for gardeners and there is none more lovely than the tiny wild pansy, or heartsease as it is commonly known, with its tricolor face. The flowers may be yellow, violet or mauve, and often a combination of all three. In fact there can be considerable variation of colour as the wild pansy crosses readily with the diminutive yellow field pansy as well as with other garden pansies. In my garden I started with three different types of pansy and the variety of face colours and combinations of colours was amazing, ranging from pale yellows, to marvellous rich purple and rust shades. By letting nature do her work and then selecting and increasing your stock by taking cuttings, you can maintain some unique faces.

Many pansies have the characteristic pollen guides on their petals – dark lines radiating from the centre of the flower to guide the pollinating bees and other insects.

Wild pansy tolerates a wide variety of conditions in the wild, and will grow well in most garden situations, particularly in the mixed border, and will establish in a gravel area. It spreads rapidly from seed and once established, flowers will appear from early spring until well into the winter.

The plant has the most fascinating seed capsules, well worth looking at closely. Each capsule splits into three little, boat-like containers when ripe, with the shiny, round honey-brown seeds arranged in two neat rows inside. The best time to collect the seeds is midday, when the maximum number of capsules will have opened.

Season: April–November **Height:** 10–20 cm (4–8 in)
Cultivation: Wild pansy is a short-lived perennial and is best considered as an annual. Sow the seed from spring to early autumn where it is to flower. Press it into the soil but do not cover it. Alternatively, broadcast the seed thinly in a seed bed, and prick out the young plants for planting into their final position. The best time for this is from May to August.
Other sites: Semi-shade.

WILD FLOWERS FOR
Semi-shady Gardens

There are many areas of dappled or half-day shade in the countryside – field and woodland edges, hedgerows, orchards, roadside verges – and the sheltered yet reasonably light conditions they provide supports a wide range of wild flowers. Many of these places are awkward sites not really worth exploiting by man – and so they represent a last refuge for many plants and animals driven out of the more profitable fields and woodlands.

Perhaps the most typical semi-shady site is the hedgerow: it is certainly the richest. I think of the hedgerow as the backbone (and indeed the ribs) of the countryside. Every hedge tells a story, and a walk around the hedgerows of a parish might well become a walk through a thousand years of history. Originally, of course, the land was covered in forest, and as the woodland was cleared boundaries of trees and shrubs were left to delineate individual fields, farms, parishes, manors and estates. Many of these ancient hedges are still in existence, following parish boundaries and ancient grass roads – they were often planted on the banks of great ditches that marked important boundaries. The open farmlands of Norman times were gradually enclosed with hedges from the thirteenth century on. This process was escalated in the eighteenth century by the Acts of Enclosure, which caused the planting of hedges on a scale never seen before or since. These eighteenth-century hedges were mostly of hawthorn interspersed with oak and ash. Many of our existing hedges date from this time.

Hedgerows have always played an important role in the ecology of the countryside, but they have never been more vital than they are now to the survival of so much wildlife, especially the wonderful songbirds whose other nesting sites, in thickets and scrub, have mostly been cleared. Hedges are often the last remaining link for wildlife between otherwise isolated habitats. They also provide a home for an enormous range of wild flowers that are often refugees from ancient woodlands long since bulldozed and hay meadows, headlands and field corners now ploughed and sprayed with herbicides year after year.

Re-creating these rich, semi-shady habitats in gardens is therefore valuable for conserving wildlife and wild flowers, and can also provide immense pleasure. Even a small area of the garden planted with a few native shrubs and climbers and underplanted with grasses and wild flowers will soon establish a thriving habitat full of birds, insects and small mammals.

The hidden world of the hedge-bottom *Clumps of primroses grow up through the moss-covered debris that provides essential shelter for wildlife in the winter.*

Hedgerow garden in spring

The hedgerow is perhaps the most exciting area of the garden in spring. Buds are unfurling and birds and animals building their nests, while the bright, low-growing spring flowers enjoy the light before the grasses and taller plants take over.

The plants on this page were all grown in gardens; wild flowers should not be taken from the countryside.

Herb-robert *(above) seeds profusely to form a carpet of seedlings with ferny leaves.*

Hedgerow crane's-bill *(left) has a mass of bright flowers.*

Ground-ivy *(below) forms a scented carpet.*

Greater stitchwort *(below) spreads vigorously.*

Primrose *(above) is a versatile plant, but flowers look best in partial shade.*

Red campion *(right). The colourful flowers appear in mid-May.*

Lesser celandine *(above) thrives in damp soil.*

Garlic mustard *(below) has edible leaves that taste of garlic.*

Sweet cicely *(left) is more creamy and robust, and smells sweeter than cow parsley.*

Cherry plum *(right) has greeny-gold fruit that makes delicious pies and jam.*

Hawthorn *(above) is the perfect hedging shrub, with sweet-smelling may-flowers and red autumn berries.*

Solomon's-seal *(left) has graceful, arching branches of white flowers.*

Hop *(left) is a vigorous climber with attractive flowers that are very fragrant and slightly narcotic!*

Blackthorn, *(left), in flower often heralds rough weather.*

Dogwood *(above) has attractive, red-coloured stems for winter interest.*

Common dog-violet *(right), once established, will form a carpet.*

White dead-nettle *(below) is attractive to bees and other insects.*

Dusky crane's-bill *(below) flowers over a long period and seeds itself readily.*

Crab apple *(right) is a good hedgerow tree, with masses of apple blossom in spring.*

Hedgerow garden in summer

The hedgerow is at its most colourful in early summer. Roses and brambles are in full flower, and vigorous climbers are well on their way to the top of the hedge.

The plants on this page were all grown in gardens; wild flowers should not be taken from the countryside.

Field rose *(above) A shrubby, often trailing, rose that has a sweet, musky perfume.*

Bramble *(left) Flower colour (pink to white) and the fruit flavour are both variable.*

Hogweed *(below) towers above the long summer grasses and its flat white flower-heads show up well against the hedgerow.*

Sweet briar *(above) The leaves have an apple fragrance, especially after a shower of rain.*

Hedge woundwort *(left) grows tall through the long grass of the hedgerow. It is a very effective wound herb which can be used as a poultice.*

Dog rose *(above) often sends long stems through the top of a hedge or high into a tree.*

Hedge-bedstraw *(left) is a vigorous, scrambling plant which enlivens any hedgerow with its mass of flowers.*

Perforate St John's-wort *(below) has masses of golden flowers. It is a valuable medicinal herb with strong healing powers.*

Rough chervil *(below) is the delicate summer equivalent of cow parsley.*

Elder *(right) has sweet-smelling flowers that make a delicious wine.*

Dogwood *(above) is a low, deciduous shrub with decorative red stems in winter.*

Blackthorn *(below left) is a spiny, suckering shrub, with fragrant white flowers and blue-black fruits.*

Wild privet *(right) is semi-evergreen, with black, shiny berries in autumn.*

Wayfaring-tree *(right) has large creamy-white flowers in spring and red seeds ripening to black.*

Grasses *(below) A good hedgerow mixture includes grasses to balance invasive plants.*

Hazel *(above) stands out in the hedgerow, with its catkins in spring and nuts in autumn.*

Common nettle *(right) This is surprisingly decorative in flower.*

Tufted vetch *(right) is a most vigorous plant that will scramble through a hedge.*

White bryony *(above) A sprawling climber for the hedgerow.*

Hedgerow garden in autumn

The hedgerow is at its most glorious in the autumn, with brilliant red hips and haws, sparkling silver old-man's-beard, purple elderberries and flourescent pink spindle berries, all set against the warm golden-brown tones of leaves and seed-heads.

The plants on this page were all grown in gardens; wild flowers should not be taken from the countryside.

Holly *(left) is a good hedging shrub. Its red berries appear in winter.*

Hawthorn *(right) provides an excellent basis for a wild hedgerow.*

Hop *(below left) This is the more decorative female plant.*

Cherry plum *(below) is a parent of the domestic plum. It makes a decorative hedging shrub.*

Sweet briar *(below) Shakespeare's eglantine — a beautiful plant with lovely apple-scented leaves.*

Black horehound *(below) is a common hedgerow flower. It has a strong scent.*

Dog rose *(below) is very vigorous, with long arching stems that can climb as high as 6 m (20 ft).*

Field rose *(above) is less vigorous and has smaller hips than other wild roses.*

Spindle (left) is brilliantly coloured throughout the autumn. The leaves make a spectacular display as they turn.

Blackthorn (below) has edible sloes and will make a dense, spreading hedge.

Field maple (above) is easy to establish in the hedge and can form a small tree.

Elder (right) A most useful hedging shrub: elderberries make a wonderful red wine and are excellent when cooked in pastry.

Dogwood (right) The leaves turn purple and the stems turn red later in autumn.

Common knapweed has decorative seed-heads (left); it can also flower into the autumn (below left).

Mugwort (right) The leaves have a silvery tinge and are also aromatic.

Ivy (right) These are young berries: they will turn black as they ripen. The flowering stems have oval leaves.

Yarrow (left) sometimes flowers very late in the year. The seed-heads that follow are brown (right).

Traveller's-joy (right) In autumn the hedgerow is lit up by 'old-man's-beard'.

Semi-shady wildflower gardens

Semi-shady gardens: the possibilities

The majority of gardens do not catch the sun right through the day. Some areas will be in the shadow of the house, or a wall or fence for up to half the day (any more, and they are true shady areas). Others will be in the light, dappled shade cast by trellises, small deciduous trees or shrubs. These areas correspond to hedgerow and woodland-edge habitats in the wild. In a small garden there will not be enough room to plant a wild hedge but instead you can encourage native climbing plants to scramble over walls and fences. Just a few shrubs in a border can imitate a woodland-edge. Whatever the scale, it is worth finding room for some of the decorative shrubs that produce edible fruits.

Shrubs for small gardens

In the smallest garden there will be room for only a few shrubs, and not very large ones either, so they should be chosen with care. The most useful shrubs are those that are of interest for more than one season.

Elder grows into a small tree but can either be cut down every few years in winter, or just cut back: it will soon grow again. The beautiful cream-coloured, fragrant flowers make an excellent wine, as do the

black autumn berries, and these are also used for cooking; the birds love them too. Dog rose and sweet briar are extremely decorative, with pink flowers followed in autumn by red hips; they make good nesting sites. Guelder-rose is also attractive, with white flowers and red berries.

For autumn to spring interest, dogwood has good autumn colour and black berries and also red stems that are eye-catching in winter and spring. Hazel is another excellent shrub for the small garden, with decorative yellow catkins and edible nuts. It can easily be kept within bounds by occasional coppicing.

To add some brilliant early summer colour to your border or thicket, broom with its bright yellow flowers is really worth growing; it will do especially well in a light soil.

Underplanting shrubs

The first choice of wild flowers for planting with shrubs in a border or small thicket must be the bulbs. These are especially valuable for providing

A semi-shady border in summer The tall-growing plants balance the backdrop of distant trees that cast half-day shade. Purple loosestrife and hemp-agrimony thrive on the damp soil, backed by willowherb and everlasting-pea.

Shrubs for year-round interest Elder is a prime example of a valuable native shrub: in late spring it bears sweet-smelling cream flowers, succeeded in autumn by bunches of berries.

colour and interest in early spring when many of the shrubs will be dormant. The cheerful yellow winter aconite (*Eranthis hyemalis*) appears first, often through the snow. This is native to much of Europe and can be found in Britain naturalized in woodland sites. It is followed by snowdrops, which will carpet the ground after a few years if they like the soil. Wild daffodils will provide a later splash of colour, as will wild tulips (*Tulipa sylvestris*) – which are occasionally found in the wild, naturalized from the Continent. All these bulbs are best planted in random drifts and will naturalize well in grass, which can be kept mown once the foliage has died down in May/June.

For later in the year, it is worth growing summer snowflake and cyclamen. Perennial flowers will mix well with shrubs and bulbs for summer interest: choose any of the flowers featured on pages 62 to 75, but remember they will look best grown in clumps or drifts to add bold splashes of colour.

There are some marvellous ground-cover plants for semi-shade. Wild strawberry spreads by runners and will carpet the ground if it doesn't have competition from grass. Bugle is really worth growing but requires moisture. In the right conditions its

shiny, purplish leaves will form a decorative carpet. Selfheal is another colourful flower, but it is usually overshadowed by grasses and larger plants. It makes an excellent ground-cover for a semi-shady border if grown without competition.

Climbing wildflowers

Climbing plants are particularly valuable for small gardens, where you can take advantage of any bare walls and fences or unsightly surfaces. Most climbers are fast-growing and if you plant them close together (30 cm/1 ft apart) and leave them to their own devices apart from occasional tying-in, they will rapidly cover any blank surface or eyesore. You will end up with good thick growth that is the next best thing to a hedge as far as wildlife is concerned.

In a larger garden you may wish to provide extra supports for climbing plants. A trellis or archway of decorative foliage and fragrant flowers will make an interesting feature and could act as a division or windbreak.

The best material to use for constructing supports is rough poles which will look the most natural in the wild garden. They can be simply pushed into the soil, propped together and lashed at the top to make a sturdy wigwam which is not only ideal for wild climbers but is superb

for old fashioned sweet peas like *Lathyrus odoratus* 'Painted Lady' or for climbing french or runner beans.

Rustic poles are also ideal for larger structures such as dividing screens. However, there is no reason why you shouldn't have a more formal screen built from sawn timber. This could be stained with dark wood preservative so that it blends into the garden more naturally. To give extra support, wires can be stretched between the uprights. A simple archway can be constructed between two trellises if you are using them to divide the garden, or it could be used as a feature on its own. An archway can be developed into a marvellous wildlife habitat. If the climbing plants are grown in profusion, creating a

Colourful ground-cover *Selfheal and wild strawberries will spread rapidly beneath shrubs or small trees. They flower (and fruit) into autumn.*

colourful tangle, birds will probably nest there. In a really large garden, you could even extend the archway to make a pergola.

Choosing climbing plants

There are some very decorative wild climbers for covering frames, fences, or any unsightly objects that you want to lose quickly. Your framework provides the same basic support for these plants as a hedge would in the wild, and you can encourage all those climbing and trailing plants that grow in the hedgerow to grow through and over it.

Traveller's-joy is always the first choice as a climber for hedgerow situations. It is vigorous and will grow to a great height or cover a wide area if you train and tie in its long main stems. In spring it bursts into fresh green leaf, followed in July by small greenish flowers. But it really comes into its element in the autumn when its flowers are followed by marvellous bearded seed-heads that light up the hedgerows.

Hop is very ornamental and will twine clockwise round anything that is handy. If left to its own devices hop will send up many shoots but if you want to train it along a fence or wall for the maximum distance you can select one or two vigorous shoots and cut the others when they are young – they can be cooked and eaten like asparagus. It is the female plants that are most decorative – from summer to autumn they carry pale-green, cone-like flowers – so always ask for them when buying hop plants.

A mixed border *Juniper and holly provide an evergreen backdrop to this border. All the shrubs have colourful autumn berries. The perennials have long flowering seasons – they could also be interplanted with spring bulbs. The border is edged by a neat row of wild strawberries.*

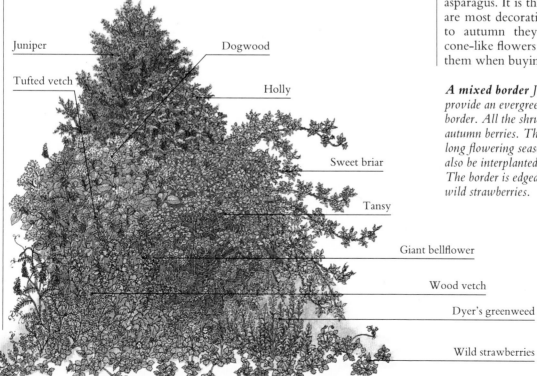

Juniper

Dogwood

Tufted vetch

Holly

Sweet briar

Tansy

Giant bellflower

Wood vetch

Dyer's greenweed

Wild strawberries

Honeysuckle is another favourite and again ideal for growing up the wigwam or over the archway – or grow it in amongst all the other climbers on the trellis. The creamy-red flowers open in summer and give out the strongest perfume after ripening by the sun, so that the scent is sweetest after dark. This would be a lovely plant to grow over a doorway or to train up a house wall so the perfume fills the bedrooms at night.

Another beautiful climbing plant for either a semi-shady or a shady situation is wood vetch. It is not a common wild flower, and I have never seen it in a garden, but it is well worth growing and should be better known. It will climb to at least 2 m (6 ft) and would look marvellous growing through shrubs or up the wigwam. Its flowers are larger than other vetches and are white with blue-purple veins.

Creating a 'woodland-edge' area

If you have the space, a woodland-edge habitat is the ideal place to grow semi-shady plants. Think of the woodland-edge as being part of a series of layers. The tall tree canopy at the heart of an established wood is represented by the larger forest trees like the oak. Beneath these is a lower layer of smaller trees such as silver birch, field maple and hawthorn. Then comes the shrubby layer which is the woodland-edge habitat. This layer is made up of small trees, which can be coppiced or trimmed to keep them to a reasonable size, and the smaller shrubs and climbers.

Many woodland wild flowers only grow on the edges of woods or in woodland glades where trees have been felled or coppiced and extra light is allowed in. Primrose and red campion are examples of plants that grow best in these lighter areas. Woodland plants that tolerate true shade will also grow well in a semi-shady situation, but many would not do well if exposed to full midday sun. All these flowers prefer the loose, undisturbed woodland floor to grow in.

A mixed border of shrubs and perennials mimics a woodland-edge on a very small scale. You can seed the area with a suitable flower and grass mix and, once the shrubs are established, encourage climbers and trailing plants such as wood vetch to scramble through them.

Coppicing in gardens

Very few gardeners exploit the possibilities of coppicing. This technique has been used for managing woodland for centuries: suitable trees are cut down to near ground level every ten to fifteen years and the poles used for tool handles, fencing or firewood. A coppiced area provides an ideal opportunity to grow many of the large forest trees that normally become too big for a garden. They can be cut down every few years to keep them at a manageable size, and allow sufficient light to reach the flowers beneath them. Such an area will be popular with wildlife, particularly birds, which will nest in the shrubby regrowth. As a bonus, the coppiced wood can be used around the garden for fencing or plant supports, or will come in handy for firewood.

Coppiced growth is often very attractive. The stems of willows and dogwood, for instance, are colourful in winter, and in spring the coppice will be a mass of fresh green buds and leaves. Coppiced trees can be incorporated into a woodland-edge area, used for screens and windbreaks, and also make natural supports for climbing plants. For information on which trees can be coppiced successfully, see the lists of trees on page 181.

The orchard garden

Fruit trees have been cultivated for hundreds of years. In large gardens they were often planted out of sight

A wild bed near trees This pink and white mixture of wild flowers and grasses includes willowherb, Himalayan balsam (a Victorian garden escape now naturalized), meadow crane's-bill, and the stately hogweed. It could be a first stop for the bees from the distant hives.

of the house, lined up in rows with military precision, but in cottage gardens they would be grouped conveniently near the house. Whether you grow a single fruit tree or plant a small orchard, make it a part of the wildflower garden. For example, it would be a natural extension of the meadow garden, or an attractive backdrop to the pond garden.

The most common fruit trees have all been derived from native trees – the plum from blackthorn crossed with cherry plum, sweet cherry from wild cherry, and pear from the naturalized wild pear. There are only three native fruit trees – crab apple, wild cherry and blackthorn. Gardeners have been 'improving' them since Roman times. The apple, for instance, has been in Britain since that time. It was developed from the northern crab apple crossed with the southern European sub-species and then with several Asian species. The Roman writer Pliny mentions twenty-two varieties of apple, and since that time something like 6,000 varieties have been developed.

The orchard will attract many unusual birds – the hawfinch, for instance, which is rarely seen in the garden, loves cherries and will crack the stones with its powerful beak.

An old fruit tree is the perfect support for climbing plants, especially traveller's-joy, hop, honeysuckle and white bryony. Dog rose growing under an old tree will often send up shoots many metres long to reach the light and rose flowers will appear tumbling from the highest branches of the tree. This has happened in my garden, which has several ancient apple trees. For year-round cover, you can grow ivy up an old apple tree that has ceased to fruit and it will eventually make excellent nesting-sites, provide flowers rich in nectar from autumn to winter for butterflies and bees, and produce its black fruits for the birds when other fruits have long since been stripped from the trees and shrubs.

If you have new and productive trees, allowing climbers into them is not recommended, but you can certainly plant the ground under the trees with a variety of hedgerow flowers. You will probably want to keep the grass short for the summer and autumn, so plant low-growing species that flower early. Grass-and-flower mixtures for hedgerow or semi-shady areas are available from wildflower seedsmen, or you could try a spring-flowering meadow mixture – in either case, it's simple to add more plants or bulbs for bolder splashes of colour. Wild daffodils look marvellous under trees, and bold patches of primroses should do well in the light shade.

Wild hedgerows

The mixed hedgerow is one of the most important wildlife habitats in the garden. Traditionally, hedges have been used in gardens as formal boundaries, usually neatly clipped and made up of a single species. These hedges can be valuable wildlife habitats, especially beech, holly and yew which keep their leaves all winter, providing nesting-sites for birds and shelter for insects and mammals. However, a mixed hedge provides

Climbing plants in hedgerows *Once the hedge is established, climbers can be added to grow through it. An attractive combination is traveller's-joy, with its cream flowers and seed-heads, scrambling over the darker hawthorn.*

the greatest range of food, looks more natural, and to my mind more attractive, for a wild garden. Even a short length of hedge, planted with a mixture of native trees, shrubs and climbers, will do more to attract a great range of wildlife into the garden than any other feature except a natural pond. A mixed-species hedge provides year-round interest with buds, catkins, new spring growth, flowers, autumn leaf colour, berries and hips. It will also provide a framework for many lovely climbing wild plants. The hedge can be kept uniformly trimmed, or individual trees can be allowed to grow to full height through it. There is no better windbreak than a deciduous hedge where the winter gales are filtered through a thick, leafless barrier.

Truly wild, mixed hedgerows are only practical in large gardens: they take up considerable space, and because their roots spread out as far as the hedge is tall they will impoverish the soil on either side.

Shrubs for single-species hedges Creating a hedge using one type of plant only will give a more formal boundary than the mixed hedgerow, but one that is still valuable for

Food from the wild garden

Shrubs with edible berries will make an interesting addition to your shrub layer. The birds will probably get most of them (which is the general idea) but there will certainly be some over for your own consumption. Bramble with its white or pink flowers and blackberries forms a good thicket. Wild raspberry (*Rubus idaeus*) is a native plant and is worth growing for its delicious fruit. Red currant (*Ribes rubrum*) and gooseberry (*Ribes uva-crispa*) are also wild plants – if you can't find the true wild species, garden varieties will do, but let them grow naturally without pruning. To complete the edible wild garden, use wild strawberries as a superb ground-cover.

A selection of wild fruits for eating, cooking or wine-making. Their sharp, distinctive flavours more than compensate for their small size.

Blackberries

Wild strawberries

Elderberries

Rosehips

Crab apples

Sloes

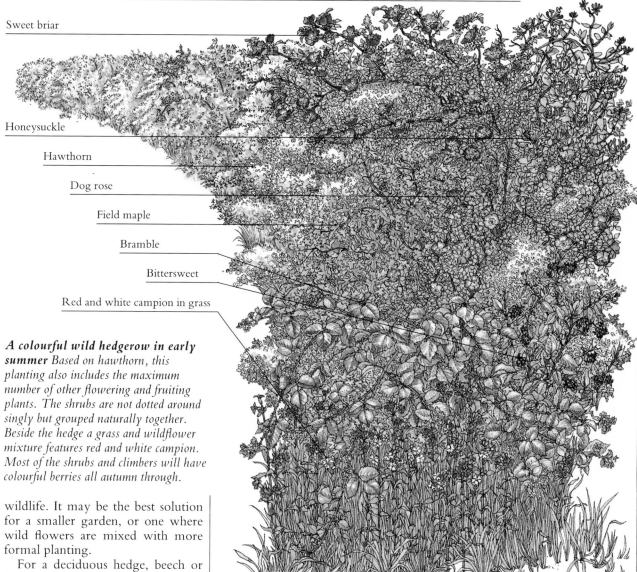

Sweet briar

Honeysuckle

Hawthorn

Dog rose

Field maple

Bramble

Bittersweet

Red and white campion in grass

A colourful wild hedgerow in early summer *Based on hawthorn, this planting also includes the maximum number of other flowering and fruiting plants. The shrubs are not dotted around singly but grouped naturally together. Beside the hedge a grass and wildflower mixture features red and white campion. Most of the shrubs and climbers will have colourful berries all autumn through.*

wildlife. It may be the best solution for a smaller garden, or one where wild flowers are mixed with more formal planting.

For a deciduous hedge, beech or hornbeam can be kept neatly clipped. Beech keeps its golden-brown leaves all winter and provides a sheltered home for birds. Hawthorn can also be kept tightly clipped, and will become very dense. Don't use blackthorn in this situation as it sends out suckers. Wild roses and some vigorous species roses (which grow wild in other parts of the world) can be used to make effective and colourful boundaries which are good for wildlife. They are very prickly, however, and not ideal for the main hedge. Roses are best mixed with other shrubs or used for a short length of hedge, perhaps for a division in the garden.

Yew makes a good evergreen hedge that does not grow too fast and needs clipping just once a year, in August. It is good for birds, who nest in it and eat the red berries. The leaves are poisonous to animals, however, especially when dried, and the berries are very poisonous to humans, so

children should be warned against them. Holly is very nasty to clip, so it is better used in a mixed hedge or as a specimen tree.

Shrubs for mixed hedges Hawthorn makes a good basis for any hedge. It forms a dense mass, produces lovely flowers and berries, and is also excellent for wildlife. I would suggest up to half the saplings in a mixed hedge should be hawthorn (you may find young hawthorns for hedging plants described as 'quickthorns' or 'quicks' in nurserymen's catalogues). Field maple is very easy to establish, and attractive too, with rich autumn colour, and could make up to twenty per cent of the hedge. Blackthorn has lovely white spring flowers, a month earlier than hawthorn, and sloes in autumn. Hazel and goat willow can be used generously as both are decorative as well as being good for

wildlife. In spring the goat willow in my garden is alive with honey bees gathering pollen.

There are many other interesting shrubs and small trees that you might include. For instance, the wayfaring-tree, or spindle, with its brilliant pink seedpods and bright autumn leaves. Buckthorn (often called purging buckthorn) is the food plant of the beautiful brimstone butterfly and should always be included. To grow a holly tree with berries, you need to plant a male (for fertilization) as well as the berry-producing female.

There is no reason why you shouldn't include some larger trees that can be kept bushy by regular cutting. The oak tree supports more wildlife than any other, so a coppiced oak is worth having. Ash, hornbeam and beech could all be introduced. If you have the space, why not allow the occasional tree to grow up through the hedge – a small one such as hawthorn or the wayfaring-tree would be suitable. This will look more natural, and also make a feature. If you plan to include specimen trees in a new hedge, buy 1–1.2 m (3–4 ft) saplings that have already been trained as standard trees, with a straight stem.

Once the hedge is established, trailing and climbing plants can be introduced. Bittersweet, bramble, hedge bindweed, honeysuckle, hop, traveller's-joy and wood vetch will all look their best rambling in or along the hedgerow just as they do in the wild.

Establishing the hedge

In order to keep the weeds down and retain moisture for the first few years after planting, mulch the ground well with plenty of organic material such as old straw, half-rotted hay, grass mowings or leaf-mould. Alternative mulches are old carpet, underfelt or roofing felt.

Trim the hedge well for the first year or two to make it bushy and thick at the base. If you cut a hedging plant back it will grow more vigorously, shooting from the base of the stem and putting more energy into root production. Always allow the hedge to establish for a few years before planting your climbers or they will tend to smother the young hedging plants.

Hedgerow wild flowers

Once your hedgerow is established and competition from weeds and grasses is no longer a threat to the shrubs, you can start to plant or sow some of the huge range of wild flowers that will thrive in the half-day shade it casts.

Grasses will probably arrive naturally, but if not, a mixture of grasses for shady sites could be sown. These grasses will not be too vigorous and will allow wild flowers to grow amongst them. Mixtures of grasses and wild flowers are also available, and will get the area off to a good start. Be sure to include garlic mustard – a major food plant for the caterpillars of the orange-tip and green-veined white butterflies, and an attractive foliage plant with roots that make an excellent substitute for horse-radish. More wild flowers can either be raised from seed and planted out when large enough to handle or bought in as small plants from specialist nurseries.

If you aim to make your hedge-bottom colourful for as long a season as possible, you will also create a habitat valuable to a wide range of wildlife. There are many lovely wild flowers that will thrive in the semi-shade of the hedge-bottom.

To start at the beginning of the season in February/March, wild daffodils will provide some cheering colour when little else is around. Primroses too flower very early in the year – and some of mine even flower in the autumn. Cowslips will grow in semi-shade as well as full sun, but they do need a moisture-retentive soil. Greater stitchwort is one of my

A springtime hedgerow mixture planted on a moisture-retentive soil features white dead-nettle, common dog-violet and water avens.

Tall-growing hedgerow flowers In summer only the most vigorous plants can compete with grasses: hedge woundwort and common poppy grow through white bryony.

favourite spring flowers, with its bright, grass-like foliage and brilliant white, star-like flowers. Herb-robert is another good plant, with very attractive foliage from spring to autumn and pink flowers for many months in the summer.

Flowers for May include red campion and bush vetch. Hedgerow and wood crane's-bill, wood avens, perforate St John's-wort, selfheal and hedge-bedstraw all begin flowering in June. By July yarrow, betony, common knapweed, meadowsweet (if there is moisture), devil's-bit scabious, goldenrod, hedge woundwort, tansy, tufted vetch and nettle-leaved bellflower are in bloom, and the summer flowers will continue to give colour until early autumn.

This hedgerow area only needs scything once a year at most, in late winter/early spring before the bulbs come up. Leave all the dead vegetation you have cut down in a pile out of sight to be colonized by wood mice, hedgehogs and maybe even grass snakes, which are quite harmless and really beautiful creatures.

Feature plants for semi-shady sites

Many of our most beautiful and well-loved flowers, such as primroses and violets,
thrive in the partial shade of the woodland edge or hedgerow bottom, areas that
are easily re-created in the garden beneath shrubs, trellises or small trees.

Bugle
Ajuga reptans

Bugle does not perhaps live up to its military-sounding name, but it is, nevertheless, very attractive and a superb ground-cover plant. The foliage is very decorative being dark green with a purplish hue, and the flowers, although normally purplish-blue, are also found in pink, pale blue and sometimes white forms.

It is a very accommodating plant as it will grow vigorously in full sun but will also tolerate quite dense shade. Grow it in the shade of taller flowers in the island bed or border, or use it as a decorative ground-cover on any soil that retains moisture. It would also thrive in a damp, boggy area near the pond, or in a hedgerow or shady woodland area.

Season: April–November **Height:** 10–15 cm (4–6 in)
Cultivation: Bugle is a perennial plant which spreads by runners. It is very easy to propagate. Simply divide the runners and plant out in autumn or spring, spaced 60 cm (2 ft) apart, as single plants spread rapidly. Sow seed in autumn or spring and cover only lightly with soil. Germination is likely to be slow and erratic. Add plenty of moisture-retaining compost or leaf-mould to the soil as this will give the plant the fertility it enjoys.
Other sites: Sun; shade; water garden.

Lords-and-ladies
Arum maculatum

This unusual and decorative plant provides eye-catching decoration from early spring, when the glossy green sheath emerges, until the bright orange berries are finally eaten by the birds in late summer or autumn. Lords-and-ladies is best grown in a hedgerow or the dense shade of a woodland garden, although it will also grow in sun. It does not like a very dry soil and requires good fertility.

This plant has always been of great fascination, especially to children. Its phallic appearance has given rise to a host of country names, ranging from 'Adam and Eve', 'ram's horn' and 'red hot poker' to 'Kitty-come-down-the-lane-jump-up-and-kiss-me!' It is no wonder the plant was considered an aphrodisiac!

Be careful, though, as lords-and-ladies is poisonous to humans. The orange berries are especially dangerous, and even the tuber is poisonous until thoroughly cooked.
Season: April–August **Height:** 30–50 cm (12–20 in)
Cultivation: Lords-and-ladies is a perennial plant growing from a short tuber which lasts for a single season. A separate tuber then develops. When ripe, the orange berries should be sown where they are to flower and covered lightly in soil. Germination should occur in spring.
Other sites: Sun; shade.

Betony
Betonica officinalis

Betony is a dense and bushy plant, producing many flowering stems covered in purple-red blooms, which are very colourful and attractive to bees. In the wild, betony is becoming quite scarce and indeed is extinct in many of its former habitats. This is rather strange as the plant seems so vigorous in the garden, growing well in light and heavy soil, and in grassland. Betony is found growing in open woodland and hedgebanks, and also in grassland and on open cliff heaths with such plants as lady's bedstraw, oxeye daisy, dyer's greenweed, burnet rose and dropwort. For centuries betony has been grown in the garden and it is very much a cottage garden plant. In the wildflower garden it looks very colourful and establishes well in the mixed bed or in grassland. It is a very accommodating plant, and will tolerate most soils; in my garden it thrives on heavy clay. It will also put up with all but the deepest shade, so is an excellent flower for the hedgerow and woodland garden. It is often added to flowering meadow seed mixtures but does not establish particularly well, except on lighter soils.

Betony used to be held in tremendously high esteem as a medicinal herb by the ancient Greeks and Romans. Sadly, however, the plant has since been proved to be of very little medicinal value!

Season: June–August **Height:** 10–60 cm (4 in–2 ft)

Cultivation: Betony is a perennial plant that grows readily from seed which it produces in abundance. Sow the seed in late summer or spring where it is to flower and cover very lightly with soil; or sow seed in trays and prick out the seedlings into small pots when they are large enough to handle.

Other sites: Sun; shade.

Hedge bindweed
Calystegia sepium

This lovely plant is our largest wild flower and the size and whiteness of these blooms make an eye-catching sight along hedgerows. Before the flowers open the buds are hidden by two green bracts and it looks as if there are no flowers growing at all. Then the trumpet-shaped flowers open, lasting all summer and well into the autumn.

It must be admitted that hedge bindweed is a rampant plant and it is best not to introduce it into a small garden unless you are prepared to control it. But it can easily be dug up if it starts to take over the garden. Its speedy growth makes hedge bindweed the ideal plant for an area that you want covered quickly, such as an old tree stump. But I would not advise growing it in a hedge unless you don't mind the hedge being taken over. The stems will climb in an anticlockwise direction so don't try to wind them the other way!

Season: July–October

Height: to 3 m (10 ft)

Cultivation: Hedge bindweed is a perennial climber that produces little or no seed. The plant is easily reproduced by the stolons (short shoots above ground that root at the tip) produced at the base of the stem. Simply peg the stolons to the soil in autumn or spring and they will produce roots.

Other sites: Sun.

Nettle-leaved bellflower
Campanula trachelium

In the wild, nettle-leaved bellflower is found growing in shady hedgerows and woodlands. Before the plant comes into flower it grows amongst the other greenery completely unnoticed, only to surprise you in July or August when the beautiful, large purply-blue flowers shine out from the deep shadows. In the garden, plant a few bellflowers in a shady spot – by a fence or garden wall or in a hedgebank – where, if allowed to self-seed, they will form a colony, providing a welcome splash of colour in late summer after most of the other plants have finished flowering. The plants will survive in a dry soil but they do need reasonable fertility.

Although it is very much at home in deep shade, nettle-leaved bellflower also thrives in the sun. However, the flowers will lose their intensity of colour in full sun.

Season: July–September   **Height:** 50–100 cm (2–3 ft)

Cultivation: Nettle-leaved bell-flower is a perennial plant which produces a lot of seed. Collect the seed in late summer by cutting off a stem and tipping it upside-down into a container, where the tiny brown seed will fall from its capsule. Sow seed in early autumn in fertile soil, either where it is to flower, or in trays; do not cover with soil. Seedlings will normally appear the following spring.

Other sites: Sun; shade.

Traveller's-joy
Clematis vitalba

Sometimes called old man's beard, traveller's-joy is one of the most familiar sights of an autumn hedgerow. The white 'beard', which is attached to the seeds, looks most decorative, and seems to light up the hedgerows in the soft autumn sun. It normally grows in great abundance on chalky soil and will often completely smother a length of hedgerow. The small, greenish-white flowers of summer are also very pretty, although less spectacular than the bearded seed-heads.

Traveller's-joy is a vigorous plant that will quickly form a dense screen if grown on a wooden trellis or, if you have space for a wild hedge, traveller's-joy grown with greater bindweed and hop can look most decorative. It is best, however, not to grow it in a well-clipped garden hedge, as its twining stems may well strangle the hedging shrubs.

Season: July–December

Height: to 30 m (100 ft)

Cultivation: Traveller's-joy is a climbing plant that can be propagated either from seed, cuttings or layering. Collect seed in November when it is easily pulled off the seed-head. It is very long-lived so it may be kept for several years. Sow seed in autumn and cover only lightly with soil. Germination is erratic but should normally take place in spring. Half-ripe cuttings can be taken from May to July and should root in about six weeks. Layering can be tried in winter by pegging down a woody stem under the soil; it should root by the spring.

Other sites: Sun.

Wild strawberry
Fragaria vesca

Snowdrop
Galanthus nivalis

Wild strawberry makes a marvellous ground-cover plant that spreads quickly by means of runners. Its dainty white flowers stand out amongst the bright green, shiny leaves which, when dry, have the fragrance of musk. This plant should have a place in every garden and will grow in semi-shade or in full sun. It enjoys good fertility and a soil that does not dry out in summer. To be able to gather the tiny, delicious fruits all through the summer is a terrific bonus. They have a marvellous flavour preferred by many to the cultivated strawberry of North America. Eaten fresh with cream, wild strawberries have no equal. The fruit also makes a delicious jam.

Wild strawberry is found in woods and hedgerows and is especially abundant on chalky soils. It also grows well on mountainsides, probably more abundantly on the continent of Europe, and especially in Sweden.

Wild strawberry has been used as a medicinal plant. The root acts as a bitter tonic and diuretic, and the dried leaves can be used to make a tea substitute. The fruit, too, has always been considered to be of great medicinal value, being good for anaemia, bad nerves and stomach disorders, so, in case you needed any more excuses for eating more strawberries, there are ample!

Season: April–September (flowers & fruit)
Height: 5–30 cm (2 in–1 ft)
Cultivation: Wild strawberry is a perennial plant that spreads rapidly by means of runners. The young plants can be transplanted in autumn or spring. Seed is also produced on the outside of the fruit. To collect the seed, leave the fruit in the sun to dry and then simply rub the seeds off the shrivelled fruits. Sow seed where it is to grow on the surface of the soil in spring. It should germinate within a few weeks.
Other sites: Sun.

Snowdrops are one of the very first spring flowers to appear, and are often seen pushing through the snow in February. The sight of their drooping, pure white blooms carpeting the ground, and their heads nodding in a cold breeze, are signs that the life of the new year is starting again. Only the little yellow winter aconite appears slightly earlier than the snowdrop but once the bees have worked this flower, they turn to the snowdrop for early nectar and pollen.

Snowdrops are flowers everyone wants to have in their gardens, but sadly they are very particular about where they grow. In my garden snowdrops grow everywhere, spreading from year to year. I have given away dozens of plants, and although in many gardens they survive, they don't spread at all. I don't know their secret but they certainly require rich soil that does not become too dry. Snowdrops establish well in short grass, and are the ideal flowers for the spring lawn as, by the time the lawn is mown in June, the leaves have died down. They will tolerate quite deep shade, however, and there is no lovelier sight than a leaf-strewn woodland floor carpeted with snowdrops. For a similar effect in your garden, plant snowdrops with winter aconites beneath the spreading branches of a tree, where the soil is rich in leaf-mould, and you will have a beautiful ground-cover display.

The flowers are worth inspecting closely, as they are so perfectly constructed. The outer petals are purest white but the inner petals are tipped with green.

Season: January–March   **Height:** 15–25 cm (6–10 in)
Cultivation: Snowdrops are perennial bulb-forming plants. Bulbs can be divided after flowering and planted out. Or sow seeds in autumn in a pot of general-purpose potting compost. The plants will flower from seed in the third or fourth season. Sowing seed outside is unwise as you may weed the snowdrops out before they become recognizable.
Other sites: Sun; shade.

Hedgerow crane's-bill
Geranium pyrenaicum

Hedgerow crane's-bill, or mountain crane's-bill as it is sometimes called, is one of many wild crane's-bills that brighten our hedgebanks and roadsides. It is probably not a true native plant but is so widely established that it can be considered as one.

Although the bright purple-pink flowers are quite small, they open in such profusion that this is a really spectacular plant. Like all crane's-bills it seeds profusely and will soon establish itself in a clump. This is the way to grow this plant to obtain its full impact. It will grow over 60 cm (2 ft) high but the stems are so thin that it will flop if not grown in a group or amongst other plants and grasses.

The beak-like seed cases spring open when ripe to project the seed several feet from the plant. Allow hedgerow crane's-bill to seed around the place and it will soon become apparent which area and association of plants suits it best. The leaves are so distinctive that it is easy to weed out if it goes out of bounds.

Scatter the seed along a hedge bottom and see what a colourful area this suddenly becomes. The jewel-like flowers are set off beautifully by a background of dark foliage and grass. Hedgerow crane's-bill also looks good on a grassy bank. Scatter some seed when the grass is cut short in the autumn, and by early summer the bank will be a blaze of colour. After flowering, hedgerow crane's-bill can be cut down and often flowers will appear again in late summer only a few inches off the ground. There is no better flower for quickly covering a dull area.

Season: June–August **Height:** 30–90 cm (1–3 ft)
Cultivation: Hedgerow crane's-bill is a perennial plant. Seed should be sown in autumn or spring where the plant is to grow. Remember that one plant in cultivated soil can grow 60 cm (2 ft) across and up to 1 m (3 ft) high. It seems to grow in almost any soil, including those that are quite acid.
Other sites: Sun.

Herb-robert
Geranium robertianum

Herb-robert is a pretty plant that provides interest and colour from early spring until late autumn. The fresh new leaves form a delicate ground cover in woodland, hedgerow or wasteland in early spring. In the garden, this adaptability makes it an excellent plant for almost any site including rock and seaside gardens. The bright flowers first appear in late spring and continue intermittently until autumn fades into winter. Then the leaves, touched with a glow of crimson, brighten the late autumn days. Herb-robert is a native of many faraway lands, including Brazil. Its other country name is stinking crane's-bill, because of its strange (but not unpleasant) scent.

Herb-robert combines well with most plants but looks especially good when taller plants, such as blue columbine, are encouraged to grow through a carpet of its filigree foliage. It is a most useful flower for growing on waste ground and heaps of brick rubble, where it will quickly provide decorative ground cover.

Season: April–September **Height:** 10–40 cm (4–16 in)
Cultivation: Sow the seed in spring or late summer where you want the plants to grow. It will grow especially well in acid soils. The seed germinates very readily. Herb-robert is an annual, but it self-seeds profusely and should be allowed to do so as the seedlings are so delicate that they won't smother other plants, and can be weeded out if necessary.
Other sites: Sun; shade; rock garden; seaside garden.

Perforate St John's-wort
Hypericum perforatum

Yellow archangel
Lamiastrum galeobdolon

There are eight or nine different St John's-worts growing in Britain and all have similar yellow flowers. Perforate St John's-wort is the most widespread of all the tribe and the one that is most adaptable to different soils and conditions. It is also a colourful flower that brightens fields, hedgerows and woodland rides in summer and early autumn.

A simple way of identifying this species is to hold the leaves up to the light to see the tiny pin-prick perforations (hence the Latin name). These are in fact oil glands that give the whole plant a strong aroma in addition to the sweet lemon scent of the flowers.

St John's-wort has been used medicinally throughout history and is still used to this day. The old herbals list dozens of uses including many 'pleasant absurdities'! As a homoeopathic tincture it is most effective in healing cuts and grazes. When the flowers are boiled with alum a good yellow dye is produced for dying wool.

The plant was associated with the vigil of St John the Baptist and the midsummer solstice, and was also used to keep away evil spirits.

Season: June–September **Height:** 30–90 cm (1–3 ft)
Cultivation: Perforate St John's-wort is a perennial plant. There is little problem growing it from seed, which can either be sown direct into cultivated soil or sown in a seed tray and pricked out when large enough. It is a good constituent of wildflower grass mixtures and suitable for establishing in meadows. It will tolerate most soils provided they are free-draining.
Other sites: Sun.

The name 'yellow archangel' conjures up attractive images even before the flowers are seen. In spring it is an insignificant, rather sprawling plant sending out runners with nettle-like leaves. Then suddenly the woods and hedgerows are lighted up with the bright golden flowers that seem to glow in the quiet shade. I love all the dead-nettle family and this is one of my favourites.

There are many areas in the garden – in the shade of hedges, fences or overhanging trees – where yellow archangel can provide the ideal ground cover with its fresh green leaves. It will tolerate deep shade, though it is happiest with more light, and its loose habit allows other plants to grow up through it.

Yellow archangel has some nice country names, amongst them weasel's snout, stingy wingles, and dumb nettle, but the sound of the Latin name brings on instant indigestion! Like all the dead-nettles, yellow archangel is a medicinal plant of some value, and Culpeper states that it also makes the heart merry, drives away melancholy, and quickens the spirits.

Season: May–June **Height:** 20–60 cm (8 in–2 ft)
Cultivation: Yellow archangel is a perennial plant. Sow seed in early autumn where it is to flower or divide plants in early spring. It likes a reasonably rich soil, with leaf mould added if possible. It will tolerate some acidity but does not like dry soil.
Other sites: Shade.

White dead-nettle
Lamium album

This is another beautiful dead-nettle in my view, but one that the gardener takes a great deal of trouble to eradicate on account of its vigorous creeping roots. And in a cultivated soil it does spread! Used in the right situation, however, this is a really lovely plant and very common as well: no one growing white dead-nettle could be accused of being a plant snob. Its great attraction is the whorls of white flowers that appear over a very long season.

Do not, of course, plant it in the herbaceous border, but in the hedgebank or any odd corner where you want some ground cover and/or good food for bees for up to six months of the year. I let it grow in a tightly packed 'wild' island bed: with competition from other plants it doesn't get out of control and it would not be too difficult to pull out if it should run riot.

It has the same medicinal properties as yellow archangel (see p. 67), and the young leaves are eaten as a pot herb by the French (although there can be nothing to beat the young leaves of the stinging nettle).

Season: May–December **Height:** 20–60 cm (8–24 in)

Cultivation: White dead-nettle is a perennial that will grow from seed (sow where it is to flower in spring and barely cover with soil), but it is not worth the trouble if you have the plant, as it divides up so easily. It will grow in moist or dry soil providing it is reasonably fertile, but it is difficult to control in cultivated soil.

Other sites: None: white dead-nettle does best in full sun.

Honeysuckle
Lonicera periclymenum

Honeysuckle, or woodbine, is probably one of our best known and best loved climbing plants. Its rich fragrance fills the air in the evening or after a shower of rain. It has inspired poets from Chaucer to Wordsworth and most of them, including Shakespeare, called this plant woodbin*d*, and with good reason. In the spring it will gently spiral up a tree – the poet Cowper claimed honeysuckle

. . . does a mischief while she lends a grace,
Slackening its growth by such a strict embrace . . .

but in fact it will not do any harm. This most fragrant of all flowers should be planted in the hedgerow if you have one, to climb through whatever is there, or against a garden fence, where it will need some support. It will flourish in the most unpromising sites – it tolerates poor, dry and acid soils and also deep shade. Besides the flowers, honeysuckle is in leaf from February through to late autumn when it produces red berries.

It is said that goats go out of their way to eat the young shoots, so be warned! The flowers can be used to make perfume and the whole plant has medicinal uses.

Season: June–September

Height: to 6 m (20 ft)

Cultivation: Honeysuckle is a perennial climber. Plants can be obtained from nurseries, but make sure you get the wild species. Seed should be sown in autumn, but it may take a long time to germinate. A good alternative is to take cuttings of non-flowering shoots in summer and root them in a cuttings compost. Honeysuckle will grow in quite poor, dry soil, and does well in acid conditions.

Other sites: Shade.

Sweet cicely
Myrrhis odorata

The large white flowers of sweet cicely decorate upland roadsides in great profusion during May and June. It is related to cow parsley, but its larger, denser flower-head and fern-like leaves make it the more attractive garden plant. The seeds are also of interest, being very large and deep, shiny, mahogany brown when ripe. They are used as a spice in Germany, and in the north of England they used to be made into polish for oak floors and furniture.

The whole plant is aromatic, with a strong scent of aniseed. The root has the strongest flavour and was taken in various forms to ward off plague or given as a tonic to teenage girls. As the boiled root was also meant to increase the lust of old people it should perhaps be taken with caution! The leaf is a salad herb and is also often cooked with sour fruit, such as rhubarb, to take away the tartness.

Sweet cicely is often thought to have escaped from cultivation after having been introduced as a pot herb from the continent long ago. It is certainly curious that whilst it is found all over the continent of Europe, from the Pyrenees to the Caucasus, in Britain it only grows wild in northern England and Scotland. The flowers are very attractive to bees.

Season: May–June **Height:** 60–90 cm (2–3 ft)
Cultivation: Sweet cicely is a perennial plant that grows easily from seed so long as it is sown where you want the plant to grow. Sow in autumn: the seeds need the winter cold and frost to germinate. Most soils are suitable, including those that are slightly acid, provided they are not too sandy. If any seedlings have to be transplanted, do this as soon as possible, before they have put down their long tap roots. You can divide mature plants in early spring.
Other sites: Sun.

Wild daffodil
Narcissus pseudonarcissus

Everyone knows the daffodil but few people have seen the wild one growing and still fewer in the profusion that Wordsworth describes in his famous soliloquy:

> *Ten thousand saw I at a glance,*
> *Tossing their heads in sprightly dance.*

I suppose the daffodil, or Lent lily, is the epitome of spring and the wonderful carpet of gold brightens the whole garden, not to mention our own spirits after a long winter. The true wild daffodil is single and a little paler than most garden varieties but is no less beautiful and welcoming for that. An old country custom was for children to gather the flowers in bunches and carry them on sticks into town singing 'Daffy-down-dilly is coming to town'.

In the wild daffodils grow in woods and thickets and also in moist meadows. In the garden they naturalize well in grass, which should be allowed to grow up until the daffodils have finished flowering. There is nothing more unnatural than daffodils in short mown grass – and when they are over the drab foliage looks awful. Daffodils look their best against a dark background, and will add a welcome splash of colour in early spring to a shady area along a hedge or fence, or under trees.

Season: March–April **Height:** 20–25 cm (8–10 in)
Cultivation: Specialist wildflower nurseries and a few bulb suppliers sell wild daffodil bulbs. Plant them 6 cm (3 in) deep in August if possible, and in any case not later than September. They will grow in most soils providing plenty of moisture is available during the spring months (this means that very light soils, especially in shady areas, may be unsuitable).
Other sites: Sun; shade.

Solomon's-seal
Polygonatum multiflorum

Solomon's-seal is a rare and elegant woodland plant. It is tall and striking, with decorative, arching stems from which hang white waxy flowers, tipped with green. The flowers are sweet smelling. The seed vessels are black berries but only a few ever seem to develop and I have never been able to collect seed.

This is a beautiful plant that looks best grown in drifts against a fairly bare woodland floor, with no other flowers or foliage to detract from it; it will lose its charm in a more cluttered garden setting.

King Solomon was supposed to have set his seal on the plant; when the roots are cut they are said to resemble Hebrew characters. The name also refers to the plant's healing properties: it is used to seal wounds.

Season: May–June   **Height:** 30–80 cm (1–2½ ft)

Cultivation: Solomon's-seal is a perennial herb with a thick creeping rootstock. It may be grown from seed sown when fresh where it is to flower, or the rootstock can be divided in autumn or spring. Soil should be light, if possible, to encourage the plant to spread. Plants can be obtained from specialist nurseries.

Other sites: Shade.

Primrose
Primula vulgaris

Primrose has suffered for its popularity. The gathering of bunches of sweet primrose flowers, or digging up plants to take home for the garden, must now be pleasures of the past. Many of its former habitats have been destroyed. Woodlands have been cleared, ditches have been filled in and hedgerows bulldozed out. Recent protective legislation (making it illegal, for instance, to dig up any wild plant) is beginning to have an effect, however, and primroses are now starting to re-establish a little. Every parish can help this process by making sure that the places where primroses grow are not mown short until they have seeded (at the end of June).

Primrose flowers are in fact of two different kinds, although only the closest inspection will reveal the differences. They are designed to be cross-pollinated by night-flying insects. On a dark night moths, for instance, have no trouble finding the mass of pale flowers on a bed of green leaves. The plants will interbreed with any other primulas in the garden, producing coloured forms—white, pink or mauve flowers are quite common.

Primroses look their best in a woodland setting, and do well in quite heavy shade. Often in a really sheltered spot flowers will open in February. Nothing is guaranteed to cheer our spirits more in the drab days of winter.

Season: March–June   **Height:** 8–15 cm (3–6 in)

Cultivation: Primrose is a perennial plant that is easily grown from seed, providing a few rules are followed. Sow fresh seed (before it is completely brown and dry), into soil or a seed tray and it will often germinate in a few weeks. Ripe, or dried, seed should be sown in autumn or early winter either where it is to flower or in a seed tray. Seeds should be pressed into the soil rather than covered. Trays should be left outside over winter in a shady spot and covered with glass. Germination will occur in spring. Primroses like a soil that does not dry out.

Other sites: Sun; shade.

Lesser celandine
Ranunculus ficaria

Lesser celandine might well be a prized garden flower if it were not so rampant in certain conditions. One of our earliest and most colourful spring flowers, with glossy dark green foliage, its brilliant yellow flowers are a welcome sight at a time of year when there is not much colour around. It will grow well (sometimes too well) in cultivated soil and also in grass. When the flowers are over and it has set its seed, grasses and flowers overtake it leaving the little tuber in the soil to store up energy for the next season. An alternative site is among the roots of a deciduous tree, which will be bare of leaves at the time the celandine is in flower. In a cultivated soil without competition it is very invasive and is difficult to eradicate once established.

Lesser celandine does need plenty of moisture early in the year; in fact it will thrive in very wet soils. Lesser celandine should not be confused with greater celandine which also has yellow flowers but is completely different in all other respects: they are not even related. The plant root used to be hung in the cow byre as the tubers are shaped like cows' teats and the flowers are the colour of rich butter. Its medicinal use is indicated by the plant's other common name – pilewort. Other, more pleasant, names include butter-and-cheese and golden guineas.

I have a particular fondness for this plant as it grows down the damp inside edges of some of my polythene propagating tunnels. In this shelter it flowers in February and makes a magnificent sight!

Season: March–May **Height:** 8–20 cm (3–8 in)

Cultivation: Lesser celandine is a perennial that requires plenty of moisture in early spring and likes a neutral soil. It can be grown from seed but it is easy to split up the small tubers and plant them into grass over the summer or early autumn. Grassy areas planted with lesser celandines can be mown once the flowers are over.

Other sites: Sun; shade.

Sweet briar
Rosa rubiginosa (syn. R. eglanteria)

Without question the loveliest of our wild roses and suitable for the smallest garden. Sweet briar flowers only once, in June/July, but what a sight that is. Red hips are produced in the autumn which stay until the birds descend on them. The great bonus though is the scent of the leaves. After a shower of rain they have an unforgettable perfume, just like fresh apples.

This rose, Shakespeare's eglantine, can be planted in a row to make an impenetrable hedge ten feet high, and also looks good in a mixed hedgerow with other shrubs, growing through trees or simply forming a natural bush on its own.

Season: June–July

Height: 1–3 m (3–10 ft)

Cultivation: Sweet briar is a perennial shrub. Seed can take a year or two to germinate. Sow seed from the hips in autumn and lightly cover with soil. You can buy plants from specialist nurseries. These can be planted at any time if they have been grown in containers; bare-rooted plants are only available for planting in spring. In either case, dig in some manure or garden compost before planting, and water well for the first few weeks.

Other sites: Sun.

Red campion
Silene dioica

Red campion comes into flower at the end of the bluebell season and goes on flowering through June and into July. There is no more stunning combination of flowers than a sheet of bluebells in a wood with a line of brilliant pinky-red campion flowering along the woodland edge, often in combination with the pure white of greater stitchwort. It is these simple combinations of colour in nature and, most important, their proportions and scale, that teach us just how to use wild flowers in the garden. The blue is the background and the red and white the jewels of colour against it, while the wonderful changing light of the woodland brings it all to life.

Often when a dense wood is coppiced and light allowed in, red campion appears in huge scarlet sheets as if by magic. Within a year or two, few flowers are to be seen as the shade returns. Red campion does well out of woodland too and looks fine in a meadow.

The colour of the flowers varies considerably through all the shades of pink to nearly white, and the plant interbreeds readily with white campion.

Season: April–July
Height: 30 cm–1 m (1–3 ft)
Cultivation: Red campion is a perennial plant and grows easily from seed sown in spring or early autumn where you want the plants to grow. It prefers a well-drained but fertile soil. It will not grow well in a heavy, wet clay soil. It naturalizes in grass if the soil is not too dry.
Other sites: Sun; shade.

Bittersweet
Solanum dulcamara

Bittersweet, or woody nightshade, is not deadly nightshade as many people imagine. Deadly nightshade looks quite different, has very large leaves and large black berries, and is a rare plant anyway. Bittersweet is poisonous, although not in any way comparable to deadly nightshade. It has been used as a medicine: however, home treatment with the plant should not be undertaken, and of course it should not be eaten! Bittersweet is of the same family as the potato, tomato and sweet pepper, and its roots smell like potato. These roots are said to be bitter on a first chewing and later sweet, thus the plant's name.

Bittersweet is a common plant of Europe and North America, growing in hedgerows and on damp ground beside ponds and ditches. In the garden it is most useful and decorative in the hedgerow where its long arching stems will ramp through the foliage and grow several feet high showing off the tiny, exotic flowers and later the glowing berries that start green then turn orange, and finally scarlet.

Season: June–September (flowers); August through autumn (berries)
Height: to 2 m (6 ft)
Cultivation: Bittersweet is a woody perennial that is best planted in a rich, moist, neutral soil. Sow the ripe berries 1 cm ($\frac{1}{2}$ in) deep in a tray full of seed compost and leave it in a shady place with a covering glass to keep the compost moist. The seed will require at least one winter outside, and maybe two, before it germinates.
Other sites: Sun; shade.

Greater stitchwort

Stellaria holostea

Greater stitchwort, or satin flower as it is sometimes known, is truly a star-like flower that appears in woods and hedgerows in April. Its pure white flowers shine out of the grass and dark woodland edges with an intensity that is not equalled by many other flowers. Greater stitchwort is very common but quite exquisite and I would bring it into any garden. Planted with bluebells and red campions, you will have a perfect colour combination. Wherever you have a hedge, fence, or shady bank, this flower will make a beautiful sprawling ground-cover, and it will enliven any area of shady grass. As its stems are very weak, it will scramble all over the grasses, using them for support. Before it flowers, its straggling stems are hardly distinguishable from the surrounding grass. Once it has finished flowering (or after shedding seed, if this is required), the grass can be cut quite short without any harm coming to the plant.

Lesser stitchwort is a similar but much smaller plant (see page 168). In the wild it is found on soils of a more acid nature, and looks beautiful scrambling amongst the leaves of other plants.

Greater stitchwort was once thought to cure 'stitches' or pains in the side. Taken with mashed acorns and wine, this was considered a standard remedy!

Season: April–June **Height:** 15–60 cm (6 in–2 ft)
Cultivation: Greater stitchwort is a perennial plant that grows readily from seed. The seed is reasonably large and can be sown in spring or early autumn where it is to flower. Cover only very lightly with soil. Seed can also be sown in a seed tray for pricking out and potting up individually. Plant out during spring or autumn. Stitchwort prefers some moisture and a reasonably fertile, not too alkaline soil.
Other sites: Sun.

Devil's-bit scabious

Succisa pratensis

A strange and not very attractive name for one of the loveliest meadow flowers. It derives from a story of how the Devil, out of envy for the many virtues of the plant, bit off the root to stop it growing. The plant survived with a root that certainly appears to have been bitten through, but which sends out lateral roots to compensate! We must be grateful that the Devil was unsuccessful in eradicating this decorative flower. There is no other plant that will attract the late summer butterflies into the garden in such profusion. I counted over forty butterflies last summer on my small patch of scabious – tortoiseshells, commas and red admirals – as well as numerous bees. I know also, to my cost when trying to produce seed, that it attracts the seed-eating birds like a magnet! It is also an important caterpillar food plant.

All the scabiouses have a place in the wildflower garden, but this one is top of the list. It is true that for some situations it grows rather tall, but it is the most adaptable, growing well in heavy or light soils; its dense, bushy shape makes it a great weed suppressor and ground-cover in cultivated soil; and it also naturalizes well in grass.

Season: July–September **Height:** 60–110 cm (2–4 ft)
Cultivation: Devil's-bit scabious may be grown from seed which should be sown in spring or autumn where it is to flower, or in a seed tray for pricking out. Cover only very lightly with soil. Germination can be slow. Plants, which may be purchased from wildflower nurseries, can be planted into meadow grass in spring or autumn. It prefers a fairly rich moist soil but will adapt to quite dry conditions.
Other sites: Semi-shade.

Germander speedwell
Veronica chamaedrys

I have one patch of grass where this flower grows and I never tire of the sight of it during spring and early summer. It is a shady spot close by a hedge and the blue of the flowers is very intense. The area needs careful management: if the grass is kept too short the speedwell hardly flowers, and if it grows too long the flowers are hidden. A reasonable, but not fanatic, mowing routine (see p. 000) will cause the plant to flower over a longer season.

This is a flower for the flowering lawn or shady hedgebank. Allow tall plants to grow up behind—red campion looks very good. Other lawn flowers that mix well with it are daisies, buttercups, black medick and dandelions. In early spring, keep the grass short and then in early May leave the speedwell to grow and flower. It also grows well in sunny grassland, where it should survive being grazed.

Germander speedwell, bird's-eye, blue-eyes, cat's-eye and eyebright are all common country names for this brightest of our speedwells. The name eyebright really refers to quite a different plant so this can be rather confusing especially as many of the poets refer to it by this name. (The real eyebright is rather like a dead-nettle and is not a very spectacular flower).

Season: March–June
Height: Creeping and to 20 cm (8 in)
Cultivation: Germander speedwell is a perennial. It cannot normally be grown from seed as this is almost impossible to collect, although the plant does produce a small amount. If you can obtain a plant or two from a friend (most gardeners will be glad to get rid of them!) they are easily split up in spring and planted out in short grass. They will tolerate almost any soil, from alkaline to slightly acid, and from heavy clay to dry and sandy.
Other sites: Sun.

Tufted vetch
Vicia cracca

All the vetches are attractive, even those with tiny flowers, like the tares, because they all have such delicate foliage. Tufted vetch has spectacular flowers in crowded spikes and even when speeding along the road, one's eyes are immediately caught by patches of purple-blue tufted vetch on the grass verge. It flowers later than most other vetches, so extending the vetch season into August. When growing in the hedgerow, tufted vetch scrambles up and over the branches to hang down luxuriantly from the highest one.

This is a flower that can be used really creatively. It is a colourful solution for the unsightly places that we would rather cover in the garden, not to mention fences of all sorts.

Tufted vetch is said to be highly nutritious to livestock, so watch out for the sheep and goats! For the smallholder, though, it could well be worth including in a meadow mixture as a potential fodder plant.
Season: July–September
Height: 60–100 cm (2–3 ft)
Cultivation: Tufted vetch is a perennial climbing plant that is easily propagated from seed. The large black seed is best rubbed between two sheets of sandpaper before sowing in spring or early autumn where it is to flower. Such large seeds may also be sown in grass, but it would be better to take out a piece of turf to give the young plants a good start.
Other sites: Sun.

Lesser periwinkle
Vinca minor

Lesser periwinkle is not regarded as a true native plant but it is very widely naturalized over the whole country and is certainly native in some areas of Northern Europe. Greater periwinkle, although very similar in appearance, comes from further south – Central and Southern Europe and North Africa. It may be substituted in the garden for the smaller flowered plant.

Lesser periwinkle is one of the oldest garden flowers – Chaucer mentions it – together with violets and roses. Being a spreading plant, it provides a most decorative ground-cover in a shady situation. Its dark green, glossy leaves are evergreen for year-round interest, and set off the blue flowers in early summer most attractively. Other flowers will grow up through the tough arching stems and provide colour later in the season. This is a good plant for growing along the base of a fence where there is dense shade and not much else will grow. Lesser periwinkle will scramble along here quite happily. You can grow it in the sun as well, where it will probably flower more freely.

Both greater and lesser periwinkle are valuable medicinal plants. They were once used to stop bleeding and to treat hypertension, and to reduce blood pressure. It is useful also as a gargle to relieve a sore throat. Periwinkle was also believed to be a herb of Venus and was taken to increase fertility. In the Middle Ages, people who were about to be executed used to wear a garland of periwinkles, as a symbol of death or immortality.

Season: March–May

Height: 30–60 cm (1–2 ft)

Cultivation: Lesser periwinkle is a perennial spreading plant that seldom produces seed. You can take stem cuttings in October or divide plants in spring. It prefers a rich, neutral soil and does well in dry conditions.

Other sites: Sun; shade.

Common dog-violet
Viola riviniana

Common dog-violet is a flower of woodland clearings and the hedgebanks of shady lanes. The word 'dog' is really a derogotary prefix to a plant meaning inferior or lesser or just plain common. That this poor *Viola* should be called common and inferior is grossly unfair for such a delightful little plant which always has happy associations of sunny spring days in a woodland glade or a quiet walk down an old shaded green lane. The inferiority presumably comes from its lack of scent compared with its relative, sweet violet.

Violets are difficult to distinguish from each other and we tend to call them all dog-violets except for the sweet violet. In fact the true dog-violet (*Viola canina*) has a paler blue flower and is only found on heaths, acid grassland, and dry woods. Another violet (*Viola reichenbachiana*) is called pale wood- or pale dog-violet and flowers earlier, sometimes in February, and prefers more open situations and woodland clearings. The violets also hybridize, so confusion reigns! Whatever violets you introduce, once established they will seed themselves profusely. Grow them in a woodland-type soil or where the grass is poor and thin. Given the right conditions you will quickly create a carpet of these lovely flowers.

Common dog-violet is an important butterfly and especially caterpillar food plant for the following fritillary butterflies: silver-washed, small pearl-bordered, and pearl-bordered, high brown, and dark green. To attract any butterflies to your garden you must have some in the vicinity in the first place, the only ones which will be drawn to the garden are those which occur locally. Don't expect some beautiful and rare species simply to appear!

Season: March–May   **Height:** 2–10 cm (1–8 in)

Cultivation: Common dog-violet is a perennial plant which grows easily from seed sown in spring or autumn, either where it is to flower or in a seed tray. It will tolerate poor soil with added leaf-mould as it requires some moisture. It will stand an alkaline or acid soil.

Other sites: Sun.

WILL FLOWERS FOR
Shady Gardens

Plants for shady gardens are found in the wild in woods and deep underneath old, wide hedgerows. Of all the areas of our countryside, woods are for many people the most magical of places, bringing back memories perhaps of childhood games or quiet walks through fragrant seas of bluebells. Our woods certainly give us a direct link with the past. Even the smallest wood might well be the last remainder of a large forest centuries old—our most ancient woods are indeed descendants of Britain's primeval forest cover.

The amazing richness of our woodland flora can only be maintained nowadays by careful management. Once the woodland canopy gets too thick and the level of light declines, the flowers gradually disappear. When the wood is thinned or coppiced again the flowers regenerate, as if by magic, from seed and roots that were lying dormant in the soil awaiting light to trigger their growth.

Woodland flowers are geared to early flowering before the leaves on the trees are fully open and the light declines. Some that flower later, like the foxglove, grow on the woodland edge or in clearings. In the summer, woodland gardens are a cool green refuge from the glaring sun. In the autumn the garden flames into colour in a blaze of leaves and berries.

Deciduous woodland not only enhances the beauty of the landscape but is a vital haven for an enormous range of wildlife. Woods and dense hedgerows act as 'corridors' for wildlife to move safely under cover from one area to another as well as providing shelter and nesting places. Now that so many old woods have gone, those that remain are oases in the vast areas of open farmland and conifer plantations.

In this countryside desert, gardens with their trees and hedges play a vital role as sanctuaries for wildlife. To create your own small patch of woodland is probably the most rewarding and worthwhile of all gardening achievements. The range of wildlife that a small group of trees and shrubs will encourage into the garden will amaze you. There are many native trees and shrubs to suit even the smallest garden, all with their special seasonal interest of catkins, buds, flowers or berries. If you have no room for trees, a few shrubs will form a shady patch, and most gardens have the shade from a wall or fence where many garden plants will not grow. Having taken the time to create a shady area, it is quite simple to introduce some of our beautiful and colourful woodland flowers. For a stunning centrepiece, encourage a single species, such as bluebell or lily-of-the-valley, to form a perfumed carpet.

An idyllic scene (left). *A sea of bluebells grows in a woodland setting alongside a mass of yellow-green spurge and white ramsons.*

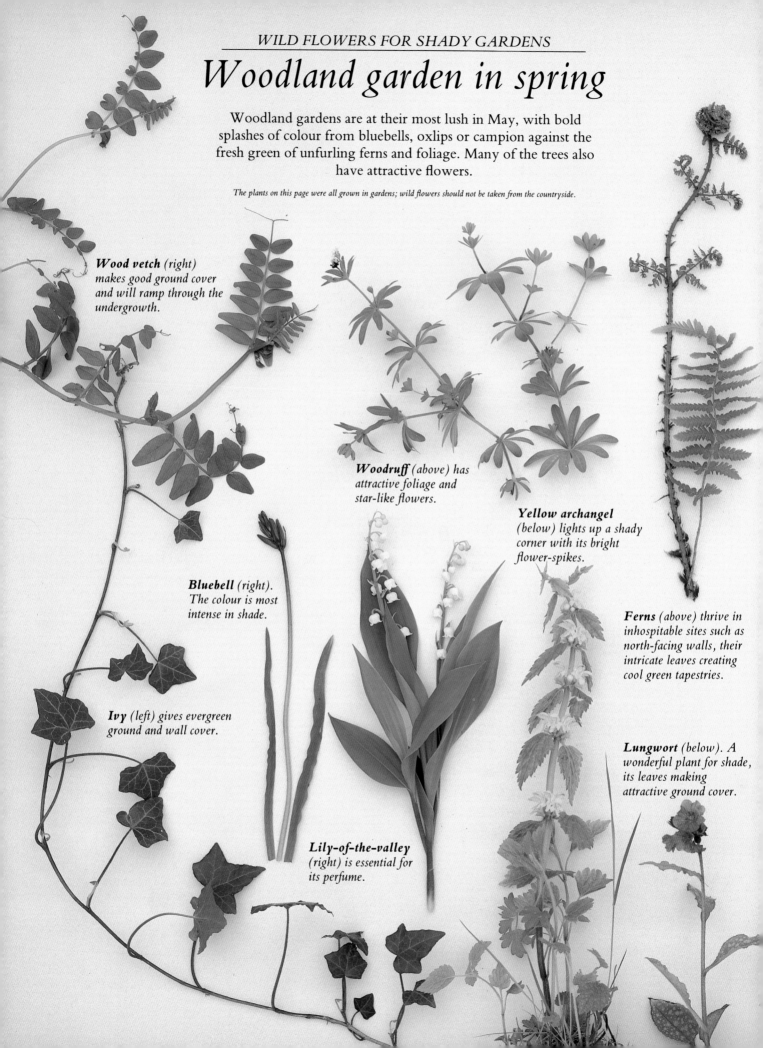

Woodland garden in spring

Woodland gardens are at their most lush in May, with bold
splashes of colour from bluebells, oxlips or campion against the
fresh green of unfurling ferns and foliage. Many of the trees also
have attractive flowers.

The plants on this page were all grown in gardens; wild flowers should not be taken from the countryside.

Wood vetch *(right)
makes good ground cover
and will ramp through the
undergrowth.*

Woodruff *(above) has
attractive foliage and
star-like flowers.*

Yellow archangel
*(below) lights up a shady
corner with its bright
flower-spikes.*

Bluebell *(right).
The colour is most
intense in shade.*

Ferns *(above) thrive in
inhospitable sites such as
north-facing walls, their
intricate leaves creating
cool green tapestries.*

Ivy *(left) gives evergreen
ground and wall cover.*

Lungwort *(below). A
wonderful plant for shade,
its leaves making
attractive ground cover.*

Lily-of-the-valley
*(right) is essential for
its perfume.*

Silver birch (*below*) *is good for small gardens, as it casts only a light shade.*

Oak (*right*). *The most valuable of all the trees for wildlife.*

Wild cherry (*right*) *in time will produce a fine specimen tree.*

Ash (*right*) *can be coppiced for the small garden.*

Bird cherry (*right*) *is an attractive tree for the small garden.*

Bugle (*above*) *spreads like mad over bare, damp ground in shade.*

Rowan (*right*) *has pretty flowers, leaves and fruit.*

Water avens (*below*). *One of my favourite wild flowers. Loves a damp, shady spot.*

Juniper (*right*). *Plant female and male for berries.*

Moss on dead wood (*right*) *is an ideal home for wildlife.*

Oxlip (*below*). *The true oxlip is a very rare flower and well worth growing.*

Jacob's-ladder (*left*) *is an old cottage garden favourite that will also grow in sun.*

Woodland garden in autumn

As the days shorten and the nights get colder the deciduous woodland prepares to rest for the winter in a last blaze of brilliant colour. Reds, golds, pinks, purples and browns, glow on the trees before the gales of autumn blow them away.

The plants on this page were all grown in gardens; wild flowers should not be taken from the countryside.

Oak *(left) supports the greatest number of insects of any native tree.*

Rowan *(above) has striking red berries that appear in late summer.*

Ash *(above) A tall, handsome tree. The fruits are known as keys.*

Hornbeam *(below) is a fine tree, with good autumn colour.*

Wayfaring-tree *(below) A shrub with red fruit, ripening to black.*

Bracken *(left) A vigorous fern that turns a beautiful golden colour in autumn.*

Bramble *(below) Autumn sees the familiar and tasty blackberries.*

Fungi *(below) live off live and decaying plant material in woodland.*

Wild cherry *(left) has attractive, reddish bark peeling off in strips. The tiny fruits are soon demolished by birds.*

Silver birch *(right) has golden leaves later in autumn. The peeling silver bark is attractive all through the year.*

Beech *(above) A magnificent tree that casts deep shade and likes a chalky soil. It also makes a good hedge.*

Wood avens *(right) will grow in the deepest shade.*

Goldenrod *(right) is a colourful flower which will happily grow under conifers or in dry shade, as well as in sun.*

Foxglove *(right) can flower into early autumn. It will grow on the thinnest soil.*

Bluebell *(left) By this time of year the plants are skeletal, and have mostly released their black seeds.*

Primrose *(below) can flower, surprisingly, in autumn, especially in a container.*

Shady wildflower gardens

Shady gardens: the possibilities

There is no hard and fast distinction between semi-shade and shade – one area will naturally blend into the other. True shady areas either receive filtered sun only (areas under deciduous trees, for instance), or are sunny only in the early morning or late evening. There is always some shade in a garden – in fact, there is often too much – and in a conventional garden such areas might prove problematic. In a wildflower garden, however, a shady area allows you to re-create a wild woodland habitat, and grow the unusual and beautiful wild flowers that thrive there.

If you have the space, you could plant a small area of woodland. In smaller gardens one tree alone provides a reasonable shady planting area, or the shade of walls and fences can be used instead. Soil near walls, trees and hedges, though, will be dry as well as shady, so make sure you choose appropriate plants: it is especially important in low-light situations to choose plants for particular soil types, whether dry or damp.

Town gardens: the urban 'woodland'

Small gardens in towns and cities, surrounded by buildings, boundary fences and walls, can be treated like a woodland or semi-woodland area. Reserve the areas of deepest shade for the true woodland species and plant areas with some direct sunlight with plants from the semi-shady section.

The softening approach is best. Cover the walls and fences with climbing plants such as wild honeysuckle, hop, traveller's-joy, hedge bindweed, bittersweet, and white bryony: if your wall or fence is in deep shade all day, ivy is one climbing plant that will thrive here. It is best to plant the climbers densely and let them grow naturally. This will help to encourage a range of wildlife to the area, in search of food from insects and flowers, and the dense foliage will give ideal protection to birds for shelter and nest-building. The climbers will also break up the hard outlines of the garden boundary.

An alternative to growing a lawn, which would not do well in a very shady situation, is to treat the area as a woodland floor and plant clumps of woodland flowers such as sweet violets, wood anemones and woodruff. These can be interspersed with spring bulbs, and for the summer and autumn columbine, martagon lily, monk's-hood and cyclamen will add

Shady town gardens are ideal for woodland plants such as these bluebells and columbines. Ferns complete the picture of a woodland glade, and a paved path seeded with wild plants winds through the area.

A new border *Young clumps of columbine, lily-of-the-valley, bugle and woodruff are surrounded by a chipped-bark mulch. The rotting branch will encourage wildlife into the garden.*

an exotic touch. Ferns make an attractive green background to the colourful flowers, with green hellebores and wood spurge filling in for them in spring. Moschatel is a beautiful plant for small gardens, with its intricate green flowers. Although its botanical name, *Adoxa*, means 'not outstanding', this only means that you might well pass it by in the vastness of a wood where sheets of bluebells capture your attention. The ground between the plants can be covered with chipped bark to simulate natural woodland leaf-mould. This also acts as a weed-suppressor.

Plants for dense shade

Areas that are permanently shady, with little light reaching them, need planting carefully. The best flowers for such areas are bluebell, giant bellflower, green hellebore, ground-ivy, herb-robert, honeysuckle, lesser celandine, lily-of-the-valley, lords-and-ladies, lungwort, monk's-hood, nettle-leaved bellflower, oxlip, pig-nut, ramsons, Solomon's-seal, stinking iris, water avens, wild angelica, wood anemone, wood avens, woodruff, wood-sorrel, wood spurge, wood vetch and yellow archangel. Take care when selecting flowers that they are suited to your site, whether free-draining or moist. For shrubs, trees and climbers try alder, bird cherry, bittersweet, bramble, buckthorn, crab apple, holly, hop, ivy,

A contrast of textures *Delicate wood anemones growing up from a bed of moss in the natural 'forest floor' conditions of a wild woodland garden.*

mezereon, wild cherry and yew. Ivy flourishes in the densest shade and climbs unaided over any surface.

There are no more decorative foliage plants than wild ferns, and most of them will thrive in deep shade. Many need moisture (but not wet conditions) and on a light soil you will have to do some watering in dry periods: it would be worth adding some compost or leaf-mould to improve water-retention. The lady-fern is a real beauty, but it should only be grown if your soil retains moisture and is neutral or acid. The male-fern (*Dryopteris filix-mas*) also likes some moisture, and is common in woods. Broad buckler-fern (*Dryopteris dilatata*), hard shield-fern (*Polystichum aculeatum*) and hart's-tongue fern (*Phyllitis scolopendrium*) are all worth growing and so is the royal fern, which prefers a wet, boggy soil.

Planting under a single tree

Even a single tree provides a woodland planting area. In the smallest garden, where perhaps there is only space for one tree, there is no better choice than a silver birch. One of the loveliest native trees, it casts only light shade, is fast growing and looks good at all times of the year. If you have the space it is worth planting a good clump of these trees.

Other trees to consider are field maple, which has autumn colour and can be coppiced; rowan, which has attractive foliage, flowers and autumn berries; bird cherry, which has lovely white flowers in spring; goat willow, with decorative catkins; and hawthorn which has flowers, berries and beautiful autumn colour. Like oak, the decorative ash tree could be planted and kept at a reasonable size by coppicing: the poles make good firewood.

Whichever tree you choose, you can plant beneath it right up to the trunk to create a miniature woodland area. Woodruff is a marvellously decorative, spreading ground-cover with attractive dark green foliage and white star-like flowers which bloom in May. Sweet violets will do well

A miniature woodland area *If you are short of space, a single small or coppiced tree can be underplanted with woodland flowers, provided it casts sufficient shade. This springtime planting could be succeeded in summer by lesser periwinkle, foxglove, wood avens and wood sage, and in autumn by a carpet of vivid pink cyclamen.*

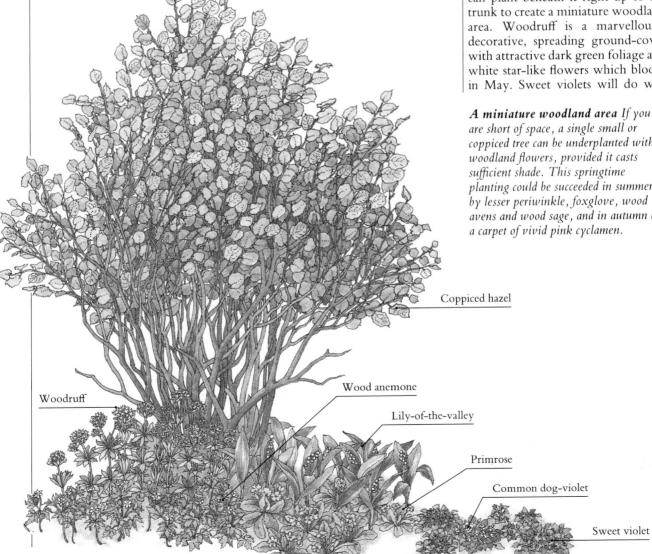

Coppiced hazel

Woodruff

Wood anemone

Lily-of-the-valley

Primrose

Common dog-violet

Sweet violet

here as will common dog-violets, primroses and ground-ivy. Other flowers to consider, especially for a light soil, are wood-sorrel and wood anemone. Both these flowers should be planted generously to form a good ground-cover.

If you have a large, old tree that casts shade so dense that grass won't grow beneath it, cyclamen, lily-of-the-valley, ground-ivy, wood avens, primroses and lords-and-ladies will thrive. If you have an area of shady ground that you want to cover but don't want to plant up with flowers then ivy does a terrific job, spreading over the most inhospitable shady ground to form a dense cover.

A wild woodland area

It is possible to include some woodland even in the smallest garden. Of course, you can never hope to re-create the wonderfully complex wild habitat that has developed over hundreds of years, but you can certainly create a small area rich in wild-life and full of woodland flowers.

If you have the space for a few trees and a hedge then you really have the makings of a miniature woodland habitat. Hedgerows on their own are semi-shady habitats, but used as a backdrop to your piece of woodland they will become shady areas that will not really be suitable for hedgerow and woodland-edge flowers.

The hedge will usually be the boundary of the garden. Several trees or groups of trees could be planted in front of the hedge and ideally this

Natural colour variations *Many wild flowers, such as these bluebells, appear occasionally in unexpected colours; such plants are often selected for gardens.*

Wildflower gardening on the large scale *If you have the space, what better than a wild woodland area to explore. Tall groups of foxgloves border a natural path through the 'forest'.*

mini-woodland would lead into a few shrubs with woodland-edge and hedgerow flowers growing between them, and then if you have the space to a small meadow area. Continuity of habitats is most important. This kind of natural progression is not only ideal for wildlife but gives the wild garden a natural look – and maintenance is much easier than if you were to have separate wild areas dotted about the garden.

If you are lucky enough to have a few established trees in your garden, these can form the basis of your woodland area. Garden trees can of course be grown with the natives, but they will support little wildlife compared to native species. Don't have too many conifers: they are not as useful for wildlife and the shade they cast is so dense that flowers will not grow beneath them.

Assuming you have no established trees, the first step is to choose your trees with care. Some trees grow very large eventually, although they will take a long time to do so. An oak, for instance, will grow very quickly upwards from a seedling, reaching perhaps 7.5 m (25 ft) in fifteen years, but it will only start to broaden out later on. You do have the option, therefore, of planting forest trees and either coppicing them after ten or fifteen years, or taking them out altogether, which is something surprisingly difficult to do if you love trees. So think very seriously about planting trees which will grow very large unless you really have the space. If you plan to coppice, don't forget that you are

trying to achieve a *shady* area: the trees can be allowed to grow much taller than they would be for a semi-shady shrub-coppice.

There are plenty of trees suitable for your small woodland that will not totally take over the garden, such as the trees suggested in 'Planting under a single tree', above. Silver birch is one of my favourites. It casts only light shade, is decorative at all seasons and supports a lot of wildlife. It is a very fast grower and thrives in most soils. Its only disadvantage is its shallow root system, which robs the topsoil of moisture and nutrients.

When buying trees remember that the smaller the trees, the faster they establish and the small ones always catch up (and often overtake) within a few years those planted at a larger size. These young trees can be purchased very cheaply from tree nurseries.

Establishing a woodland needs patience. It is best to keep the area immediately around the trees weeded for several years, until they have grown to about 1.5 m (5 ft) tall. Vigorous grasses and mature plants and bulbs will compete with the young tree roots. There is no reason though why you should not grow wild flowers in between the trees, so long as they are not too close. Some of the woodland-edge flowers, suitable for semi-shade, would be best

Woodland harmony *Fresh green wood spurge sets off the intense colour of the bluebells. Both plants look best planted in bold clumps and drifts.*

until the trees start shading out the light, and then your woodland flower planting can begin in earnest. It will not harm the trees to sow a woodland mixture or individual species around them the first spring or autumn after planting. If you sow bluebell seed, for instance, you will have bluebells in flower by the time your saplings are starting to look like trees.

When planting wild flowers in woodland, remember that most of them look much better *en masse*, and it is only the larger, more spectacular flowers that should be planted singly or in very small groups. Complicated planting tends to look fussy and not so effective, so be bold and plant large groups of perhaps two or three species

The woodland floor *(above)*
Untidiness is essential to both plants and animals in woodland areas. Here an early purple orchid has seeded itself in the loose debris; oxlips and dog's mercury are thriving; and even 'dead' wood is sprouting again.

only in an area, possibly with an occasional colour accent. Bluebells, for instance, should be planted in a dense mass, and for a really spectacular colour combination a few red campions added. Another wonderful plant for these shady areas is wood spurge, which seems to light up any dark corner with its bright yellow-green flowers and is a marvellous foil for bluebell. Ramsons is an excellent ground-cover plant for wet shady areas and is a lovely sight in flower. The only problem is the strong garlic scent, so I don't recommend it for a small garden unless you are hooked on garlic!

Beneath the tree canopy of a wild woodland is the shrub layer. This provides a different nesting level, to attract a wider variety of birds. Don't fill the whole woodland area with shrubs, or there will be no room to grow flowers. One or two small groups of shrubs, perhaps with a climbing plant growing through them, will look natural and still allow plenty of open areas for woodland flowers. There are many suitable native shrubs to choose from. Hazel is the most important, producing nuts which are loved by birds and small mammals. It is an easy shrub to coppice, and will make a bushy shape

good for nesting. Dogwood, spindle, wild privet and elder are all shrubs valuable to wildlife, and thickets of wild roses are a marvellous sight in June when in full flower, or in autumn when covered with red hips. Roses provide food for wildlife and make good nesting-sites for birds.

Undergrowth is an important part of the established woodland. Some clearing and coppicing will be necessary from time to time, but this should always be done a bit at a time, not all in the same season. There should always be plenty of dense wild growth for the benefit of wildlife. A clump of bramble is a marvellous wildlife habitat and the blackberries are always welcome.

Gradually, after a few seasons, leaves will build up a good layer on the woodland floor. Don't clear them up as they are essential for your wildlife and form a good mulch over the ground, conserving moisture. As they rot down they return nutrients and minerals to the soil.

Dead wood hosts a wide range of insects and fungi. If you are doing some clearing, keep a few logs and maybe a tree stump, pile them up and you will be amazed how quickly they are colonized. Peel off a piece of bark and you will find it alive with insects. Under the logs you may even find newts enjoying the moist conditions. Wood-boring beetles will bore their way into the wood; mosses and fungi will start to grow. As the logs decay further, plants will invade. Herb-robert and ground-ivy will flourish – I even have a log with a healthy silver birch growing out of it! Eventually the pile will rot down and you will be left with rich, crumbly compost.

One word of warning, though, about the honey fungus (*Armillaria mellea*). This golden-yellow fungus appears on dead wood and the base of infected trees in September. It is a very common fungus of woodland and often inhabits gardens without doing any damage; some strains are not at all harmful. Suddenly though, for no apparent reason, it will strike – usually old and sickly trees, but sometimes healthy specimens too. It spreads by underground black laces. To be on the safe side, remove it if you see it on your dead logs, especially if they are within 3 m (10 ft) of a favourite tree or shrub, and don't pile logs up near living trees.

Feature plants for shady sites

Even the smallest garden will have at least one shady spot where our lovely
woodland flowers can find a home. Why not plant your own 'secret' garden under
an existing tree or in the shade of a wall, and transform a once-dreary site.

Wood anemone
Anemone nemorosa

Wood anemones, like bluebells, never seem to do things
by halves: when you come across them they usually form a
great carpet. The delicate, nodding flowers are sometimes
pink rather than white, and even when the flowers are
over the intricately cut foliage is attractive.

In the wild, wood anemones grow in deciduous woods
and open sites with low fertility. They are often seen
growing along hedge-banks, usually with primroses,
perhaps indicating that the bank was once part of a nearby
wood. Unusually, they are also natives of North America,
where they often grow beside dusky-pink wood crane's-
bills—an arrangement worth imitating.

Wood anemones are also known as windflowers: an apt
name, as they grow on many a windswept hilltop or
mountain in the north of England, and they flower at the
windiest time of the year. The French also call them
windflowers—*les herbes au vente*—and the Italians, *fiori
stella:* star flowers.

Season: March–April   **Height:** 15 cm (6 in)
Cultivation: Wood anemones are perennial plants that
grow from underground rhizomes. They do best in a well-
drained site without other plant competition. Add plenty
of leaf mould to the soil and plant them about 20 cm (9 in)
apart: they should spread readily. Although they produce
seed it is difficult to collect by the time it is ripe and the
plant can be divided so easily that this
is a better way to increase it.

Other sites: In sun or semi-shade on
banks with poor soil where grass is
sparse and not vigorous.

Columbine
Aquilegia vulgaris

Columbine is one of our most familiar cottage garden
flowers and has been 'improved' out of all recognition for
modern garden cultivation. The simple charm of this
favourite wild flower of intense blue cannot be compared
to modern multi-coloured hybrids. Few people have seen
it growing truly wild although it often escapes from
gardens. It is certainly one of the old garden flowers and
was recorded as early as 1580. When growing wild it
favours shady woodland situations. The flowers have
always been likened to doves and birds. Its Saxon name of
culverwort came from *culfre,* a pigeon.

Most gardeners only use columbines in the sun, but they
look lovely in dappled shade. Pink- and white-flowered
forms occur, and are often seen in gardens. The young
leaves are most attractive in spring, when tinged with pink.

Season: May–July
Height: 30–90 cm (1–3 ft)
Cultivation: Columbine is a perennial plant easily propagated from
seed. Sow the seed where it is to
flower during spring or early autumn. Ideally, the soil should be fertile
and alkaline. Columbine will survive
in quite dry soils.
Other sites: Sun; semi-shade.

Lily-of-the-valley
Convallaria majalis

Lily-of-the-valley is a quiet, gentle plant that thrives in the shade. It certainly does not always grow in valleys as the name suggests and in fact it prefers the drier areas of woods. This is a plant traditionally associated with modesty and purity. It has some lovely country names including lady's tears, fairies' bells and may lily. The pure white flowers, which look like drops or maybe tears, are very sweetly scented; indeed they are used to make perfume.

This is a valuable medicinal plant, having properties similar to foxglove as a cardiac tonic: it is said to be safer though not as strong. It was recommended by the old herbalists for a number of complaints and was thought very good for strengthening the memory.

Lily-of-the-valley will naturalize easily in a shady spot under trees or in the shade of a fence, provided there is not much vegetation to compete with it. The plants spread by means of creeping rhizomes if given a well-drained soil with plenty of leaf mould added. There is room for them in the smallest garden, and they may even be grown in a half-barrel on the patio. When the flowers are over, the leaves provide dense ground cover until winter.

Season: May–June **Height:** 10–20 cm (4–8 in)

Cultivation: Lily-of-the-valley is a perennial plant with creeping rhizomes. Ripe seeds are seldom formed, but plants are widely available from nurseries, or you can divide an existing plant once it has finished flowering. For the best flowers, double-dig the soil before planting and add plenty of compost or leaf mould. Plant in late September 15 cm (6 in) apart in well-drained, rather sandy soil, burying the crowns (where the leaves grow from the roots) just below the soil surface.

Other sites: Semi-shade.

Foxglove
Digitalis purpurea

Unlike so many of our wild flowers, which are quiet and subtle in their beauty, the foxglove is bold and bright and tall.

In the garden foxgloves can be grown in many different situations: in the shade of trees; along a fence or wall; along a shady hedgerow; or in the sunny flower border. If you have very light, sandy soil then try naturalizing them in grass.

Foxgloves are poisonous if eaten; they form the basis of a strong drug used to treat heart disease.

Season: June–August

Height: 30–120 cm (1–4 ft)

Cultivation: Foxgloves are biennial plants, normally flowering the year after sowing. Sow seed in spring or late summer where it is to flower, or in trays, and cover lightly. Foxgloves will grow in most garden soils but to naturalize well they require the soil to be well-drained, and preferably acid.

Other sites: Sun; semi-shade.

Bluebell

Endymion non-scriptus (syn. *Hyacinthoides non-scripta*)

Although bluebells are found on the continent, the great woodland carpets of blue, unbroken save for the thrusting trunks of trees with often no other flowers to be seen, are a very British scene. By the time the bluebells have set their seeds, the foliage has often disappeared under a sea of bracken, giving the clue to the rather light and slightly acid soil they prefer.

The flowers can be white or even pink, and they have a marvellous spicy perfume like their oriental cousins, the garden hyacinths. The white bulbs used to be harvested for the starch they contain.

In the wild, bluebells grow in woodlands, grasslands and even on cliffs. In small gardens, a clump under a tree or in the shade of a hedge looks good, with primroses nearby; or grow them massed closely together in short lawn grass. A mixture of blue, white and pink forms looks particularly striking growing between the bricks of a path.

Season: May **Height:** 30 cm (12 in)

Cultivation: Bluebells are perennial plants that grow from bulbs. They are easy to grow and prefer a well-drained, and ideally slightly acid, soil. Plant the bulbs in autumn 15 cm (6 in) apart and 5 cm (2 in) deep. Bluebells self-seed profusely, but the seeds need the winter frosts to break their dormancy and will take several years to form flowering plants.

Other sites: They will grow happily in semi-shade or sun, but the more light they receive, the less intense their colour will be.

Wood spurge

Euphorbia amygdaloides

All the native spurges have great decorative value, and none more so than wood spurge, which grows quite large and almost illuminates the areas of woodland where it grows with its brilliant, lime-green flowers. It seems to prefer ancient woodlands.

In the garden it needs to be grown in shade, even deep shade, and shown off against a dark background. Grow a clump in the shade of a fence or wall, or to light up a dim corner. It makes a magnificent foil for intensely coloured flowers such as oxlips or bluebells.

The spurge family is very large: it comprises nearly a thousand species including both herbaceous plants such as wood spurge, and succulents from hot desert areas. Most of them, including wood spurge, have a milky sap that can be used (depending on the species) either medicinally or as a poison. But, to be on the safe side, it is best not to eat any spurge at all!

Season: April–May **Height:** 30–80 cm (1–2½ ft)

Cultivation: Wood spurge is a perennial. It will grow easily from seed which should be sown in spring or early autumn 1 cm (½ in) deep where it is to flower; or plants may be purchased from specialist wildflower nurseries. Wood spurge does best in a woodland-type soil with plenty of leaf mould and some compost added. It does not like an acid soil and does not require a lot of moisture except during early spring.

Other sites: Semi-shade.

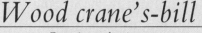

Woodruff
Galium odoratum

This is a flower of the deep woods and a flower of joy and good spirits and even amorous encounters (it is supposed to be slightly aphrodisiac!). Its country names are sweet woodruff, kiss-me-quick, ladies-in-the-hay. The whole plant is scented, and when dried the leaves have a strong scent of new-mown hay.

I like to think of this plant as 'star-of-the-woods'. The pure white flowers are star-like against the dark woodland floor and the interesting leaf formation is star-like in whorls. Woodruff is closely related to lady's bedstraw, and to that menace of hedgerows and shrubberies, cleavers or goose grass. Except for the leaf formation, woodruff has none of the undesirable characteristics of cleavers!

Try to grow this plant in the shade as it really loses so many of its virtues in the sun: the leaves are bleached a yellow green and the star-like flowers do not show up very well. This is a plant for difficult places as it loves growing in the dry shade of trees, right up to the trunk. It makes a dense and very decorative ground cover with its rich green leaves, and its underground runners spread rapidly in the right situation.

Harvest some of the plants as they do in Germany on May Day and steep them in a Rhine wine to make the delicious drink *Maibowle* (literally, May bowl). Dry the leaves to place in linen cupboards or drawers. The dried leaves were once used to strew on floors and to fill mattresses and pillows, and they are still used in pot-pourri.

Season: May–June   **Height:** 15–30 cm (6–12 in)

Cultivation: Woodruff is a perennial that is easily propagated from underground runners. Split these in early spring and plant out: every little piece will grow. Woodruff likes a rich alkaline soil and some moisture especially during the spring. The plant does not produce much seed, but if seed is collected it should be sown fresh and not kept until the following year.

Other sites: Semi-shade.

Wood crane's-bill
Geranium sylvaticum

Wood crane's-bill is one of our prettiest crane's-bills, so vivid that a photograph cannot really do it justice, and it should establish easily in the garden.

Most of us have shady areas in our gardens, and wood crane's-bill is a lovely flower to fill them with colour and attractive foliage. It can also be used in the open bed or border. Group several plants together to extend the flowering period as no two plants flower exactly together.

Like all crane's-bills it distributes its dark round seeds over a considerable distance by the use of its own catapult mechanism. If you ever try to collect the seed of a crane's-bill you will soon discover that timing is all-important. One day the seed is there and seems to be not quite ready, the next it has gone! The answer, to catch just a few seeds, is to tie a paper or muslin bag over the flower-head, or pick the heads just before ripening and put them in an open container covered in muslin.

Season: June–July   **Height:** 30–80 cm (1–2½ ft)

Cultivation: Wood crane's-bill is a bushy perennial plant that is easily grown from seed. Before sowing, rub the hard seed between two sheets of sandpaper to speed germination. Sow in spring or early autumn 1 cm (½ in) deep either in a seed tray or where it is to flower. Cover trays with glass until germination. The soil should be rich and moisture-retentive. It does best in acid conditions but will tolerate a moderately alkaline soil.

Other sites: Sun; semi-shade.

Green hellebore
Helleborus viridis

This quiet and lovely plant is a good example of how every wild flower has its appropriate time and place. When the bright bluebells and campions are in full flower it would hardly be noticed, but set against the dark woodland only just awakening from winter it is a real gem. Plant green hellebores in a clump against a dark background for a lovely splash of fresh green. They also look attractive, if not so dramatic, in association with snowdrops or blue and pink lungwort.

Green hellebore dies down in autumn and appears again in early spring, but the other native hellebore, stinking hellebore, is an evergreen plant large enough to be mistaken for a small shrub (it grows to 60 cm/2 ft). Its leaves are finger-like and make attractive year-round foliage; its flowers are smaller than those of green hellebore, and each one has a dark brown-purple rim. It can flower as early as December in a mild winter, and its spray of flowers can last for several months. Its smell is not as unpleasant as its name sounds – but avoid crushing the leaves, as they are much more potent! The smell attracts bees and other insects, making it a valuable early-season nectar plant.

In the wild both green and stinking hellebores are rare plants. Both grow normally in chalk and limestone woodlands, where they favour steep slopes. It would be reasonable to suppose therefore that they require sharp drainage, but they have also been found growing in damp valley bottoms, making them versatile plants for the shady garden. Stinking hellebore will also tolerate sun.

Season: February–March **Height:** 45 cm (18 in)

Cultivation: Hellebores are perennials, and will grow happily in either well-drained or damp soil. Add plenty of leaf mould to the soil. If you use peat instead, make sure the soil does not become acid, as hellebores prefer alkaline conditions. Plant them about 20 cm (8 in) apart. They should readily self-seed if the soil and situation are to their liking, or you can sow seed in early autumn for flowers a couple of years later. Green hellebore dies down in early summer.

Other sites: Semi-shade.

Martagon lily
Lilium martagon

Botanists have mixed opinions on whether martagon lily is native to Britain. It is widely distributed over central and southern Europe but in Britain it is only found apparently growing wild in the chalk woodlands of Kent and the Wye valley, though it has become naturalized in woodlands over much of the country. Martagon lily was once very popular among gardeners – Gerard mentioned it in his list of garden plants in 1596 – and it has been maintained in many old cottage gardens.

The plant's other common name is purple Turk's-cap, from the unusual, turban-shaped flowers. It is a most graceful plant, producing on its long stem as many as thirty spotted purple flowers. The stamens protrude from the flowers in a distinctive feather.

Martagon lily is a very easy plant to grow and provided the soil is not acid it grows equally well in sun or shade, although I recommend it for woodland planting as it looks so good in this situation.

Season: May–July

Height: 1 m (3 ft)

Cultivation: Martagon lily is a perennial bulb that grows best in well-drained soil. Plant the bulb 15 cm (6 in) deep. Martagon lilies produce a lot of seed and the best method of increasing them, as with all wild plants, is to allow them to self-seed. Alternatively, sow seed in spring where the plant is to flower. Lilies like potash, so an organic potash feed is beneficial when planting.

Other sites: Sun; semi-shade.

Wood-sorrel
Oxalis acetosella

Wood-sorrel is a wonderful surprise when it is first encountered. The name suggests a rather dull and ordinary plant, but this is one of the most delightful and delicate of the woodland plants. Dainty is perhaps the adjective to use. In spite of its name it is not related to the sorrels, but it has a similar, acid taste. The leaves are a light, clear green, and there has always been speculation that this leaf is the true Irish shamrock.

The whole plant is exceedingly sensitive. The leaves close up if exposed to direct sun; if touched; in wet weather; and at night. They fold in on the stem and form a pyramid to prevent evaporation. The flowers also close before rain and at night, and when the blooms fade the flower stem curves down and the seed-head is concealed inside the leaves. Once ripe, the stem straightens up again and the seeds propel themselves several feet from the pod.

The leaves of wood-sorrel were traditionally used in small quantities as a salad vegetable and to make a green sauce. The acid taste would take the place of vinegar and lemon. The plant is also medicinal and is used today as a gargle and externally to treat scabies.

Wood-sorrel should always be grown in shade, and in a rich woodland-type soil it will spread rapidly. It makes lovely early spring ground cover around a tree trunk or on a fairly dry piece of ground, and looks especially good on a shady bank or mound. It needs to grow without competition from grasses or other plants and will grow in alkaline or acid soils.

Season: April–May   **Height:** 5–10 cm (2–4 in)

Cultivation: Wood-sorrel is a perennial plant which will grow from seed, but this is not always available owing to the difficulty of collecting it. Plants are best purchased from a wildflower nursery, and will establish easily if planted in a shady situation in autumn 15 cm (6 in) apart.

Other sites: Semi-shade.

Oxlip
Primula elatior

Oxlips are charming, delicate flowers, with a scent that has been likened to ripe apricots. They are frequently confused with cowslips (whose much smaller, golden flowers have distinct orange dots at the centre) and false oxlips (which have a bunch of large, golden, primrose-like flowers, and are a cross between cowslips and primroses). Oxlips were not recognized as a distinct species until the 1840s, when Henry Doubleday established their distinct identity after studying the large oxlip population around Great Bardfield in Essex. The true oxlip is often known as the Bardfield oxlip.

Because the wild primulas cross so readily it is best not to grow more than one species at a time if you want them to seed true to type. Of course, it can be fascinating to see what natural hybrids are produced if oxlips are mixed with cowslips, primroses or coloured garden forms. The naturally occurring false oxlip was the parent of the many modern varieties of garden polyanthus.

In this country, oxlips grow only in the ancient coppiced woodlands of East Anglia, but they are more common in the rest of north-west Europe, often growing in damp meadows.

Season: May   **Height:** 30 cm (12 in)

Cultivation: Oxlips are perennials. Plant them 20 cm (9 in) apart in soil that is moist all year round. Seeds need the winter cold to germinate, so you should sow them in early autumn. Really fresh seed can come up very quickly, but older seed may be more erratic. Oxlips take two or three seasons to reach flowering size.

Other sites: Sun or semi-shade, but the soil must never dry out.

Lungwort
Pulmonaria officinalis

Lungwort is a striking plant that naturalizes easily in a woodland or shady situation where the growth of grass is not too vigorous to compete with it. The flowers are deep pink in bud opening to a violet blue, a contrast which inspired the old country name of soldiers and sailors. Other descriptive names include Abraham-Isaac-and-Jacob, and Lady-Mary's-tears. Because the form of the flowers resembles that of the cowslip, the plant was often known as Jerusalem cowslip. The reference to Jerusalem is obscure but it is said to refer to the Virgin's milk spilling on the leaves, making pale blotches, a superstition that arose as the plant grows wild in Palestine.

The most common name, lungwort, relates to the plant's supposed medicinal properties: according to the sixteenth-century doctrine of 'signatures', the blotches on the leaves resemble lungs and therefore indicate that the plant should cure lung ailments.

In the wild, lungwort grows in woods and along hedgebanks, but is now quite rare. It is a most useful garden plant: even when the flowers are over, the foliage makes superb ground-cover. There are many decorative garden forms, including white, pink, and rich purple-flowered varieties.

Season: March–May   **Height:** 30 cm (12 in)
Cultivation: Lungworts are perennial plants, and should be planted in spring or autumn 30 cm (1 ft) apart in a rich soil with plenty of leaf-mould for added fertility and moisture. They will quickly spread to provide dense ground-cover. Lungwort seldom produces mature seed, but you can increase your stock by dividing plants in the autumn.
Other sites: Semi-shade.

Sweet violet
Viola odorata

Sweet violets are one of our best loved wild flowers. Their popularity is due as much to their delightful scent – they are the only scented wild violets – as to their lovely deep purple flowers, which sometimes appear in white or pale mauve forms. Sweet violets really herald the advent of spring and by the time their flowers are over, spring is with us. A mass of sweetly scented violets makes a wonderful woodland carpet with their large, heart-shaped leaves covering the ground. They also look lovely growing in combination with primroses, as they often grow together in the wild woodland.

The violet flower is full of nectar, but because the flowers are open so early, when the weather is usually cold and no bees are about, the flowers are hardly ever pollinated. Seed is more likely to be produced in the autumn from the secondary flowers which form amongst the leaves and are self-pollinating. However, as the plant sends out runners which root and form new plants, there is not much necessity for seed.

Sweet violets have always been used medicinally and have long been used to make scent and syrup of violets. Violets were grown very extensively for the perfume industry and at one time cut blooms were taken to market.

Season: February–April   **Height:** 10–15 cm (4–6 in)
Cultivation: Sweet violets are perennial plants that spread easily by means of runners. Divide plants in spring, or transplant new plants developed from runners in early spring in a rich soil with reasonable moisture. Plants appreciate the sun early or late in the day. Alternatively, sow seed in trays in autumn and leave them outside over winter, covered with glass. Germination is very erratic.
Other sites: Semi-shade.

WILD FLOWERS FOR
Water Gardens

A wild pond *Meadowsweet, greater spearwort and purple loosestrife thrive on the pond-edge.*

Until quite recently there were many sites in the countryside where the large and varied wetland flora could flourish. If you look at a map of only fifty years ago you will often see hundreds of ponds marked in a single parish, and there were streams, ditches and undrained meadows as well. Nowadays, water supplies are managed on a larger scale and many ponds and wet meadows have either been drained deliberately for agriculture or, in the case of many clay ponds, have cracked and dried up without proper maintenance and been overrun by shrubs and trees.

A wild pond or wetland area will be a haven for the wildlife whose habitats have been destroyed. You will find that many more animals and birds are attracted to a garden with a guaranteed water supply. The smallest pond will be a focus of interest all year round, even after the spring and summer flowers are over.

In addition to, or instead of, a pond you can create a wetland area to grow the bold and colourful plants that thrive in reasonably fertile, waterlogged soil. Even a small area, formed with a pond liner, can look effective. Why not capitalize on a naturally waterlogged area and plant a wetland meadow as well as a pond and marsh area, to grow the full range of wild water plants.

Pond garden in summer

Many different types of wild plant will thrive in or near a pond. They are at their most colourful in the summer months, but the wildlife a pond garden will attract makes it fascinating to watch throughout the year.

The plants on this page were all grown in gardens; wild flowers should not be taken from the countryside.

Common club-rush *(below) The dried stems are used for thatching.*

Meadowsweet *(above) is a fragrant, well-loved flower of streamsides and wet meadows. It looks attractive grown in groups.*

Small-reed *(right) looks decorative planted at the edges of a pond or lake. It will also grow in moist woodland.*

Branched bur-reed *(left) is a decorative plant, but it can be invasive: its roots can damage a pond liner.*

Common water-crowfoot *(above) floats on the water.*

Common valerian *(right) is a tall marshland plant.*

Water-plantain *(below) likes to have its roots in very wet soil.*

White water-lily *(below) will pattern the water-surface with its glossy leaves.*

Hemp-agrimony *(below) is a colourful, tall, bushy plant.*

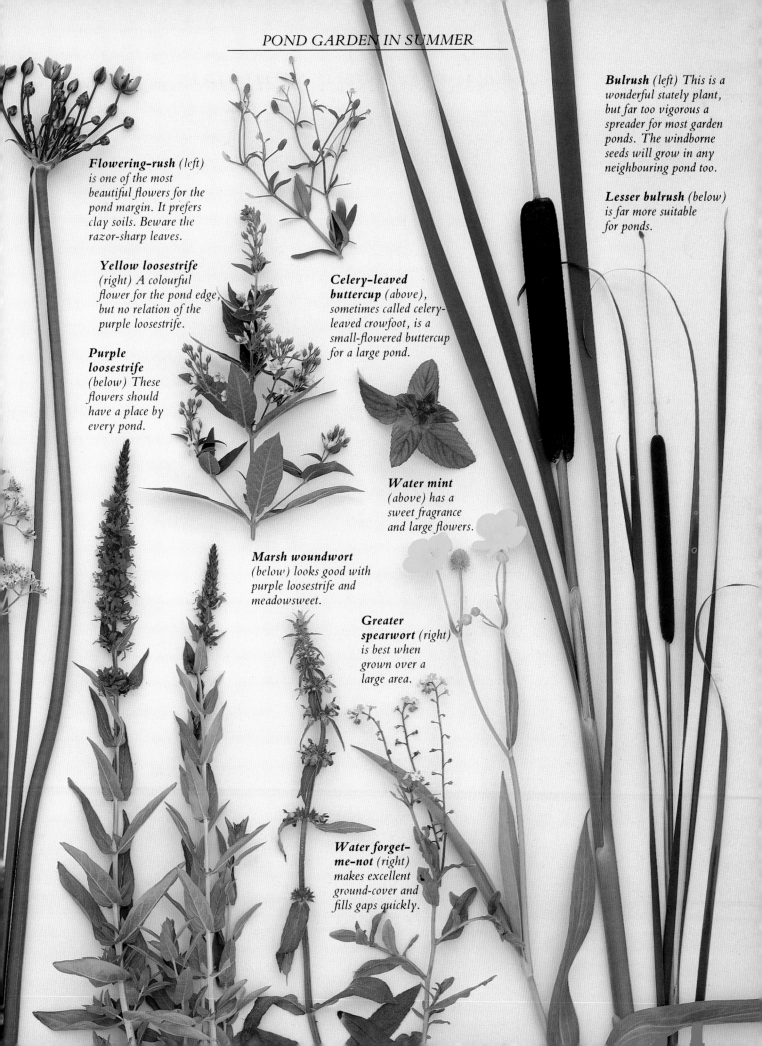

Flowering-rush (left) is one of the most beautiful flowers for the pond margin. It prefers clay soils. Beware the razor-sharp leaves.

Yellow loosestrife (right) A colourful flower for the pond edge, but no relation of the purple loosestrife.

Purple loosestrife (below) These flowers should have a place by every pond.

Celery-leaved buttercup (above), sometimes called celery-leaved crowfoot, is a small-flowered buttercup for a large pond.

Water mint (above) has a sweet fragrance and large flowers.

Marsh woundwort (below) looks good with purple loosestrife and meadowsweet.

Greater spearwort (right) is best when grown over a large area.

Water forget-me-not (right) makes excellent ground-cover and fills gaps quickly.

Bulrush (left) This is a wonderful stately plant, but far too vigorous a spreader for most garden ponds. The windborne seeds will grow in any neighbouring pond too.

Lesser bulrush (below) is far more suitable for ponds.

Wildflower water gardens

A small pond gone 'wild' This formal pond is now surrounded by vigorous clumps of garden yarrow, purple loosestrife, yellow chamomile and pink willowherb.

A pond often becomes the main feature of the garden; there is no area that is so rich in wildlife and so colourful from spring to late summer. Any garden pond makes a worthwhile contribution to conservation as so many thousands of ponds and wetlands have gone from the country-side together with their wildlife.

Making a 'wild' pond
Formal, carefully tended ponds surrounded by mown grass and filled with goldfish look out of place in a

Small-scale detail A clump of bright marsh-marigolds on the edge of a still pond. Sawn logs act as stepping stones across the water.

wildflower garden and are of little benefit to wildlife. A natural-looking pond, with shallow-sloping sides and vegetation growing up to the water's edge will encourage wildlife to move freely from water to land. The pond should be related to the rest of the wild garden. Don't think of it as a separate feature but rather a part of a complete habitat. The deep water at its centre blends into shallow at the pond edge, the shallow water into bog and wetland. The wetland might lead into a dryer meadow and then shrubs and trees. Another part of the pond might lead into shingle or gravel and then a rocky feature. Of course, very small gardens won't have room for all these different habitats but you can at least allow an area of wild vegetation to lead up to the pond.

The planting suggestions for ponds also apply to streams, although water-lilies and other surface-covering plants aren't practical. An attractive arrangement is to have a wetland area, with its lush vegetation, one side of the stream and a spring meadow or flowering lawn on the other side.

Planting the pond
Once you have filled your pond, let it settle for a few days before you start planting. This is essential to allow any chlorine in the water to evaporate. If the pond is made of concrete it will need to be rinsed out several times over three or four weeks before it is filled permanently to remove the free lime from the new concrete.

It is important to remember that a pond and its surroundings, once es-tablished, will form a virtually self-contained community or ecosystem. In order to achieve this, the widest range of water plants, insects and amphibians should be encouraged or introduced. Plants provide oxygen, nutrients, food, shelter and support for animals, and breeding-sites and escape routes for emerging insects such as dragonflies.

Wildlife for ponds
By the time you have planted your pond and introduced a good mix of plants you will without doubt have quite a range of pond-life already establishing itself as if by magic. Even

Pond life *Ponds repay close observation. These two frogs coming up for air are only just visible through the lush vegetation.*

fish can find their way to a new pond by means of eggs carried by birds, and certainly many of the insects will arrive with no assistance. If you are in the right area frogs and even toads can appear. If you want to keep decorative fish, you will need two ponds – they will live on the tadpoles and spawn in a wildlife pond, destroying the natural balance that can otherwise be established even in a small area such as this.

Pond maintenance It is essential for the plants, animals and insects that live there that the pond is never drained. Water plants are generally vigorous and invasive, however, and it is important not to let them get out of hand so that the pond becomes choked up with vegetation. Every few years, as soon as the mass begins to look impenetrable, wade in and pull out all the excess.

A miniature pond in a tub

If you don't have room in your garden for a pond, a half-barrel makes a fascinating mini-habitat. Old wooden barrels will be the most hospitable containers as far as wildlife is concerned, although you could use a plastic barrel if you can't get hold of the genuine variety. A wooden barrel should be well washed out and then soaked for several days. This should swell the wood and seal it. If not, you will have to plug the gaps with a waterproof sealant. Cover the bottom with an 8 cm (3 in) layer of sand and gravel and fill with water. If you use tapwater, wait for forty-eight hours before planting.

You will need to choose plants in scale with your container. Frogbit, for instance, is an attractive miniature floating plant. Upright plants such as water-plantain, arrowhead and water-mint will give height to the arrangement. You can accommodate marginal plants such as flowering rush by standing the pots on stones so that they are barely submerged. Water forget-me-not will trail over the side of the barrel, softening the hard edge.

There is not room for many plants in the barrel – five or six would be about right – and they should all be kept in the containers they are supplied in, or planted in suitable pots, to keep them under control. Keep a close eye on the plants and cut them back or remove some if they begin to fill the tub – you will probably have to do this about once a year.

You can encourage wildlife to establish in the barrel by putting a few stones and rocks on the bottom to provide shelter, and planting plenty of water weeds such as hornwort and water milfoil, as oxygenators. Wait for a few weeks for the plants to establish and things to settle down before introducing any wildlife. Add some water snails and fresh water winkles (available from specialist suppliers) and the rest of the wildlife will arrive naturally.

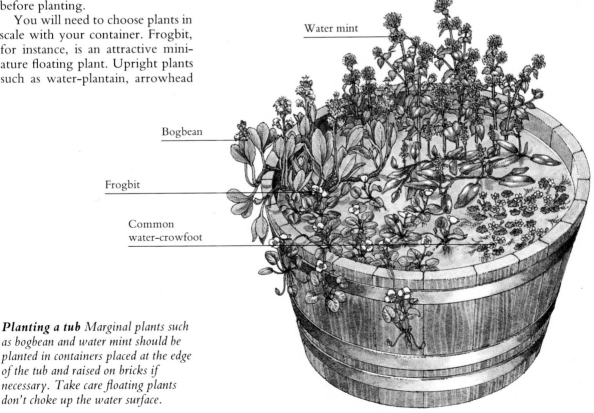

Water mint

Bogbean

Frogbit

Common water-crowfoot

Planting a tub *Marginal plants such as bogbean and water mint should be planted in containers placed at the edge of the tub and raised on bricks if necessary. Take care floating plants don't choke up the water surface.*

Water meadows *support some of the most unusual and colourful wild flowers. Here marsh orchids grow between yellow iris and cow parsley at the edge of the lake at Scotney Castle.*

The range of water plants

Water plants can be divided into five categories that relate to the depth of water in which they will grow.

Submerged plants or oxygenators produce oxygen for the pond organisms and help to prevent excessive growth of algae. They should be planted abundantly. The best are water-starwort (*Callitriche* spp.), rigid hornwort (*Ceratophyllum demersum*) and spiked water-milfoil (*Myriophyllum spicatum*).

Floating and floating-leaved plants like the water-lily grow in water up to 3 m (10 ft) deep. They root into the pond bottom, their leaves floating on the surface. Frogbit can be substituted for water-lilies in a small pond.

Emergent plants have normal stems and leaves that can be seen above the water-surface, but they will grow in water several feet deep. Arrowhead, flowering-rush and water-mint are worth planting. Whatever you do, keep the invasive bulrush, or greater reed-mace (*Typha latifolia*), out of your pond, as it will take over.

Marginal plants grow in the shallow water up to 15 cm (6 in) deep around the edge of the pond. Besides being decorative they are useful for introducing some shade to the water. For colour and interesting foliage try marsh-marigold, water forget-me-not, water-plantain, yellow iris, bog-bean and brooklime.

Wetland plants grow in ground that is permanently wet. They are very colourful plants. Ragged-robin

flowers early in the season together with marsh-marigold (which grows in shallow water as well as wetlands) and cuckooflower. Bugle is a very decorative low ground-cover, flowering from early summer onwards; it prefers a shady situation. For July/August flowering, meadowsweet, purple loosestrife, yellow loosestrife (no relation to the former) and hemp-agrimony are colourful and attractive to butterflies and other wildlife. Common valerian is also a beautiful, tall plant that flowers in early summer.

Grasses, rushes and sedges are important for wildlife and should form the basis of your wetland and bog areas. The following are worth obtaining: common sedge (*Carex nigra*), hairy sedge (*Carex hirta*), and lesser pond-sedge (*Carex acutiformis*) (sedges); common spike-rush (*Eleocharis palustris*), galingale (*Cyperus longus*), and soft rush (*Juncus effusus*) (rushes); brown bent (*Agrostis canina*), meadow foxtail (*Alopecurus pratensis*), purple moor-grass (*Molinia caerulea*),

The pond-edge *This planting shows how one habitat can blend naturally into the next. A mown grass path skirts a wetland area planted with greater spearwort and flowering-rush, and is bordered on the other side by grassland.*

tufted hair-grass (*Deschampsia cespitosa*), and wood small-reed (*Calamagrostis epigejos*) (grasses).

A wetland or boggy patch

There are many colourful marginal and wetland plants and these can be grown in an area next to a pond or stream; or it can be a separate site (see p. 135). The area must be kept moist during the summer (just a trickle through a hosepipe is sufficient) as many of the wetland plants are in full flower in August. They look best in a bold, simple planting scheme: let nature complete the design by means of self-seeding.

A wetland meadow area

If you have an area of naturally poorly drained land, where the soil is wet for much of the time, you can create a wetland meadow area. Seed it with a wetland meadow mixture; you can then add in any of the wetland plants and also devil's-bit scabious, water avens, common comfrey, fritillary, grass-of-Parnassus and bird's-eye primrose.

Your wetland meadow will dry out on the surface over the summer (although there must be plenty of moisture underneath) and by autumn it should be dry enough to scythe.

Feature plants for water gardens

Water has an endless fascination for everyone, and even a small pond in the garden,
planted with some of the many colourful native plants – such as flowering-rush
and water-lily – can provide a stunning focal point.

Flowering-rush
Butomus umbellatus

Flowering-rush is a magnificent plant for the pond edge,
growing up to 150 cm (5 ft) tall. When seen in all its glory
in late summer, after the water-lilies have faded, the
beautiful rose-pink flowers, with their dramatic red
stamens, are spectacular. The flowers have a lovely
almond scent, and, when they fade, they are followed by
attractive purple fruits. The three-sided rush-like leaves
are razor sharp and you would be well advised to leave
them alone. This flower might have been picked out of
existence in many areas if it was not for these green swords
guarding the plants.

In the garden flowering-rush
should be planted at the edge of the
pond, with its roots in the water,
alongside such plants as bogbean,
yellow iris, and water-plantain.

Season: July–September
Height: to 150 cm (5 ft)
Cultivation: Flowering-rush is a
perennial plant growing from a rhizome. Plants can be propagated easily
by dividing lengths of the rhizome
containing an 'eye' or shoot in the
spring; or collect seeds in late autumn
and sow them in a shallow pot filled
with seed compost and cover lightly.
Stand the pot in a saucer filled with
water to keep the compost wet. Seedlings can be transplanted to the pond
edge the following spring.
Other sites: Sun.

Marsh-marigold
Caltha palustris

This is a lovely plant to establish in the wet areas of the
garden. It will be the first of the wetland plants to flower,
producing a golden mass of flowers with glossy, bright
green leaves, and will continue flowering into the summer. Marsh-marigold will be happy in any waterlogged
ground, provided there is plenty of fertility, and it enjoys
all but the deepest shade. In a shady garden it would look
particularly attractive growing with ferns and golden-
saxifrage. In a more open site, plant marsh-marigold with
yellow iris, wild angelica, meadowsweet and ragged-
robin for an attractive combination of flowers that will
bloom over a long period.

Marsh-marigold is a plant of very ancient origin.
Before the first Ice Age, it grew on vast areas of bog and
wetland making the landscape look as if it was carpeted
with gold. In the wet meadows that still remain today
marsh-marigold glows with brilliant colour in the spring
sunshine. Grazing cattle fortunately leave the plant well
alone on account of its acrid juice. It also grows on stream
banks, in ditches and most luxuriantly in wet woods.

Season: March–May **Height:** 30–40 cm (12–16 in)
Cultivation: Marsh-marigold is a perennial plant that
grows from a thick rhizome. Rhizomes can be divided up
in spring and after flowering in the summer, and planted
out in wet soil. Sow seed in a pot of
peat-based seed compost and place it
in a dish filled with water to ensure
that the compost remains wet. Seed
should be sown in late summer and
covered lightly with soil.
Other sites: Sun; semi-shade; shade.

Hemp-agrimony
Eupatorium cannabinum

Meadowsweet
Filipendula ulmaria

Hemp-agrimony is a marvellous sight in full flower, with large heads of the softest pink flowers. Each flower-head consists of many separate small flowers, each made up of florets of a pink-mauve colour, or sometimes much paler, giving the head its distinctive look. The plant's most appealing country name, 'raspberries and cream', describes the colour of the flowers very accurately.

When the flowers are over, tiny seeds form; each one has fine feathery hairs attached to it, which gives the seed-heads a fluffy appearance. This 'fluff' blows away in the slightest breeze and if you don't wish the plant to establish all over the garden it is wise to cut the heads off before they reach this stage!

In the wild, hemp-agrimony grows in marshes, fens, on the banks of streams and in wet woods, with some of our most colourful wild flowers, such as purple and yellow loosestrife, marsh valerian, and greater spearwort. You could plant hemp-agrimony in the marshy area near the garden pond with a similar combination of wild flowers, and a grouping of grasses, reeds and sedges. Hemp-agrimony also grows in very deep shade, so it is useful for filling a dark corner in the garden.

Season: July–September
Height: 30–120 cm (1–4 ft)
Cultivation: Hemp-agrimony is a perennial plant which can be divided up in autumn or spring; or sow the small seed on the surface of the compost in a seed tray in autumn or spring. Cover the tray with glass to keep the compost moist.
Other sites: Sun; semi-shade; shade.

Meadowsweet, or queen-of-the-meadows, is indeed a lovely flower. Its white blooms, tinged with yellowish-green, grow in crowded clusters, and they are so light and feathery that the slightest breeze will ruffle them. Its leaves, which are delightfully fragrant, are dark and shiny and almost fern-like.

Meadowsweet is a flower of late summer, found growing along streams and ditches and in wet meadows. In the garden it grows in any soil that is fertile and remains moist in summer. A drift of meadowsweet looks attractive on its own, though it also grows well with ragged-robin, and purple and yellow loosestrife.

The flowers have a wonderful sweet fragrance, sometimes described as almond-like, but this can be very overpowering in a confined space. In the sixteenth century the plant was used as a strewing herb and was the favourite of Queen Elizabeth I. In centuries past the flower was called meadsweet or meadwort which referred not to its meadow habitat but to its use in flavouring mead and other wines. Meadowsweet leaves and flowers are an important addition to pot-pourri, and the plant has been used medicinally to cure fevers.

Season: June–September
Height: 60–120 cm (2–4 ft)
Cultivation: Meadowsweet is a perennial plant that produces plenty of seed. Sow seed in moist ground in autumn or spring, and cover only very lightly with soil. Mature plants can be split up easily in the autumn and planted out in moist soil.
Other sites: Sun; semi-shade.

Water avens

Geum rivale

Water avens is an unusual and delicate plant to grow in the wet soil by the side of the pond. Its drooping, bell-shaped flowers appear in a subtle combination of purple, pink and orange, which look particularly striking when set off by the dark green leaves. It is often found growing in the wild in wet meadows, or in shady damp woods, and is a close relative of yellow-flowered wood avens. Although wood avens does not normally grow in wet soils, the two plants do sometimes grow together, and when this happens they readily cross, which can be confusing, as the resulting plants usually have more characteristics of wood avens, including the yellow flower.

Water avens is best grown as a dense ground-cover on the pond margin, where its unusual nodding flowers will look marvellous reflected in the water. This plant particularly likes shade, especially deep shade, so if you have a suitable area, you could grow water avens with wood crane's-bill, red campion and oxlip. In deep shade, water avens can be grown amongst wood spurge, lady-fern and royal fern for a cool and pleasing effect.

Season: May–September **Height:** 45–60 cm (1½–2 ft)

Cultivation: Water avens is a perennial plant which produces lots of small seeds. Sow seeds in autumn or spring where they are to flower and cover lightly with soil. Germination in spring will take a few weeks. Seedlings may be transplanted when they are large enough to handle.

Other sites: Sun; semi-shade; shade.

Water-violet

Hottonia palustris

This is a lovely and elegant flower that should have a place in every pond. Its name is most misleading as it is not related to the violets at all, and is in fact a member of the primrose family and the only native member of this family to grow in the water. Its delicate, pale mauve flowers with a yellow throat look like a paler version of bird's-eye primrose, and its leaves are particularly decorative being very finely cut, like a yarrow leaf. This has given the plant the country names of 'featherfoil' and 'water yarrow'.

The plant grows from long, thread-like, black roots which are tipped with white. Some roots are free-floating while others penetrate into the soft mud at the bottom of the pond. Only the flowering part of the stems stay above the water, the remaining stem and leaves being submerged. Water-violet is rapidly becoming scarce in the wild, largely as a result of pollution in the rivers.

Water-violet is easy to establish in a pond and should be allowed to increase naturally. Seed can be collected in late summer and kept moist until sown.

Season: May–June **Height:** 30 cm (1 ft) above water

Cultivation: Water-violet is an aquatic perennial. Sow seed thinly, when fresh if possible, into pots of seed compost. Stand the pots in a container of water, so that the water comes above the level of the pots. Ideally they should be kept at a temperature of 15°C (60°F) until the seeds germinate.

Other sites: None.

Yellow iris
Iris pseudacorus

Yellow iris, or yellow flag as it is commonly known, is a handsome and stately plant of marshes, wet woods and the margins of ponds, rivers and ditches. With large, bright yellow flowers and long sword-like leaves, this is a magnificent plant for the shallow edge of the garden pond. It will grow in water up to 15 cm (6 in) deep. The large flowers are veined with purple and are pollinated by honey bees and hoverflies. The plant secretes a lot of nectar which gives it a lovely sweet scent. Yellow iris is one of only two irises native to Britain, the other being the much less spectacular stinking iris.

Yellow iris should be grown by everyone who has a pond or ditch or piece of boggy ground. Although it grows happily in semi-shade, it needs full sun in order to produce the maximum blooms. In deep shade it will not flower at all, but it will spread quickly by stout, underground rhizomes, so a certain measure of control will be necessary.

Season: May–July

Height: 40–150 cm (1½–5 ft)

Cultivation: Yellow iris is a perennial wetland plant that grows from a thick rhizome. This rhizome can be divided up in spring or autumn and planted out in wet ground; or sow seeds in autumn in a pot of seed compost. Stand the pot in a dish of water to keep the compost very moist, then cover the pot with glass and leave it outside in a sheltered spot over winter. Germination should take place in spring.

Other sites: Sun; semi-shade.

Yellow loosestrife
Lysimachia vulgaris

This is a tall and handsome plant with cheerful, bright yellow flowers growing in clusters amongst the large, lance-shaped leaves. In the wild, it grows on the banks of rivers and streams and on wet and marshy ground. It is often dwarfed by much taller rushes and grasses and it seems to thrive in this semi-shady situation.

In the garden, yellow loosestrife will grow in any soil that remains moist during the summer. A wetland area by a pond would be ideal, especially if the site is in some shade. Although yellow and purple loosestrife are not related to each other they will grow very well together in the garden and produce a most eye-catching and striking combination of colours.

Although not used by modern herbalists, yellow loosestrife was considered at one time to be a valuable medicinal plant. It was also said to have a calming effect on oxen and horses, and used to be burnt in the house to deter insects.

Season: July–August

Height: 60–150 cm (2–5 ft)

Cultivation: Yellow loosestrife is a perennial plant that grows from a spreading rootstock. This can be split up in spring or autumn and planted out; or sow seeds in autumn or spring and cover lightly with soil. Sometimes with an autumn sowing seedlings do not appear until the spring, so mark the spot well.

Other sites: Sun; semi-shade.

Purple loosestrife
Lythrum salicaria

Purple loosestrife is a brilliantly colourful flower which sends up tall spires of reddish-purple flowers from June through to August. It can grow up to 120 cm (4 ft) tall, hence the descriptive country name of 'long purples'. The plant grows in rich, marshy areas, by streams and lakes and may occasionally be found with yellow loosestrife, hemp-agrimony and greater spearwort. These tall flowering plants would also look most colourful growing together in the marshy area of the garden.

Purple loosestrife will grow in semi-shade but flowers more profusely in full sun. The plant produces an enormous quantity of seeds which require strong light (preferably direct sunlight) to make them germinate.

At one time, purple loosestrife was used for tanning leather as it has a high tannin content. Now it is used medicinally to clean wounds, as a gargle and as an eyewash.

Season: June–August
Height: 60–120 cm (2–4 ft)
Cultivation: Purple loosestrife is a perennial plant. Divide rootstock in March or take cuttings of new shoots in April and insert them in cutting compost, which should be kept damp until the shoots have rooted; or sow the tiny seed thinly on the surface of the compost in a seed tray in spring. Give the tray maximum light and place it in a tray of water to keep the compost moist.
Other sites: Sun; semi-shade.

Water mint
Mentha aquatica

Water mint – the prettiest of all the mints – is a wonderful, fragrant, spreading plant that produces a profusion of lilac-type blooms late in the summer. The flowers are usually covered in butterflies and bees as water mint is a favourite nectar plant. Its leaves are soft and downy and have a strong scent that seems to differ from one plant to another: sometimes the scent is fruity, and sometimes it is a little like peppermint.

Water mint is commonly found growing by streams, ponds, in fens, marshes and other wet places, including woods. In the garden it is a beautiful plant to grow along the side or in the shallows of the pond. It could also be allowed to scramble amongst other flowers in the marshy area or in other moist soil. A particularly attractive combination of flowers would be water mint, devil's-bit scabious and grass-of-Parnassus; but bear in mind that mint plants are very vigorous and spread by underground runners, each runner producing many roots and shoots. Growing mint in a container is a good way to keep it within bounds and it would make a beautiful show in full flower, growing in a decorative pot on the patio.

Season: July–October
Height: 15–60 cm (6 in–2 ft)
Cultivation: Water mint is a perennial plant with a creeping rootstock. Division of this rootstock is simple. Bury pieces of root, a few centimetres long, in moist soil to a depth of 2 cm (1 in), where they will quickly root and produce leaves. Seed may also be sown in moist ground and should not be covered.
Other sites: Sun; semi-shade.

Bogbean
Menyanthes trifoliata

This beautiful flower is a must for the water garden. Not only is it very attractive, flowering over a long period of time, but it is also very easy to grow and spreads quickly. Before bogbean flowers open, the buds are a bright rose-pink colour, and when fully open they look like white stars. Each petal is fringed with delicate white threads which give the flowers the beauty of frost crystals in the sun. The leaves are like those of the garden bean, hence the name of the plant.

Bogbean grows in the wild in marshes, bogs, ditches, reed beds, and even on ground as high as 1000 m (3000 ft). Its fibrous roots form a raft on soft, boggy ground but as the plant often floats in a dense mat in deeper water, it could be very treacherous to step on such an area. The roots can float freely as well as rooting into the mud.

In the garden it will grow best in shallow water or boggy ground. It can probably withstand rather dry conditions in late summer, provided it has plenty of moisture during its main growing season in spring and early summer. The plant will quickly spread to form a dense ground-cover, which, when in flower, will be quite a stunning sight.

Bogbean was once a popular medicinal plant, good for treating liver and skin complaints and as a tonic. The leaves have been used in brewing, and were also once smoked as a tobacco substitute.

Season: May–July   **Height:** 10–30 cm (4 in–1 ft)
Cultivation: Bogbean is a perennial aquatic plant with a creeping rhizome. The rhizome may be divided during spring and summer and pressed into moist ground, where it will soon root. Sow seed in spring and press into the wet soil or compost; do not cover.
Other sites: None.

White water-lily
Nymphaea alba

White water-lily is the most exotic and perhaps the most perfect of all our native wild flowers. In some lakes huge areas of the water are completely covered with the shiny leaves, justifying its other common names of 'queen-of-the-waters' and 'lady-of-the-lake'. The flowers are sweetly scented but this is only really noticeable in the sun; they open late in the morning and close up again and partly submerge in the evening.

White water-lilies are lovely flowers for garden ponds, but they are large and vigorous and need to be kept under control so that they do not cover more than a quarter of the surface. They will grow in water up to about 3 m (10 ft) deep. The seed capsules appear above the water after flowering and then submerge to ripen before bursting underwater to liberate the small, pink seeds.

Season: July–August   **Height:** Floating
Cultivation: White water-lily is a perennial plant which grows from a stout rhizome that is easily divided before regrowth starts in March. You can prevent the plant spreading too vigorously by planting it in a plastic basket. Cover the rhizome to a depth of 25 cm (10 in) with good rich soil and then sand, to anchor the plant. Set the basket in a minimum of 30 cm (1 ft) of water. Renew the soil in the basket every three to four years.

Seeds are difficult to collect as they ripen underwater. They should be buried when ripe in rich soil in a small container submerged in water. Trans-plant seedlings into individual containers of rich soil when large enough. These should also be kept submerged.
Other sites: None.

Grass-of-Parnassus
Parnassia palustris

This rather rare plant, growing mainly in the north of England, has exceptionally pretty, creamy-white blooms with a green veining. It needs to be seen at close quarters for the exquisite detail and subtle colouring of the flowers to be made apparent. It is a flower of marshes, fens and moors and prefers alkaline soil. Grass-of-Parnassus is not, of course, a grass, and since its leaves are not remotely grass-like it is difficult to understand how it received its name! Even the reference to Parnassus is rather obscure as the plant certainly doesn't grow profusely, if at all, on the holy mountain of Apollo.

But whatever its origins, grass-of-Parnassus is a lovely delicate flower to grow in the garden and would look most attractive growing in a damp, marshy area at the edge of a pond, along with water mint, devil's-bit scabious, lesser spearwort and yellow iris.

The flowers have a faint scent of honey and this, together with the green veining on the petals, attracts many insects to them.

Season: July–October   **Height:** 10–30 cm (4 in–1 ft)
Cultivation: Grass-of-Parnassus is a perennial plant which, once established, may be easily increased by division in the spring and planted out in wet soil. Seed can sometimes be obtained and should be sown in wet soil in the spring.
Other sites: Sun; semi-shade.

Common comfrey
Symphytum officinale

In the wild, common comfrey is often found growing by rivers and streams and in damp ditches, and it makes an attractive plant for the edge of the garden pond. It can grow quite tall and produces delicate sprays of nodding bell-shaped flowers. These are usually cream, but pink or mauve flowers are sometimes found. One word of warning though – be sure of a permanent site before you plant comfrey, as it can establish itself very quickly and is difficult to eradicate.

Common comfrey has, for at least 2,000 years, been one of the most valued medicinal plants. Its common names of 'knitbone' and 'boneset' indicate its properties for setting broken bones. Comfrey ointment is also remarkably effective for healing cuts and sores. It is also a valuable organic fertilizer for the garden as its leaves contain a large amount of potash.

Season: May–July
Height: 30–120 cm (1–4 ft)
Cultivation: Common comfrey is a perennial plant that grows from an extensive, fleshy rootstock. It is easily propagated by breaking off a section of root, preferably one with a growing point, during the growing season (March to September) and planting it 2 cm (1 in) below the surface of the soil. Sow seed in spring in a tray of compost and cover lightly. Germination is slow and erratic
Other sites: Sun; semi-shade.

Common valerian

Valeriana officinalis

Brooklime

Veronica beccabunga

Common valerian is a very versatile and adaptable plant and can be grown successfully in almost any garden soil, in sun or deep shade. It is the earliest flowering tall wetland plant and its heads of beautiful, delicate pink flowers give some early summer colour to pond edges. Plant common valerian in a clump and it will look spectacular when in flower. It may also be grown in grass and looks very decorative in a mixed border or bed of wild flowers.

In the wild, common valerian is often found growing in marshes, on stream banks, in moist woods in the deepest shade, and sometimes on sea cliffs.

Common valerian also has many valuable medicinal properties. It is a powerful nerve stimulant and antispasmodic and is especially valuable in cases of strain, neuralgia and migraine. Cats love the plant; they are attracted by the strong smelling roots.

Season: June–July

Height: 30–120 cm (1–4 ft)

Cultivation: Common valerian is a perennial plant that may be divided by splitting the rootstock in spring or autumn and planting out. Alternatively, sow seeds in spring where the plants are to grow, or in a seed tray, and cover lightly with soil.

Other sites: Sun, semi-shade; shade; seaside garden.

Brooklime is a pretty, creeping plant to grow on the banks of the pond or in the pond shallows. Its bright blue flowers with a white eye and dark veins, and dark green, shiny leaves grow from succulent stems which spread rapidly along the ground, sending out roots and upright shoots at intervals. The flowers, which are occasionally pink, go on flowering all through the summer. Honey bees are frequent visitors to the plant. Brooklime will rapidly cover any unsightly areas of wet, muddy ground in the garden, but it is so easy to pull up that there is little danger of it getting out of control.

Brooklime, water forget-me-not and water mint look attractive growing together, especially as ground-cover between taller plants such as yellow iris, purple and yellow loosestrife and common valerian.

Brooklime used to be eaten as a salad vegetable, often with watercress which grows in the same wet areas, but the taste is really too pungent to be very palatable. (Indeed the Latin name *beccabunga* means 'smarting mouth', referring to the taste of the acrid leaves.) At one time brooklime was taken as a cure for scurvy.

Season: May–September   **Height:** 20–30 cm (8 in–1 ft)

Cultivation: Brooklime is a perennial plant with prostrate rooting stems. These stems can be divided during the growing season and planted out into wet soil. The stems will root in mud or float in water. Seed may also be collected and sown in spring into wet soil or compost and firmed in. Do not cover the seed with soil.

Other sites: Sun; semi-shade.

WILD FLOWERS FOR
Rock Gardens

Re-creating a mountain landscape *In a mature rock garden, the plants will spread naturally over the rocks.*

There are many beautiful, delicate flowers that thrive in the extreme conditions to be found in high hill and mountain country. These areas of unspoiled wilderness hold a fascination for many people, living as most of us do in the overpopulated lowlands. Compared with the heavy interference of man on the rest of our landscape, the mountains and their flora are to our eyes natural, although in times past man has altered the mountain landscape by clearing the original forest cover and grazing sheep.

The alpines have adapted themselves beautifully to the difficult conditions in which they live. Winters are long and summers short, so most mountain plants flower in early summer and have often produced seed within a few weeks of flowering. Insects are scarce at high altitudes, so many plants are self-pollinating, or rely on rhizomes and runners to propagate themselves rather than seeds.

In the mountains there is a wide variety of different habitats, and for this reason it is difficult to define an 'alpine' plant. Plants can be found growing in pockets of rich, moist soil; perched in crevices; amongst loose scree; and on mountain meadows, wetlands and heaths. Any one of these habitats makes a fascinating feature for the smallest wildflower garden.

Rock garden in summer

No garden is too small to grow some of the lovely colourful alpine plants, many of which we don't get the chance to see in the wild. Most of them can be grown in stone sinks, in cracks in drystone and brick walls, and on gravel or scree.

The plants on this page were all grown in gardens; wild flowers should not be taken from the countryside.

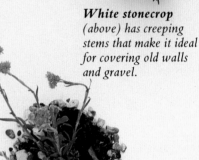

White stonecrop *(above) has creeping stems that make it ideal for covering old walls and gravel.*

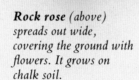

Shrubby cinquefoil *(above) grows naturally on damp rock in mountain areas.*

Rock rose *(above) spreads out wide, covering the ground with flowers. It grows on chalk soil.*

Mountain everlasting *(above) produces leafy rooting runners from creeping stems.*

Tormentil *(left) is a delicate and graceful plant with attractive foliage and long flower stems.*

Chalk milkwort *(above) is a beautiful flower of short grassland on chalk. Its neat form makes it a good plant for the rock garden.*

Wild thyme *(above) is an excellent carpeting plant with aromatic foliage that is loved by bees. It likes a hot, dry situation.*

Heather *(below) is a well-loved flower of moors and heaths that likes acid soil. It tolerates some shade.*

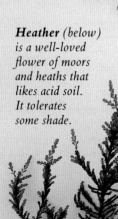

Londonpride *(below) is an established garden escape. It is easy to grow, preferring some moisture to do well.*

Clustered bellflower *(below) is an exquisite flower of chalk grassland that makes a colourful feature plant.*

Spring squill *(below) is a lovely and rare native bulb from the west coasts of Britain, France and Norway.*

Alpine lady's-mantle
(above) has very
attractive foliage for
ground cover. It prefers
sun or semi-shade and
acid soil.

Roseroot (right).
The large, fleshy
root enables the
plant to survive in
dry conditions. It
prefers poor,
neutral soil.

Pebbles (above) keep
down the weeds, and can
be mixed with the soil to
ensure good drainage.

Ivy-leaved toadflax
(above) will spread into
all the cracks of a brick
or stone wall. It seeds
freely and often has
white flowers.

Bloody crane's-bill
(right) loves semi-shade
and some moisture: it is
found near woods as well
as on high ground.

Chives (below) is a rare
native plant of chalk and
limestone grassland and
sea cliffs. It requires
moderate moisture and a
sunny site.

Reflexed stonecrop
(above) has creeping
stems that enable it to
spread into an attractive
clump. It will survive
dry conditions.

Rock cinquefoil (right)
is a rare native for
growing in hot, dry
situations. It prefers an
acid soil.

Pasqueflower
(right) is a rare
plant of chalk or
limestone.
Striking purple
flowers precede the
silky seed-heads.

Wildflower rock gardens

Rock gardens: the possibilities

The beauty of growing alpine and rock plants is that they take up little space. There is no need to import tons of rock or create an artificial hillside in order to grow them. With a little imagination and ingenuity, you can re-create several different mountain habitats in the smallest garden. Walls and gravel paths are excellent sites for mountain plants, and you can integrate the area into the rest of the wild garden by introducing some of the many other wild flowers that will enjoy the sharp drainage and poor soil conditions, in particular herbs and chalk downland flowers.

Native alpines, in contrast to many of the usual garden alpines, grow in areas of high year-round rainfall. So if you live in the south or east of the country, or if there is a particularly dry summer, you will need to do some watering. Covering the soil surface with gravel or stone chippings is invaluable in conserving moisture in the soil beneath.

A traditional rock garden

Unless your garden includes a natural hillside, one of the best positions for a rock garden is next to a pond. If you are digging a new pond, you can use the soil to make a mound that will serve as an ideal base for a rock

Using rocks naturally *This large-scale wild rock garden shows how rocks can be built up to resemble a natural outcrop. The 'faults' all run the same way.*

garden; and wildlife, particularly the amphibians, will enjoy the shelter it provides. There are also other, more technical, considerations that apply when siting a rock garden. In high rainfall areas it should be in full sun, but in drier parts of the country it should be shaded from the midday sun. Don't site your garden in a draughty spot – between two buildings, for instance – or in a damp hollow. If it is too close to trees the branches will drip on the plants; the roots will rob the soil of valuable moisture in the summer; and fallen leaves will be a nuisance.

The basic construction is the same for all rock gardens (see p. 136): it is when you reach the stage of adding the rocks that imagination and skill come into play! Local stone will look most natural if you can get it; otherwise, weathered limestone is best, but sandstone, granite and tufa (see 'Sink gardens') are all suitable. Rocks dotted around like currants on a bun don't look convincing. Try to imagine how the rocks would look in their natural setting. They would be arranged in definite layers – not rigidly horizontal like bricks in a wall, but in a general line with the occasional vertical break, like a fault line.

A wide range of plants can be grown in the rock garden, including bloody crane's-bill, carline thistle, chives, goldenrod, horseshoe vetch, maiden pink, mountain avens, mountain pansy, pasqueflower, purple

Siting a rock garden In my garden, which is flat, I grow wild rock plants in a special bed at the front of a cottage-garden border. Reflexed stonecrop, ivy-leaved toadflax and yellow corydalis grow from a low brick retaining wall, backed by thymes and hyssop.

saxifrage, rock cinquefoil, roseroot and thrift. Jacob's-ladder is an old cottage-garden favourite and very rare in the wild: it will grow in the rock garden or in scree. Bird's-eye primrose is especially beautiful but requires a soil that retains moisture.

If you have a shady spot in the rock garden, it's worth adding some leaf-mould or compost to the soil to help the moisture-retention. Several plants would then thrive there, including the exquisite wood-sorrel, and the colourful wood crane's-bill and Welsh poppy. Ferns would also do well, especially maidenhair spleenwort and parsley fern.

A simple rock outcrop

This takes up very little space and looks good cut out of a flowering grass area. A slope is an ideal site, and several separate outcrops would be quite dramatic. Start with an interesting, preferably large, rock, and build around it, adding smaller rocks and stone chippings. You should try to achieve the effect of underlying rock being exposed above the ground by the action of the weather. Some of the scree plants (see p. 111) can be grown here; and any crevices in the rock can be filled with rock-garden soil mixture and planted with small wall or rock plants.

A scree garden

A simple and attractive way of growing rock plants is on scree, and with its perfect drainage it is ideal for plants that are prone to neck rot. It should be built in the same way as a rock garden (see p. 136), but on top of the rubble there should be a 15 cm (6 in) layer consisting of a mixture of 5 parts of 1 cm (½ in) stone chips or gravel and 1 part of soil and peat mixed together in equal quantities.

Plants that particularly enjoy scree include alpine lady's-mantle, Jacob's-ladder and wild thyme. As a surprise addition, you could include red campion. This flower is normally associated with lowland habitats, and will grow on scree and cliffs up to 1,000 m (3,500 ft) high. Once the area is planted, finish off with a layer of stone chips and a few larger pieces of rock, for a natural effect.

Gravel paths

Paths make an ideal setting for a wide range of plants. The basic gravel path (see p. 137 for construction details),

---

Sink gardens

Growing alpines in a sink is very rewarding, particularly for those without the space for anything larger. The ideal containers, if you can get hold of them, are old stone sinks or troughs, but they must have a drainage hole – if not, you will have to drill one. The next best option is an old white glazed sink. The shiny outer surface can be disguised by coating it with PVA adhesive, extending the coating over the edge and a few centimetres down inside the sink. The whole surface should then be covered with hypertufa, which can be made by thoroughly mixing 2 parts of moist sieved sphagnum peat, 1 part fine grit or coarse sand and 1 part cement, and then adding sufficient water to form a stiff paste. Cover the sink with a minimum 1 cm (½ in) layer, and then work the material to the texture of weathered stone (this is where artistic ability comes into its own!). You can cast a whole sink in this material, using a home-made wooden mould, although this requires a good deal of expertise. If you do make your own 'sink', take the opportunity to form several drainage holes in the bottom. Sink gardens can be appreciated best if they are raised off the ground on supports constructed of flat stone or old brick.

Fill the container with a shallow layer (5 cm/2 in or so) of broken pots or gravel (there must be crocks over the drainage holes). On top of this place inverted turf (short mown, of course, with no docks, thistles or bindweed!) or instead use coarse peat, having sieved out the fine stuff. Top up with soil-based potting compost or a mixture of 3 parts loam, 2 parts sphagnum peat and 1 part grit or coarse sand. Some ½ cm (¼ in) limestone chippings will give especially sharp drainage, but they are not essential. Firm down the soil as you fill, otherwise it will settle later and your plants will be hidden behind the rim of the sink.

It is best to have one large rock in the sink, with smaller ones clustered near it, rather than odd bits dotted about. Any kind of rock will do, but the best type for sinks is tufa. This is very porous and can be drilled to make planting holes (you could even try using a piece on its own as a truly miniature rock garden!).

The majority of plants in a sink garden should be low-growing, with some trailing over the edge. One or two taller plants could be used for a vertical accent, and a small shrubby plant such as common rock-rose will add a different texture. Any of the smaller rock plants would be suitable, and it is worth including some small bulbs for spring interest – try snowdrops, winter aconites (*Eranthis hyemalis*), spring squills and chives. You could vary the planting conditions by using acid soil (omit the limestone chippings and add 3 parts, not 2, of sphagnum peat) or by making a miniature scree garden.

A slab garden is an interesting and simple variation on the sink. Start with a paving slab set on a short pillar of stones or bricks. Place small pieces of rock around the sides to hold the soil on the slab. The rocks can be anchored with a little cement, but don't overdo it. More rocks can be used in the middle and the spaces filled with rock-garden soil (p. 136).

A miniature rock garden *Don't overcrowd a small sink with plants: they will look unnatural and will compete for the limited space.*

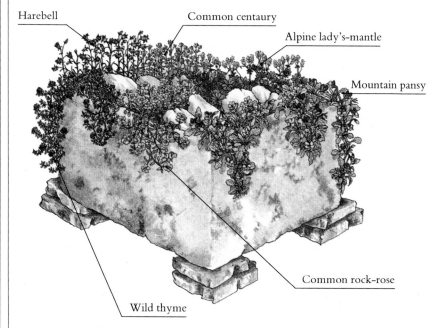

Harebell

Common centaury

Alpine lady's-mantle

Mountain pansy

Common rock-rose

Wild thyme

with soil fairly near the surface, will be both moisture-retentive and fertile. It can be planted with a terrific range of wild flowers, including some seaside plants. You will find flowers seeding themselves there and taking over the whole path if allowed! Herbs in particular will mix well with the wild flowers here – try scented ones such as basil, coriander, fennel, hyssop, marjoram, pot marigold, sage, thyme, and winter and summer savory. An occasional giant such as great mullein will add another dimension to your path!

If you want to grow a full range of rock-garden plants in gravel, you should use a minimum of 15 cm (6 in) gravel mixed with sharp sand (the amount is not critical). It is well worth forking over the soil first and mixing in some gravel before adding the gravel-and-sand layer. Wild flowers that like scree will grow particularly well here, as will the small, carpeting plants – try chamomile (the non-flowering 'Treneague' variety) and wild thyme for a fragrant, cushioned walk.

A wall garden

Existing drystone walls and even old brick walls can be adapted for growing quite a range of plants by making use of natural faults and missing bricks; rock-garden soil (see p. 136) can be added to crevices.

If you are starting from scratch, the best type of wall to build, providing that the rock is available locally, is a drystone one. This can be a single wall with plenty of gaps for plants, or a double wall which will also allow you to grow plants along the top. Plants rooting in the side of the double wall will have the middle filling for their roots to run along, which means a far greater variety of plants may be grown. If you have a bank or want to create another level, retaining walls have great possibilities for planting, but they must be skilfully constructed on a solid foundation.

Unless you are experienced at building walls, I suggest you limit yourself to a low one – say 60 cm (2 ft) or so. Dig out a shallow trench twice the width of the wall (if the ground is soft, dig down to solid soil). The stones should be angled into the centre of the wall, or into the bank if it is a retaining wall, as you lay them. A single wall could be two stones wide

Walls as backdrops Often the soil next to a wall will be dry and fast-draining, since much of the moisture is absorbed by the wall. If the site is not too shady a wide range of rock plants can be grown there. Here crane's-bill and chives going to seed are backed by yellow mullein.

Planting a wall Herb-robert and ivy-leaved toadflax scramble up this drystone wall at Benthall Hall, while a yellow daisy-flowered garden Senecio leans down from the top of the wall.

at the base, narrowing to a stone's width at the top; a double wall could be about 1.2 m (4 ft) at the base and 1 m (3 ft) at the top with a central filling of rubble or stones mixed with soil, added as you build the wall, and topped with a layer of rock-garden soil. Ram stones or brick rubble into the trench to hold the first layer of stones in position. Use soil between the stones in place of mortar as you build: although not a true drystone construction technique, it will help

greatly to stabilize the wall if you are not an expert – and also provide the maximum planting opportunities.

Wild flowers worth planting in walls include biting stonecrop, ivy-leaved toadflax, wallflower, wall germander, wild thyme and yellow corydalis; herb-robert will flourish in particular on the shady side of a wall. Three ferns that are particularly suitable for walls are maidenhair spleenwort, parsley fern and wall-rue (*Asplenium ruta-muraria*).

Feature plants for rock gardens

A rock garden, be it a stone sink or an area of scree, provides plenty of scope for growing some of the daintiest and most delicate wild alpine plants, found in the wild growing on windswept upland pastures and mist-covered rocks.

Alpine lady's-mantle
Alchemilla alpina

This is an especially lovely foliage plant with the most beautiful leaves of any wild flower. The leaves are made up of five or seven segments, glossy green on the top and silver underneath, each one covered in silky down and bordered with silver. After rain, when the drops are still on the leaves, the plants sparkle in the sun. The tiny, yellowish-green flowers grow in dense and pretty clusters above the leaves.

In the wild, alpine lady's-mantle grows on mountain grasslands, in rock crevices and on screes, and it looks perfectly at home in any kind of rock garden. If you let it self-seed, the seedlings will start to emerge in all sorts of places amongst the rocks. The foliage will also look delightful against the stone chippings of a small scree, or gravel path. It is a useful ground-cover plant with a creeping rootstock. In a suitable situation the silver-edged evergreen foliage will carpet the ground and look decorative in both winter and summer.

Alpine lady's-mantle can be grown in short grassland. Once the flowers are over, the grass should be kept cut as short as possible without cutting into the foliage.

Season: June–August　**Height:** to 20 cm (8 in)
Cultivation: Alpine lady's-mantle is a perennial evergreen plant with a woody stem. Plants may be divided in spring or autumn. The tiny seed should be sown in autumn or spring in a seed tray. Press into the soil and do not cover. Germination may be slow.
Other sites: Sun.

Mountain avens
Dryas octopetala

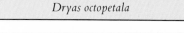

Mountain avens is a beautiful alpine plant that will grow in any well-drained, poor, alkaline soil, whether in a rock garden or a raised bed. Its flowers are white with a gold centre, rather like white pasqueflowers, and are quite large in relation to the plant itself. The most decorative aspect of the flowers are its long, white, silky awns (fluffy hair), to which the many seeds are attached. When the seed is ripe, the awns carry it away in the mountain gales. The leaves are evergreen, and covered on the underside with a soft white down. Mountain avens looks attractive growing in combination with the lovely blue flowers of spring gentian and with purple saxifrage.

Mountain avens spreads quickly and will rapidly form a carpet over the rocks. In some places, if allowed to do so, it can grow into an extensive heath. Although the plant is very low-growing in the wild, this characteristic will often disappear to some extent when it is grown in a 'luxurious' garden situation.

Season: May–July　**Height:** 2–7 cm (1–3 in)
Cultivation: Mountain avens is a woody, perennial undershrub. It may be divided in early autumn or spring; or sow seed in spring (with the feathery awn attached if possible) and cover lightly with soil, leaving the awn uncovered. Germination may be erratic.
Other sites: Sun.

Bloody crane's-bill
Geranium sanguineum

Bloody crane's-bill is a most adaptable plant and will settle into the garden in many different situations. If you only have one crane's-bill in the garden this is the one to choose for its brilliant colour and compact habit. Bloody crane's-bill is not a common plant in the wild, but it does grow in some profusion in the north of England, on the Scottish coast and on the Burren of County Clare. It grows on alkaline soils in upland meadows, on rocks, by the sea, and even in woods.

Unusual wild plants such as bloody crane's-bill are particularly interesting additions to the wildflower garden. By having them close where you can appreciate them you can get to know them and appreciate their particular beauty and how they grow. If you are then lucky enough to come across them in their natural habitats it is like meeting old friends and, like people, it is often suprising to see the differences when they are on their home ground. Growing wild plants in the garden should really be an encouragement for us to go out and discover them in the wild and appreciate them the more for it.

In the garden, bloody crane's-bill grows best in the sun or light shade in a well-drained, fertile and alkaline soil. It makes a lovely plant for the rock garden and will also establish well in a hedgebank or other semi-shady situation. It is happy growing in grass, and young plants should be introduced from autumn to spring into grass that has been cut short.

Season: June–August   **Height:** 10–40 cm (4–16 in)
Cultivation: Bloody crane's-bill is a perennial plant that may easily be grown from seed. Rub the seed between two sheets of sandpaper to speed germination. Sow the seed in spring or during September either where it is to flower or in trays, and cover with soil. Thin plants to 30–45 cm (1–1¼ ft) apart.
Other sites: Sun; semi-shade.

Common rock-rose
Helianthemum chamaecistus (syn. *H. nummularium*)

Rock-rose, sun-rose, beauty-of-the-sun or, best of all, *l'herbe d'or*, is truly a flower of the sun. Its delicate golden blooms close up when the sun goes in and the plant becomes insignificant, so small are its leaves. In its season, when the sun is out, the rock-rose is a blaze of golden blooms, a really marvellous sight and very attractive to bees. Common rock-rose is also a food plant of the green hairstreak butterfly. There are several garden forms of the rock-rose, including one with red flowers, but the wild plant has a charm that is hard to beat.

As its name suggests, it is a rock plant and a plant of chalk soils low in nitrogen. It will thrive on a bed of gravel a few inches deep with its roots growing down into the soil, so is ideal for decorating a gravel path or drive. It would feel at home too in a chalk or shingle garden. If you grow it in grass then the soil should be stony and poor on top so that the fine grasses sown will never grow very vigorously. Normally when it grows in grassland, sheep keep the grasses grazed around the plant. This is the problem with keeping some of the smaller and often colourful wild flowers flourishing in grass: the slightest fertility and the grasses grow too vigorously and swamp the flowers.

Season: May–September   **Height:** 5–30 cm (2–12 in)
Cultivation: Rock-rose is a shrubby perennial plant. Seed is difficult to germinate and should be rubbed between two sheets of sandpaper before sowing. Sow in a seed tray in spring or autumn and leave in a shady place till seed germinates, which might take several months. Plant out in spring or early autumn. (Plants for grassy sites should be planted in autumn after the grass is mown).
Other sites: Sun.

Bird's-eye primrose
Primula farinosa

Bird's-eye primrose grows high up in the hills of northern England. It is a little more widespread on the continent, but most people will never see it in its natural habitat.

I first grew this flower, never having seen it in the wild, from a little packet of seed sent to me by a friend. Like common primrose seed it needs to be sown in the autumn and germinates after the cold of winter in March or April. The first surprise was the tiny leaves that were so pale they were nearly white. The following year a few plants flowered. No picture had prepared me for the delicate beauty of these flowers. I have been growing them ever since, and hope soon to have enough seed to be able to supply it to other gardeners. The plant requires moisture but reasonable drainage and finding a suitable place in the garden will need some experiment. It will grow in grass but the grass needs to be very low-growing, and without the benefit of grazing animals this is difficult to maintain.

Season: June–July **Height:** 10–20 cm (4–8 in)
Cultivation: Bird's-eye primrose is a perennial plant that grows easily from seed. Sow in a tray of ordinary seed compost in autumn (the seeds need winter cold to germinate) and barely cover with soil. Cover the tray with a sheet of glass until the seed has germinated. Plant the young plants in full sun in a moist, alkaline soil that is not too fertile.
Other sites: Sun.

Pasqueflower
Pulsatilla vulgaris

Pasque-, or Easter, flower is rare in the wild but it has long been established in gardens in several forms. It grows on the chalk of the Chilterns and Cambridgeshire, on the limestone of the Cotswolds, and in a few other areas on the east side of the country. This plant was probably rather more widely distributed before the chalk grasslands were brought into cultivation. In the rest of northern Europe it is much more frequent on dry upland pastures.

Pasqueflower is a most valuable medicinal herb and is a standard homeopathic remedy, being a specific for measles but having many other applications as well. It is also a dye plant, the flowers yielding a bright green dye and the leaves also giving a green. The plant was often used to stain Easter eggs.

The plant is very attractive at all stages. The leaves are decorative—feathery and silky—the young flower buds are also silky, and the open flowers of rich purple gleam like satin in the sun. Then the beautiful silky seed-heads appear, each seed attached to a feathery plume which carries the seed on the wind when ripe.

Pasqueflower is a member of the buttercup family, and like buttercups has an acrid taste. It is avoided by cattle but goats seem to like it quite well!

Season: April–June **Height:** 10–20 cm (4–8 in)
Cultivation: Pasqueflower is a perennial plant that requires a well-drained, alkaline soil in full sun. The seed is best sown when ripe, in June–July although, contrary to popular belief, the seed still germinates reasonably well after several years if stored in conditions of low humidity. Sow in trays and barely cover with soil. Germination may be slow and patience is required.
Other sites: Sun; semi-shade.

Roseroot
Sedum rosea

There are so many lovely alpine flowers that selecting the best is an impossible task! Many of the alpines or rock plants available are not of course native to the UK, so these cannot come into such a selection. Of the native sedums or stonecrops, roseroot has many points in its favour and would always be on my top list of good alpines. The silvery green succulent leaves stand out against the darker rocks or soil and give year-long interest. The large, orange-yellow flower-heads appear in May–June and like all sedums attract the bees and butterflies. But roseroot has a fragrant surprise up its sleeve (so to speak!). Cut the plant and the scent is of damask roses! Plants are full of surprises.

Roseroot is native only to the north and west of England and mainly the north of Scotland, so although it enjoys sharp drainage, it is used to a high rainfall.

Roseroot is so called on account of its very thick rose-coloured rootstock which stores a considerable supply of nutrients for the plant.

Some other plants from the same family which are well worth growing are biting stonecrop (*Sedum acre*), orpine (*Sedum telephium*), reflexed stonecrop (*Sedum reflexum*) and white stonecrop (*Sedum album*). These are all attractive and suitable to grow in a sharply drained situation in full sun. Some do well in an acid soil and others prefer extra moisture. (See p. 156 for growing instructions and a full description of biting stonecrop.)

Season: May–August   **Height:** 10–30 cm (4 in–1 ft)
Cultivation: Roseroot is a perennial plant that may be propagated either by stem cuttings inserted into a gritty compost or by division of the root. Take cuttings in August or September. Roots should be divided in spring and each piece should include an 'eye'.
Other sites: None.

Wild thyme
Thymus drucei

Wild or creeping thyme is a plant of pure air and unspoilt places, and is very much associated with the hills and rocks of Scotland and the chalk downs of southern England. However, thyme does in fact grow in a very wide range of habitats, from high rocks and mountains to dry lowland grassland and even in many damp areas.

This is a lovely plant to use in the garden in conjunction with many of the other decorative and culinary thymes which are available from herb suppliers and garden centres. The wild variety is certainly hardier and more adaptable to different soil conditions than many of the non-native ones, and does not die out as readily as the others after a hard winter on heavy soil.

Wild thyme does not usually have such a strong scent as the culinary thyme and comes into flower later in July, whereas most of the decorative carpeting thymes come into flower in June. There are so many ways to use creeping thyme. Its pale purple flowers will make a soft, fragrant path, small lawn or even a seat! Grow it in gravel or sharp sand, or in a rock garden. Remember when walking on it in bare feet on a sunny summer day (which is lovely to do) that bees love the flowers! Alas, ants also like setting up home amongst it. Wild thyme also looks charming planted between bricks or paving and forming a carpet over them. It is a good plant to grow in a wall, and it will also grow in lawns which are kept well cut.

There is some confusion over the Latin names of this thyme. Often it is called *T. serphyllum*, or *T. praecox*.
Season: June–July   **Height:** Low
Cultivation: Wild thyme is a perennial plant that is easily propagated either by cuttings, or by cutting off the rooted stems and growing them on in a gritty soil and then planting out. Seed is not often available.
Other sites: None.

WILD FLOWERS FOR
Seaside Gardens

A windswept habitat *Bell heather and gorse growing by the sea at Minsmere in Suffolk.*

Whether you garden by the sea or simply want to grow seaside flowers, the wild plants of our coasts include some beautiful flowers that are well worth considering. Unless they are on inaccessible cliffs, seaside plants are threatened in several ways. Wonderful seaside salt marshes rich in wildlife have been drained for agriculture or development; and caravan parks and holiday camps have taken their toll. Thankfully there are still long stretches of unspoiled coastline, many of them now owned by the National Trust or otherwise protected and thus, hopefully, safely preserved for future generations.

Seaside plants are able to establish themselves in very unstable habitats as many of them have long roots. Where they grow in the wild, shingle is constantly moving, sands are shifting, and sea cliffs are constantly crumbling. A little further inland, where the sand dunes are stabilized with grasses, the alkaline, shell-rich sand supports a rich and colourful flora that is similar in many ways to a chalkland flora. Legumes, with their ability to fix nitrogen in the nutrient-poor sand, are represented by common bird's-foot-trefoil, white clover and common restharrow. Other colourful flowers might include hound's-tongue, viper's-bugloss, lady's bedstraw, biting stonecrop, common centaury and wild thyme.

Seaside garden in summer

Many seaside plants are attractive all year round, but they are most colourful in the summer, when a seaside patch is a welcome addition to inland as well as coastal gardens. Sea-holly, for instance, adds a dramatic focal point to any border.

The plants on this page were all grown in gardens; wild flowers should not be taken from the countryside.

Frosted orache
(left) has mealy, silvery foliage.

Annual sea-blite
(below) is a low growing, succulent plant.

Biting stonecrop
(below), or wall-pepper, is a fleshy, evergreen plant that will grow in sandy or gravelly soil.

Shells and pebbles
(above) will add an attractive finishing touch to a collection of seaside plants.

Wild carrot
(below) thrives in sandy soils. The dried seed-heads are also attractive.

Sea-holly *(right) is a superb foliage plant, metallic, spiny and very beautiful.*

Sea wormwood
(below) is a lovely, fragrant plant that spreads quickly and grows in any garden soil. It is much finer than common wormwood.

Lady's bedstraw
(below) spreads rapidly in sandy soil.

Sea campion
(below) is similar to bladder campion but smaller. It grows well in shingle.

Sea rocket *(left) is a pretty, sprawling plant bearing lilac, pink or white flowers on succulent stems. It grows well in sand.*

Sea sandwort *(below) forms a bright green carpet over shingle, binding the stones together.*

Narrow-leaved bird's-foot-trefoil *(right) has wiry stems and distinctive narrow leaves, and often grows in sand on the coast.*

Musk thistle *(below) has large, drooping, cup-shaped flower-heads which have a musky aroma.*

Slender thistle *(left) is common near the sea but it also grows inland. Insects love it.*

English stonecrop *(above) bears white flowers in June and then the whole plant turns red.*

Fennel *(below) is a lovely foliage plant with a characteristic aniseed scent. It thrives in sandy soil by the sea.*

Sea pea *(left) is a beautiful, large-flowered pea that is quite rare. It is deep rooting and grows on shingle.*

Thrift *(below) forms bright cushions of pink blooms, followed by decorative, papery seed-heads.*

Common centaury *(below) is a beautiful, sweet-scented miniature flower.*

Common sea-lavender *(left) looks best growing in drifts. It also makes a decorative dried flower.*

Wildflower seaside gardens

Many seaside flowers are most beautiful plants and well worth trying to grow in any garden. Just because they have adapted themselves successfully to such a specialized habitat doesn't mean they won't grow away from the sea; indeed most will thrive in any well-drained garden soil. They will look best, however, in a seaside-like habitat, and it is fun to try and create such an area in the garden. There is a list of plants suitable for seaside gardens on page 155.

Gardens near the sea

For those who actually live within sight of the sea and have to contend with the salt-laden air, prevailing

Seaside shrubs *This burnet rose, though low-growing compared to inland roses, will make an effective windbreak. It has black hips in autumn.*

winds and even sea sprays, quite another problem exists: that of trying to create a garden at all in such an inhospitable site. The most important element will be windbreaks, and burnet rose and sea-buckthorn (*Hippophae rhamnoides*) are both suitable and decorative.

The first piece of advice to any wildflower gardener is look around you and make a note of what is growing in nearby wild areas. This will give you the basis for a collection of wild flowers that will survive in your conditions. Unless you live very near the sea you should have few problems growing a wide range of wild flowers, and as wildflower gardening is new and experimental, the way to find out what you can grow is by trial and error.

A shingle garden

Coastal gardeners are at an advantage when it comes to creating a shingle garden. Inland gardeners will have to transport shingle from the nearest seashore if they want to be really authentic – otherwise, use 1–2 cm ($\frac{1}{2}$–1 in) stones from your local gravel pit.

The shingle garden doesn't have to cover a large area. It will look best sited next to the rock garden, if you have one, or bordering a gravel path. In any case, it must be in full sun. Dig out the area to a depth of at least 15 cm (6 in) – more drainage may be necessary in clay soils – and fill it with small stones.

The most beautiful and unusual of the shingle plants is the yellow horned-poppy. This could be combined with biting stonecrop and sea

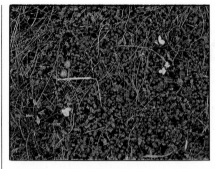

Carpeting plants *English stonecrop, with its rosy new shoots, makes a dense ground-cover for sandy soils or shingle, enlivened by common bird's-foot-trefoil.*

wormwood for a yellow/silver scheme; common restharrow or red valerian would add a splash of brighter colour. If you want to grow a wider range of plants, you can mix the shingle 50:50 with sand and grow all the sand-garden plants as well.

A sand garden

This is made in the same way as a shingle garden, but sand is used instead of shingle. A few stones and shells scattered round the plants make a decorative finishing touch.

There is a wide range of flowers liking sandy soils and these can be mixed together to provide colour from spring through the summer. A blue, pink and white scheme could include spring squill, thrift, sea-holly and sea campion. Sea-holly is particularly valuable: its spiny, metallic leaves are always spectacular and last right through winter. Other flowers well worth growing are carline thistle, fennel, sheep's-bit, lady's bedstraw and hound's-tongue.

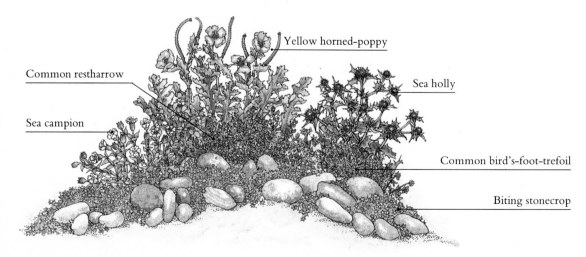

Yellow horned-poppy

Common restharrow

Sea holly

Sea campion

Common bird's-foot-trefoil

Biting stonecrop

Techniques of Wildflower Gardening

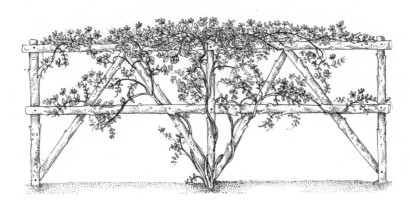

Collecting seed and raising new plants

How seed is spread in the wild

Unlikely as it may seem, blackberries, dandelion clocks and bristly teasels have something fundamental in common – these seeds are all designed to be distributed over the countryside by various means, so helping to guarantee the survival of the species. An appreciation of how some of these systems work will help you when collecting seeds and also with wild garden planning. Seeds that are carried by the wind must be collected just as they ripen but before the wind disperses them. Seed that relies on gravity, on the other hand, is often held safe in a capsule.

Seeds dispersed by gravity

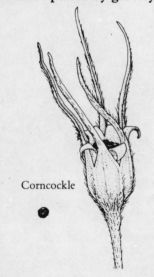

Corncockle

A very large range of plants from all families distribute their seed by simply shedding them, or, if held in a capsule, by tipping them directly on to the ground when stems are broken. Some lighter seeds may be blown a little way by wind, but most will land near to the parent plant and so give rise to a closely spaced colony. Excessive over-crowding does not occur though, because many seeds remain dormant in the soil for one or more seasons or are scavenged by mice and birds. Although most of the seeds eaten are completely digested, there is always a proportion that will come through intact and it is these seeds that are responsible for starting new colonies further afield. Seeds that are distributed by means of gravity are often easy to collect – especially those held in capsules, like corncockle.

Seeds dispersed by wind and water

Rough hawkbit

Seeds dispersed by wind are among the most attractive seed-heads, the best known example being the dandelion clock. Each seed is attached to a parachute-like device or has a wing-like appendage (such as ash keys) for catching air-currents.

Some seeds are designed to be carried by water currents and are light enough to float across a pond or stream. Germination may take place while the seeds are still floating, or it may not occur until they are grounded on the muddy shore-line.

Seeds dispersed by ejection

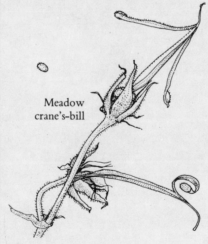

Meadow crane's-bill

While most plants rely on an external source of energy to spread their seed, some give their seeds a head-start by launching them into the surroundings. Meadow crane's-bill (above), for example, can fling its seed several feet by means of a trigger mechanism. Ejected seeds may germinate where they land or they may continue their journey by another means.

Seeds eaten by animals

Wild strawberry

These plants have attractive, tasty and usually soft-fleshed fruits surrounding their hard-coated seeds; wild strawberry (above), hawthorn, holly, roses, blackberries, honeysuckle are all good examples. The fruit is eaten, acted on by the animal's digestive system, and then the undigested material – including the seed – is passed out in the droppings often miles away from the parent plant. Seeds from plants using this method of seed dispersal are always germinated more easily after they've been eaten by animals. Even so, they can take a year or eighteen months to germinate and may require stratification to break their dormancy (see p. 127).

Seeds carried by animals

Agrimony

Some plants have prickly or hooked cases enclosing their seed. These attach themselves to anything that happens to pass by the plant, especially animal fur, and seeds are thereby carried along until they fall. This method of seed dispersal has been evolved by several members of the carrot family and also corn buttercup, agrimony (above) and wood avens, for example.

Modern-day life has brought with it many more opportunities for distribution of seeds. They can gather and lodge themselves in anything, from trouser turn-ups and jacket pockets to the tread of lorry tyres. By these means plants have found new and sometimes unlikely habitats – in city centres, on roof tops, and even in foreign countries.

Plant families

A plant family is a group of plants that is judged by botanists to have evolved from common ancestors. They don't necessarily look similar – for example, germander speedwell (a tiny-flowered ground-covering plant) and the towering foxglove both belong to the Figwort family – but they do have certain key characteristics in common; plants within the same family have essentially the same reproductive structure.

Although you can learn about wild flowers without knowing which family they belong to, this knowledge can help the wildflower gardener in seed collection and germination since many close relations have similar requirements. The lists below shows those plants featured in the book grouped together in their families.

Amaryllis family
(Amaryllidaceae)

Snowdrop
Summer snowflake
Wild daffodil

Bedstraw family
(Rubiaceae)

Hedge-bedstraw
Lady's bedstraw
Woodruff

Bellflower family
(Campanulaceae)

Clustered bellflower
Giant bellflower
Harebell
Nettle-leaved bellflower
Sheep's-bit

Bogbean family
(Menyanthaceae)

Bogbean
Fringed water-lily

Borage family
(Boraginaceae)

Common comfrey
Hound's-tongue
Lungwort
Viper's-bugloss
Water forget-me-not

Buttercup family
(Ranunculaceae)

Columbine
Corn buttercup
Globeflower
Green hellebore
Larkspur
Lesser celandine
Marsh-marigold
Meadow buttercup
Monk's-hood
Pasqueflower
Pheasant's-eye
Traveller's-joy
Wood anemone

This family has several methods of seed dispersal: monk's-hood and columbine seeds are dispersed by gravity; anemone has wind-dispersed seed; buttercups have an uncovered seed-head crowded with seed; and some plants in the family have hooked seed, designed to be caught on the fur of passing animals and carried along. Seed from any member of this family is best sown freshly harvested.

Campion family
(Caryophyllaceae)

Bladder campion
Corncockle
Greater stitchwort
Lesser stitchwort
Maiden pink
Ragged-robin
Red campion
Sea campion
Soapwort
White campion

Plants belonging to this family have seed contained in a toothed capsule. Harvest the seed as soon as it is dry and shakes out of the capsule cleanly. The seed stores well and is easy to germinate.

Carrot family
(Umbelliferae)

Burnet-saxifrage
Fennel
Pignut
Rough chervil
Sea-holly
Sweet cicely
Wild angelica
Wild carrot
Wild parsnip

Most plants in this family have a very similar way of carrying their flowers and seeds. They form umbels, attractive branching heads rather like umbrellas. Among the exceptions are sea-holly and field eryngo, both with seed-heads more like teasels. Both the umbel and the teasel types are ripe when they look dry. Seeds often don't keep well. Germination can be rapid when freshly harvested seed is sown; after storing, stratification may be required (see p. 127).

Crane's-bill family
(Geraniaceae)

Bloody crane's-bill
Dusky crane's-bill
Hedgerow crane's-bill
Herb-robert
Meadow crane's-bill
Wood crane's-bill
Wood sorrel

Most members of this family have distinctive 'beaked' seed-heads containing five hard seeds. These are catapulted from the plant when ripe so to catch them, gather the seed-heads or place a paper bag over them just as they turn from green to brown. Crane's-bill seed lasts for years and requires scarification for quick germination (see p. 127).

Daisy family
(Compositae)

Autumn hawkbit
Carline thistle
Cat's-ear
Chamomile
Chicory
Common knapweed
Cornflower
Corn marigold
Cotton thistle
Daisy
Dandelion
Elecampane
Feverfew
Goat's-beard
Goldenrod
Greater knapweed
Hemp-agrimony
Milk thistle
Mouse-ear
hawkweed
Musk thistle
Oxeye daisy
Rough hawkbit
Saw-wort
Scented mayweed
Scentless mayweed
Sea wormwood
Tansy
Wormwood

One of the largest families of flowering plants, with more than 14,000 species, and also one of the most evolutionarily advanced. Many of the daisy family's seeds are plumed to facilitate wind pollination, although some species have hooked seed for clinging to animal fur. Collect the daisy-flowered types by removing the seed-head when the petals have withered. The dandelion types can be easily picked off into a paper bag when they're ready. Cut knapweeds when the heads have turned brown – don't leave the ripe heads for long or birds will get the seed. Thistle heads, with a short stem, are cut when fluff appears; hang them with their heads in a paper bag to catch the seed as it ripens and falls. The seed of members of the daisy family keeps well and germinates readily.

Dock family
(Polygonaceae)

Amphibious bistort
Chalk milkwort
Common sorrel

Figwort family
(Scrophulariaceae)

Brooklime
Common toadflax
Dark mullein
Foxglove
Germander speedwell
Greater mullein
Ivy-leaved toadflax
Purple toadflax
Slender speedwell
Yellow rattle

The seeds of most species belonging to this family are held in seed capsules – usually remaining on the plant for several weeks – so immediate collection is not necessary. Their seed is very small and keeps well.

Fumitory family
(Fumariaceae)

Common fumitory
Yellow corydalis

Grass family
(Gramineae)

Quaking-grass
Silver hair-grass
Wavy hair-grass
Wood millet

Heath family
(Ericaceae)

Bell heather
Heather

Honeysuckle family
(Caprifoliaceae)

Elder
Honeysuckle
Wayfaring-tree

Iris family
(Iridaceae)

Yellow iris
Stinking iris

Labiate family
(Labiatae)

Basil thyme
Betony
Bugle
Gipsywort
Ground-ivy
Hedge woundwort
Lesser calamint
Marjoram
Red dead-nettle
Selfheal
Wall germander
Water mint
White dead-nettle
White horehound
Wild clary
Wild thyme
Wood sage
Yellow archangel

This family contains many herbs and medicinal plants. The figworts are sometimes confused with the labiates, but all members of this family have square stems, opposite leaves and (usually) two-lipped flowers; and the seed is always in the form of four one-seeded nutlets. The seeds tend to be shed easily (as they are not contained within a seed case), so the timing of seed collection is quite critical. As soon as the seeds have turned black or dark brown, cut off the seed-head and shake it into a paper bag or container. Seeds can be stored successfully, or you can plant them immediately. They will germinate normally within a few weeks.

Leadwort family
(Plumbaginaceae)

Common sea-lavender
Thrift

Lily family
(Liliaceae)

Bluebell
Chives
Fritillary
Lily-of-the-valley
Martagon lily
Ramsons
Solomon's-seal
Spring squill
Star-of-Bethlehem

Seed is contained either in a capsule (bluebell) or in a berry (Solomon's-seal). It is easily collected as the capsules dry out or the berries ripen and are then ready to pick. Lily seeds normally have a short life and some need to be stratified before they will germinate (see p. 127).

Mallow family
(Malvaceae)

Common mallow
Marsh-mallow
Musk-mallow
Tree-mallow

Mignonette family
(Resedaceae)

Weld
Wild mignonette

Mustard/Cabbage family
(Cruciferae)

Cuckooflower
Dame's-violet
Honesty
Wallflower

Pea family
(Leguminosae)

Black medick
Broom
Bush vetch
Common bird's-foot-trefoil
Common restharrow
Common vetch
Dyer's greenweed
Greater bird's-foot-trefoil
Hare's-foot clover
Horseshoe vetch
Kidney vetch
Meadow vetchling
Narrow-leaved everlasting-pea
Red clover
Ribbed melilot
Sainfoin
Smooth tare
Spiny restharrow
Tufted vetch
White clover
Wood vetch

Most plants in this family have small pea-like flowers and large seeds contained in a pod. The pods eventually burst, releasing the seed when it's ripe, so pick them as their colour fades to brown and they'll ripen off the plant. Other legumes, such as clovers, hold their seed in soft, fused sepals known as the calyx. This will stay attached to the withered flower-head for a short time after ripening. There's no need to remove the calyx before sowing. All legume seeds are long-lived and hard and may require scarification to aid germination (see p. 127).

Polypod fern family
(Polypodiaceae)

Lady-fern
Maidenhair spleenwort
Parsley fern

Poppy family
(Papaveraceae)

Common poppy
Welsh poppy
Yellow horned-poppy

Members of the poppy family have tiny seed that is held in attractive capsules for many weeks. You can simply tip the seed out into a paper bag anytime after the seed-heads have dried. This seed keeps for very long periods and often needs stratification before germination will occur (see p. 127).

Primrose family
(Primulaceae)

Bird's-eye primrose
Cowslip
Creeping-jenny
Cyclamen
Oxlip
Primrose
Scarlet pimpernel
Water-violet
Yellow loosestrife

A small but very diverse family, so few general rules apply. The most widespread characteristic is a capsule-like seed-case at the base of the flower.

If the stems arch over (as in primrose), collect the seed-case just as it turns brown. Timing is not so crucial with cowslip, since the stems hold themselves upright for several weeks after they've ripened. Bird's-eye primrose, cowslip, oxlip, primrose and cyclamen seed requires stratification (see p. 127).

Rose family
(Rosaceae)

Agrimony
Alpine lady's-mantle
Blackthorn
Bramble
Burnet rose
Dog rose
Dropwort
Hawthorn
Lady's-mantle
Meadowsweet
Mountain avens
Rock cinquefoil
Salad burnet
Silverweed
Sweet briar
Tormentil
Water avens
Wild strawberry
Wood avens

A very diverse family that includes small herbaceous plants, shrubs, and trees. The plants have no common features obvious to the naked eye, although some have rose-like flowers. The seed of many species is contained in berries and is designed to be eaten by birds. The seed of some plants requires stratification before it will germinate (see p. 127).

St John's-wort family
(Hypericaceae)

Perforate St John's-wort
Square-stalked St John's-wort
Tutsan

Saxifrage family
(Saxifragaceae)

Meadow saxifrage
Purple saxifrage

Stonecrop family
(Crassulaceae)

Biting stonecrop
Roseroot

Teasel family
(Dipsaceae)

Devil's-bit scabious
Field scabious
Small scabious
Teasel

Valerian family
(Valerianaceae)

Common valerian
Red valerian

Violet family
(Violaceae)

Common dog-violet
Mountain pansy
Sweet violet
Wild pansy

Water-lily family
(Nymphaeaceae)

White water-lily
Yellow water-lily

Water-plantain family
(Alismataceae)

Arrowhead
Water-plantain

Collecting seed

In general, collecting seed from the wild is not to be encouraged. Excessive trampling, and careless harvesting, can easily damage the parent plant or its neighbours – in fact, it is illegal to harvest seed from some rare species (see p. 182). However, where a large colony of quite common wild plants is thriving then little harm can be done by gathering a few seed-heads in a paper bag.

When to harvest

The great majority of seeds are harvested when the seed-head has dried and turned brown. If the seeds are contained in capsules, like poppies and corncockles, you can take one off the plant and tip it up: if ripe, the seed will fall out cleanly into a container. Some capsules won't empty by tipping and they may need crushing to release their dark, ripe seed inside. (If you are collecting harebell, take your glasses because the seed is like dust!) If the seed is still green or moist, leave it for another week or so. Thistles are ripe when the seed-heads start to open and the seed can be gently pulled out by the fluffy tail (called the pappus) attached to it.

Cowslip and oxlip are easy as the seed containers are held upright, so you can see the ripe brown seed inside. The seed-head can be cut off and the seed just tipped out. Primrose is trickier as the seed-head is on a long stalk which bends over on to the soil and you have to look carefully to see which heads have turned brown. Collect these seed-heads just before they open – otherwise the seed will just fall to the ground.

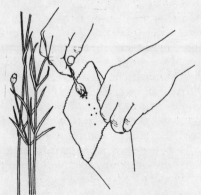

Collecting corncockle seed Bend the stem over and shake the dried seed capsule into a bag.

There are very many other seeds that are collected when their seed-heads are brown and dry – and not all are held in containers or capsules. The carrot family has attractive branching seed-heads. It is obvious when the seeds are ripe as they look dried and

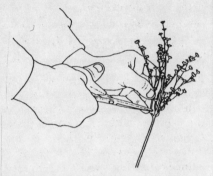

Harvesting dropwort seed Snip off the short, dried stems and store them in a cool, dry place.

will readily shake off the seed-head. Cut the dried seed-heads and rub off the seed between the hands.

Dandelion-like seed-heads, such as hawkbits and cat's-ear, are easy to collect (pull the 'parachutes' off gently, and put them into a paper bag for storing), but of course you must watch them as once ripe it doesn't take much wind to blow them away. The fluff doesn't need to be cleaned off the seed before sowing.

Plants that should be harvested before they're fully ripe

With some plants it is wise to harvest the seed before it is fully ripe. If you want to propagate scabious, for example, the seed-heads should be harvested just before they turn brown, when the green colour has nearly faded from them. At this stage, if you rub a seed-head in your fingers it will break up into individual seeds, ready for storing or sowing. (In fact, you can't see the actual seed, but no further extraction is required.) Don't harvest all the seed-heads of scabious, though, since they do look beautiful in the garden, and goldfinches love to eat the ripe seed, especially the devil's-bit scabious.

Common knapweed seed-heads open when they're ripe, but if you wait until then, the seed will have escaped; instead, cut a bunch of heads just after they've turned brown and put them head-first into a paper bag. Hang the bag up, in a dry airy place.

The members of the crane's-bill family are something of a challenge! Ripe seed is catapulted quite a distance, so the best solution is to tie a bag (not plastic) over the seed-heads once the flowers are over to catch the seed as it ripens. The other way is to cut the heads when they begin to turn brown but before they are ripe and ripen them in a container in the sun. Cover the container with a stocking or piece of muslin to stop the seed flying out. Hedgerow crane's-bill is easier than the other crane's-bills as the ripe seed stays on the plant for some time before being catapulted, allowing you simply to cut a branch and shake it into a bucket.

Vetches, peas and other podded seeds are quite simple if you only want a few seeds, but if you want to harvest on a large scale, their uneven ripening will cause problems. The pods turn brown when ripe, but often on a hot, sunny day they burst open and the seed is gone. Collect the pods just as they're turning brown and keep them in a bucket in a warm, dry place.

Wild pansy is really fascinating to watch as the seeds ripen. Each fat little capsule ripens quickly, turning paler green as it does so, and then splits open to reveal three slim pointed 'canoes' with the seed arranged along each one in a neat row which will be brown when ripe. Once the capsule is fully open the seed will drop out within the day, so daily collection of pansy seed is essential.

Deceptive plants

There are some oddities to remember when it comes to seed collection, and the more collecting you do the more exceptions you'll discover.

There is one plant that seems to disobey all the rules on seed and that is the green hellebore. The seed of the green hellebore is difficult to see, as the flowers hang down and the green petals (strictly sepals) remain attached to the seed-case and are still green when the seed is ripe. Keep an eye on the plant towards the end of May and check whether the seed has gone brown. If you cut the head with a length of stem then it can be cut a bit early and kept in a paper bag to ripen.

The sage and borage families contain some tricky plants to collect seed from. The plants in both families have seeds that drop out when ripe and are not held in a capsule. You can try putting a muslin bag over the whole stem to catch the seed as it ripens and falls. Alternatively, when some seeds are ripe and black cut the stem and allow other seeds to ripen off the plant. Seeds could be caught on the ground as they drop but the birds and mice will usually get them before you. With luck, and a piece of fine muslin (to allow rainwater through) spread under the plant with a sprinkling of chilli pepper to discourage the mice, you will manage to collect some seed. Viper's-bugloss makes life more difficult by ripening its seeds to a light grey colour, so don't wait for them to go black.

Storing seed

The best advice to the wildflower gardener is not to store seed unless there is a good reason for doing so. If you are sowing your own seed, sow it after harvest, as would happen in nature, or keep it in a paper bag or envelope for sowing in autumn. If you wish to keep seed until spring, then keep the seed envelopes in a drawer or tin where they will be dark, dry and at an even temperature. The garden shed is not a good place to keep envelopes of seed as it is far too damp – the house is much better, and there is less risk of mouse damage. If necessary there are two methods of keeping seed for longer periods.

Seeds that have been collected after they have ripened can be packeted (well labelled of course) and placed in a plastic bag or other container in the fridge (the lower half is best). This method is also good for any bought, packeted seed that you have to keep for next season. If the bought seed is sealed in a foil packet then cold storage is unnecessary and the seed should last for several seasons.

Although some seed, like parsnip, dandelion and chives, goes off after a season or two, most wildflower seeds will last for several years and hard-coated seed, like that of the clovers and vetches, is especially long-lived. Remember, though, that no seed will keep for any length of time unless it is kept dry.

Sometimes bought seed will germinate less readily than seed freshly collected from the same species. This is because the seed has been dried down for commercial storage and, with some wildflower seeds, this can induce a state of dormancy. If the packeted seeds were viable when they were packeted they will certainly grow, but they might take longer to germinate or perhaps need the winter cold treatment (stratification) to break their dormancy.

Which seed to buy?

Native seed is vital for any wildflower seeding that is to be of any value for conservation, whether in the garden or in the countryside. Often people ask if there is any difference between the seed of a named native UK species and the seed of, for instance, the same species (with exactly the same botanical name) grown in Europe.

Take, for example, marjoram. There are many forms of this plant, coming from many different parts of Europe – the variation within the species is enormous. Botanically they have great similarities so at present they are classified together as the same species – *Origanum vulgare* – (although in time this is surely going to change). The variants all look and often taste quite dissimilar; they have various coloured flowers, some are prostrate and some erect. Wild marjoram seed from the Continent, therefore, may produce plants which look completely different from our native species of marjoram.

The other difficulty with wildflower seed from abroad is that there is no guarantee it is wild. Take the example of the Cheddar pink *(Dianthus gratianopolitanus)*. This is a very rare and protected species in Britain, but is more common in Europe. Seedsmen buy seed from the Continent and sell this as a British wildflower seed. The plants can often turn out to be a cultivated form and nothing like the wild species. Not only is this in contravention of the Trades Description Act, but if these plants grow vigorously and reproduce prolifically, they may even threaten the balance of the native flora.

Other non-wild seed is sometimes sold as native seed – the agricultural crops such as common bird's-foot-trefoil and kidney vetch, for example. These are native plants that have been especially bred for agricultural use: their size, yield and rate of germination have all been 'improved'. This makes them very much more vigorous than the native species. As butterfly-attracting plants or garden flowers they are suitable enough but they are not wild flowers and shouldn't be sold as such.

In order to be sure of growing true native species, you should buy wildflower seed only from those specialist seedsmen who guarantee their seed to be of native UK origin. These seedsmen take much care to sell only authentic native seed and most of the seed is produced either by them or for them by specialist growers (see list of suppliers on pp. 183–4).

Germination

It's usually assumed when you buy a packet of seeds they will grow without trouble if you simply place them in the soil. With most cultivated plants this is largely true. Plant breeding and selection goes on all the time, with the aim not only of producing better varieties but of making them more reliable to germinate and grow.

In nature things are very different and seeds often have a struggle to find the right conditions for germination. It is marvellous to think that inside a seed such as a foxglove—a seed much smaller than a pinhead—there is a life-force that will, within two years, produce a flower of great size and beauty that will itself produce literally thousands of seeds.

Seed is an incredibly efficient method of reproduction. Some seeds will find ideal germinating conditions soon after falling to the ground. Others might wait years before they germinate. In order to ensure survival of the species many seeds go into a state of dormancy shortly after ripening. For instance, primrose seed when fresh and moist will germinate readily. Once dried, as it would be for storage or packaging, the seed becomes dormant and will not awaken until it has experienced a period of cold or freezing temperatures. This cold treatment is called stratification.

Common poppy seed will remain in the soil for fifty years or more. The seed is buried when the soil is ploughed, and only a proportion is near enough to the surface at any one time to germinate. Remember this fact when cultivating an old garden. Just because you start with a beautifully clean soil don't be misled into the idea that there are no weeds! All those dock and thistle seeds that have been buried for years were just waiting for you to bring them up to the light! Some seeds do last as long as 100 years but the popular myth that seed from ancient Egyptian tombs has grown is sadly untrue. Seeds of this age are almost always totally dead.

When you sow wildflower seed it will often germinate patchily. But wait a few weeks, or until next season, and up will come the rest! It just is not in a wild plant's interest to encourage all its seed to germinate at once – one bad winter, disease or cultivation might wipe out the whole colony.

Special techniques to assist germination

Unfortunately there are no hard and fast rules about which seeds require special treatment to assist them in germination. However, knowing which family a plant belongs to (see pp. 123–24) will give you a rough idea, and further details are supplied in each plant article.

Scarification This involves rubbing hard-coated seeds between two sheets of sandpaper: once the coat has been weakened in this way, the moisture essential for germination can penetrate the seed. It is necessary for many seeds of the crane's-bill and pea families.

Stratification Sometimes called vernalization, this involves subjecting the seeds to a period of cold of from one to six months. Seeds may be sown in the autumn – either in the ground or in seed trays left outside. Alternatively, seed can be mixed with damp sand or peat and kept in the fridge but it seems in many cases that a fluctuation in temperature, as would occur outdoors, is important.

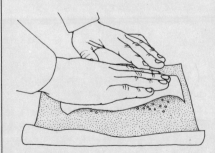

Scarifying seeds Rubbing seeds between sheets of sandpaper will speed up germination.

As some seeds that require stratification also need a period of warmth before the cold, it is a good idea to sow these seeds in August or September. Stratification is often necessary for seeds of the poppy, rose, carrot, primrose and lily families. Seeds of other families don't normally require this treatment but it never hurts to sow in autumn, and if in doubt it is a good rule to do so. Some plants have very complicated seed dormancy systems; lily-of-the-valley and Solomon's-seal, for example, require a period of cold (six months), warmth and then a further winter before they will germinate – this is known as double-dormancy.

How to sow seeds

The main seed-sowing times are autumn and spring, but detailed advice is given in the individual plant articles. Wildflower seed can be sown either in the soil where it is to flower, or in a seed tray. As a general guide, large seed is more easily sown in the soil, while small seed (easily lost outdoors) should be sown in a seed tray.

Wildflower seeds generally require light to germinate, but they also need moisture. A simple rule is to scatter small seeds on the surface of moist compost or soil; press medium-sized seeds into the surface with your hand or a flat piece of wood and cover larger seeds very lightly. The scale drawings on p. 122 give an idea of the range of seed sizes that can be found.

Moisture is particularly important. The general rule is to sow into moist compost and then water as little as possible, never letting the surface dry out. Lack of moisture can prevent the seed germinating and can kill seedlings, but too much water excludes essential oxygen and encourages disease. Use a fine spray in order not to disturb the seed, but make sure the water soaks well into the compost.

Sowing directly into the soil

It is important that the seed-bed is well prepared (see p. 129). Scatter the seed thinly on the soil and press it into the surface or cover lightly, depending on the size of the seed (see above). Mark the spot carefully with sticks and label with the name and the date they were sown. You can give some protection from birds by stretching a criss-cross of fine black thread between the sticks. Inspect the area every week and keep it weeded. If you are not sure whether the seedlings that appear are weeds or flowers, leave them to grow a bit to make identification easier.

Sowing in a seed tray

Fill the seed tray with compost up to 1 cm ($\frac{1}{2}$in) below the rim and firm it down. This gap prevents seed and compost being washed over the edge when watering, as well as providing a little room for growth to occur if the tray is covered with glass.

The easiest compost to use is a peat-based seed compost out of a bag. For most seeds (those belonging to the *Primulaceae* family being an exception) some sand mixed into the compost is beneficial, though not essential. The compost should be slightly moist from the bag and is easy to wet using a watering can with a fine rose. If the compost is at all dry then several waterings will be necessary to moisten the bottom layer. A disadvantage of peat-based compost is that moss and lichens might grow on the surface if the tray has to be left for a long period. This layer can, however, be removed if germination has not started, but be careful not to pick up any seeds with it. Soil-based seed compost made up to the John Innes formula is recommended for very slow germinating or larger seeds.

Spacing your seed

There is always a tendency to sow small seeds too thickly. This results in overcrowded seedlings having to fight for space, and the danger of disease spreading. A fungus disease, known as damping-off, can spread rapidly through a tray of overcrowded seedlings and causes them to go limp and die.

For the best results, take a pinch of seed at a time and sprinkle evenly over the surface of the compost. For larger seeds, space them 1 cm ($\frac{1}{2}$in) apart each way. This spacing allows the seedlings to grow on in the seed tray for far longer than usual.

Covering the tray

Cover the seed tray with a small sheet of glass or plastic. This keeps in the moisture, ensuring that the seed and compost never dry out – the cover also stops mice from taking the seed.

Sowing seed

1 *Fill the seed tray with compost up to 1 cm ($\frac{1}{2}$ in) below the rim. Tip a few seeds into one hand and, with the other, take a pinch of seeds, sprinkling them thinly over the compost.*

2 *Water in the seeds and then cover the tray with a sheet of glass or plastic. Leave in a lightly shaded, sheltered spot, outside or in an unheated greenhouse or frame.*

3 *When the seedlings look quite vigorous and have developed plenty of roots, gently tease each one out separately, taking care not to break the delicate roots.*

4 *Transplant each seedling into a small pot of soil-based compost. Insert the seedlings into an indentation large enough for the roots, add more compost, and firm it down well.*

Leave the seed tray in a lightly shaded and sheltered spot outdoors or in a shaded, unheated greenhouse.

Pricking out
If your seeds have been sown thinly don't be in a hurry to prick them out. Wait until they look quite vigorous and have developed plenty of roots and are large enough to be handled easily. Then, using a flat knife or spatula, gently tease out each seedling, taking care not to break off the root. Transplant each seedling into its own small pot, about 4–6 cm (2–3 in) in diameter, containing soil-based compost. The plants can then become accustomed to the soil and develop a stronger root system before they are planted out in the garden. For tiny, slow-growing seedlings, such as harebells and primroses, it is a good idea to prick out the seedlings into another tray filled with soil-based potting compost before transplanting into individual pots. Instead of bought compost, you can use weed-free garden soil mixed with some peat to give better drainage.

Growing on
The pricked-out seedlings should be left to grow on in their individual pots over the summer. The earliest time to plant out is when the roots look vigorous and start coming out of the bottom of the pot. Keep your eyes on the roots and not on the greenery, as a lot of green growth can be produced before there is very much root growth.

Hardening off
If the seedlings or small plants have been raised in a greenhouse over winter, they must be hardened off before being planted out. This means they must be acclimatized to the cold wind and rain and especially the cold nights. It is done by gradually increasing the length of time the plants are left outside. The best method is to move them from the greenhouse into a cold frame. Wild plants are pretty tough but a sudden change of temperature will set them back, so they should be hardened off slowly.

Planting out
The best times for planting out are in autumn or spring. In early autumn the soil is warm and this allows the roots to grow a little before winter.

Plants can be planted during winter in mild weather provided that the soil is free-draining. However, frost tends to lift winter-planted plants above the soil level; if this happens firm them back in again.

Planting in the spring is best if you have very heavy soil. If you want to plant during the summer the plants should be watered in thoroughly and then will require extra watering until they are established.

First dig a hole easily large enough to accommodate the plant. When planting out remove the pot and place the plant in the hole making sure that it is set at the same depth as it was in the pot. Loosen the roots from the rigid shape of the pot, water in around the roots to settle the plant, and then fill in the hole with soil and firm in.

Raising ferns

Raising ferns Instead of seeds, ferns have spores enclosed in spore cases on the back of their fronds.

From June onwards, cut off a frond with well-developed spore cases. Wrap it in paper for a week or so until the spores are shed. Sow them on special fern compost in a tray and treat as you would seed. Spores should germinate in six weeks. For more information, see the bibliography (p. 184).

Sowing seed mixtures

There are many different seed mixtures available, including meadow, wetland, hedgerow and woodland grass and flower combinations. They are ideal for seeding large areas, and will enable you to grow a far wider range of plants than is possible by simply choosing a variety of individual species. A good mixture may include up to about 30 different species. Many mixtures are tailored to particular situations and different types of soil, so it is worth looking at 'How to assess your site', pp. 131–2, before buying.

The great advantage of any grass plus wildflower seed mixture is that you achieve complete ground-cover. Maintenance is reduced to three cuts a year, or less, and most nasty weeds will be suppressed by timely cutting (see 'Maintaining flowering lawns and meadows', pp. 144–45). This type of mixture also supports the maximum amount of wildlife.

Mixtures without grasses are also available, of which the most popular is the cornfield flower mixture (or farmer's nightmare!). This consists of colourful annual flowers that were once common in cornfields (although they would not normally have grown all together). All the previous categories described are also available without grasses. These mixtures are mostly composed of perennial flowers. There are also special seed mixtures compiled to attract butterflies and seed-eating birds.

Mixtures without grasses that contain perennial flowers would normally be sown in an island bed or border. A certain amount of selective weeding is necessary, firstly to keep unwanted plants already in the soil under control, and secondly to keep a balance between the mix of newly sown species. Cutting some flowers before they seed themselves will also regulate the balance.

The soil

For the best results from your wildflower seed mixture, the poorer the soil you have the better. It is always well worth considering removing a good, rich, loamy topsoil to another part of the garden where it can be better used (for growing raised-bed vegetables, perhaps). A poor soil is not a disadvantage for wildflower growing, since a very fertile soil always encourages grasses to grow at the expense of flowers.

Clearing the ground of weeds

For seed mixtures without grass, the ground should be prepared very thoroughly and must be really weed-free before sowing.

Don't be fooled by a lovely, freshly dug, clean area of soil, for lurking beneath there are thousands of weed seeds just waiting for you to prepare a seed-bed for them. All they'll need then is a shower of rain, and your clean patch will be green in no time, covered with unwanted weeds! In the old days every field on a farm was fallowed or left bare for a season on a regular rotation. If you can wait a whole year before seeding, this is the best way to clean a piece of ground.

A fallow season Cultivate the ground well in spring or autumn and, if the soil is very heavy, repeat several times to get a good seed-bed. Hoe the weeds out and fork out the roots of the real nasties like docks, creeping thistle and couch grass. Keep on weeding until you are ready to sow in the autumn or spring. Don't forget that every time you cultivate you bring more seeds to the surface.

A short fallow The cleaning process can be speeded up. Allow enough time after the initial cultivation to let the weed seeds grow back a little. Then clear the weeds with a hoe — don't use a cultivator since this will bring more seeds to the surface. Fork out any docks or thistle roots. Then you'll be ready to prepare the seed-bed (see below) and sow your seed.

A mulch of black plastic sheeting This is a very effective way of clearing a small area of ground of most weeds and is particularly good for preparing an area of lawn for wildflower and grass seeding. Thin black plastic sheeting is obtainable from horticultural suppliers and builders' merchants. First cut the area as short as possible with a rotary mower and then anchor the sheeting down with bricks, logs or turf. Leave it for a season, and then take up the sheeting. The soil will have been beautifully worked by worms and possibly moles, and all vegetation will be dead. Of course some of the perennials with deep and creeping roots will still be present but these can now be easily

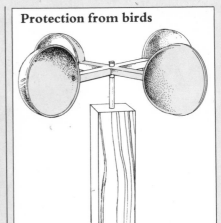

Protection from birds

A bird-scarer This ingenious wind-blown device was made out of two old ball-cocks, each surface being painted alternately red and white.

Birds can be a problem with newly seeded areas. An assortment of moving, glittering things will help (birds quickly get used to conventional bird-scarers) or try stretching a net over the area.

removed. The soil will most likely be loose enough to rake over; if not, rotovate it. For the best results put back the black plastic sheeting for a few weeks after raking or rotovation to encourage further germination of seedlings which, as before, will die as soon as they germinate.

Herbicides Herbicides are very much a last resort as there is no knowing what harm they can do both in the short and the long run. However, if you are starting off with a really horrendously weedy area then try a herbicide containing glyphosate. Spring to early summer is the best time to apply it, when growth is at its most vigorous. Two separate applications may be necessary for nettles, thistles, and other really tough plants. When the weeds have turned brown, seven to ten days after application of glyphosate, the foliage should be taken off and the land given a thorough cultivation. Any weed seedlings that then appear should be hoed off in the normal way. This chemical breaks down very quickly and seeding can take place in a few weeks.

Preparing the seed-bed

The seed-bed needs to be prepared thoroughly so there is a moderately fine, firm and even surface for sowing. Never prepare a seed-bed when

Sowing meadow mixtures

1 *To sow seed in situ prepare the ground well; first cultivate, then rake and tread the soil, until it's firm and smooth.*

2 *Mark out the site into equal-sized areas, then divide the seed into the same number of parts. Scatter the seed evenly.*

3 *If sowing a grass and wildflower mixture, sow the grass seed first, and then sow the wild flowers.*

4 *After sowing, lightly roll or tread the ground.*

the soil is wet; the soil should not stick to your boots as you walk over it. In the early spring or autumn, after clearing the soil of weeds, rake over the surface until it is reasonably smooth and quite firm.

Marking out the plot
Wildflower mixtures are seeded at about 4g per square metre/yard for grass and flower mixtures and 1–2g per square metre/yard for flowers only. To distribute seed evenly, divide the plot up into equal parts with string. Then divide and weigh your mixture into the same number of parts, being careful to keep it well mixed all the time. It is more important to sow the grasses evenly than the wild flowers, as these will look more natural if they are not spread evenly.

Sowing the mixture
Some people recommend mixing the wildflower seed with sand to bulk it out and make it visible and easier to spread evenly. This seems to me a lot of unnecessary messing about! The thing to do is to pour the seed into a container (a cup for a small packet or tub for larger quantities) and just broadcast (the farmer's word for scattering) the seed very thinly by picking up a small amount of seed in the palm of the hand, closing the fingers over it and then swinging the hand from side to side, allowing the seed to

slip slowly through the fingers. It is not nearly as difficult as it sounds – if you don't feel confident, practise with some dry sand before you start!
Sowing wild flowers and grasses
Flowers and grasses usually come separately packaged and this is the best way to sow them. Broadcast the grasses first and then rake them well in. Next, broadcast the flowers. Don't rake the soil again but roll or tread the area, so the flower seed is just pressed into the soil surface.

Sowing wildflower beds or borders
Again, broadcast the seed on the surface and roll or tread it in. If wildflower seed is raked in, much of the really tiny seed just gets buried and doesn't grow.

Watering
It is best not to water an area sown with a mixture but to allow seed to germinate when the soil moisture conditions are naturally right.

Maintenance
In terms of maintenance, a lot depends on your soil and how the mixture is developing.

First of all a common myth must be exploded – that it harms meadowland plants to mow them. Quite the opposite is the case! Cutting at a minimum height of 3 cm (1½ in) every two months or so during the initial year can only do good. Encroaching weed species will be deterred, the fine grasses will be encouraged to establish well and the flowers will put their energies into root and leaf production. The snag is that many mixtures will contain annuals for first year colour and you might also be impatient for a few flowers to show for your efforts (and financial outlay). So normally no harm will be done by letting the mixture grow the first year until July (after an autumn or spring sowing). By this time you will have had some flowers. One more cut in the autumn will probably be all that will be needed until the following spring. See pp. 144–45 for routine annual maintenance of flowering grassland, and p. 144 for maintaining flower-only areas.

Problems
The most frequent cry is 'there is nothing except weeds coming up!' By far the most common cause of this situation is poor soil cleaning and preparation, but whatever the cause, all may not be lost. Remember the golden rule: to improve a meadow mixture, mow it! You will find that many weeds will not survive this decapitation and many hundreds of seedlings will come up to replace them – almost certainly wildflower ones. Maintain as normal the following year and if a few nasties have crept back in then you can get rid of them by hand-weeding. Be patient: you can't expect to have an instant meadow garden.

The annual cornfield patch
The area to be sown should be seeded like any other type of mixture. In theory, the patch will be self-perpetuating if you cut it down each September. The ground is then lightly cultivated or rotovated to produce a seed-bed for the fallen seed. In practice, however, many unwanted plants creep in and after a few years these can take over as they will seed themselves in the same way as the cornfield flowers. So you may have to clean up the ground after a few years and start again.

The groundwork

How to assess your site

The first thing to do if you want to create a really successful wildflower garden, is to take a good look at the site and consider the type of environment that your garden will provide. Wild flowers are remarkably adaptable, but, like all plants, they do best in a position that imitates their natural habitat as closely as possible.

The importance of light
In most gardens, the deciding factor in determining which plants will flourish is the amount of sunlight the area receives – few of the flowers found in a sunny meadow will grow in woodland shade. For this reason, the three main sections in **Creating wildflower gardens** (pp. 15–120) deal with sunny, semi-shady and shady situations. The definitions below will help you decide where these lie in your garden.

Soil and drainage
The most important aspect of soil analysis as far as growing wild flowers is concerned, is drainage. This may vary considerably over the whole area of your garden. If water stands on the surface during wet weather for days on end, making the soil unworkable, you have a drainage problem. A good test is to dig a 30 cm (1 ft) hole in the wettest spot and see whether it fills or nearly fills with water. If it doesn't then you don't have much of a problem. Once you start to grow plants the deep-rooting ones will break up the subsoil naturally.

If your hole does fill with water, the first thing to do is to find out why the soil isn't draining well. In a new garden it might be that a load of clay subsoil has been dumped and consolidated and topsoil spread on top. This clay will have to be broken up and mixed with topsoil.

Another common problem is a solid, inpenetrable layer of clay or perhaps a mixture of clay and soil which has been inadvertently 'panned' by a mechanical cultivator run at the same fixed depth for many seasons. You may well find that you can fork through this layer, or run the cultivator over it at a deeper setting, and the soil will start to drain.

If neither of these solutions applies, you will have to decide whether you want to provide proper drainage for the whole garden – a job that may need to be done professionally.

There are many wild flowers that will thrive in poorly drained soil (see pp. 95–107), so I suggest you work

Sun and shade

Sunny Areas that are in full sun at midday and are, at most, shaded only early or late in the day.

Semi-shady Areas close to walls, fences or hedgerows that are shaded for up to half the day, or any area in very light, dappled shade all day long. Plants in semi-shady situations are able to thrive on less than maximum light levels.

Shady Areas that are under deciduous trees and therefore shaded from late spring to autumn; or any area that is shaded throughout the year for most of the day, perhaps being in the sun only in early morning or evening. The ideal for shade-loving plants is that they should receive no direct sun during the summer months except in early morning or late afternoon. Most shade loving plants produce flowers early in the year.

Deep shade Areas under densely-foliaged trees such as conifers, or in day-long shade from a solid barrier such as a wall or fence, can support very little plant life. Try growing ivy, wood-sorrel, wood anemone and woodruff, and encouraging any mosses or ferns that are present.

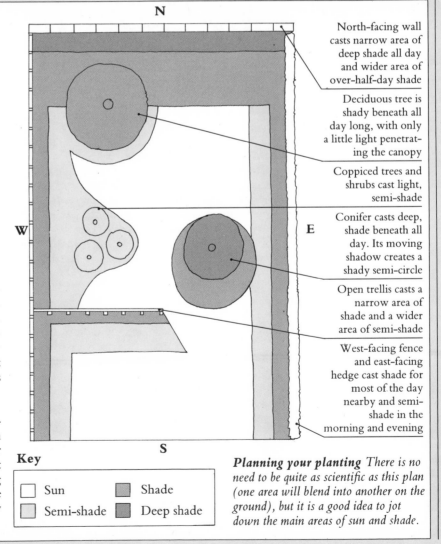

North-facing wall casts narrow area of deep shade all day and wider area of over-half-day shade

Deciduous tree is shady beneath all day long, with only a little light penetrating the canopy

Coppiced trees and shrubs cast light, semi-shade

Conifer casts deep, shade beneath all day. Its moving shadow creates a shady semi-circle

Open trellis casts a narrow area of shade and a wider area of semi-shade

West-facing fence and east-facing hedge cast shade for most of the day nearby and semi-shade in the morning and evening

Key

☐	Sun	▨	Shade
☐	Semi-shade	▨	Deep shade

Planning your planting There is no need to be quite as scientific as this plan (one area will blend into another on the ground), but it is a good idea to jot down the main areas of sun and shade.

with what you have, perhaps building a better drained bed as a feature (see p. 136, but use ordinary soil).

Soil types

For the purposes of growing wild plants in the garden, soils can be divided into three basic types: light (or sandy), medium (loam), and heavy (clay).

Light soils Because of the very free-draining nature of these soils, all nutrients are quickly leached out by rainfall and the soil is often slightly acid as well. For the wildflower gardner, light soils support a large range of very attractive flowers and grasses and the low fertility is a benefit. (They are not such good news for the conventional gardener as they need a lot of feeding and watering to support cultivated flowers and vegetables.)

If you have a very light, sandy soil, you can grow rock garden and seaside plants (see pp. 107–116 and 154) and also meadow flowers suitable for light soils. To grow a wider range of plants, you would need to dig in plenty of bulky organic material, such as compost, manure, leafmould or peat, since many wild flowers will not survive the summer drought without the help of such moisture-retentive material.

Medium soils These are the most usual garden soils and cover a range from light loams, which are free-draining but have more fertility than sand, to heavy loams, which are very fertile and retain moisture. Medium soils support the widest variety of wild flowers, including those that require some moisture in summer.

Heavy soils These are soils with an underlying layer of clay sometimes only a few inches under the topsoil but more usually 30 cm (1 ft) or more down. Heavy soils are fertile and moisture-retentive but do not drain after heavy rainfall. They can get very waterlogged in winter and spring and are therefore slow to warm up and get going. Heavy soils are ideal for a wide range of attractive wild flowers including all the wetland plants (see pp. 95–107). Ponds can be made without using a liner, by simply 'puddling' the clay (see p. 135).

Acid and alkaline soil

Most soils are acidic, and many wild flowers tolerate quite acid conditions, but if you want to grow the very

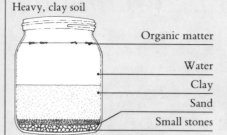

Heavy, clay soil

Organic matter
Water
Clay
Sand
Small stones

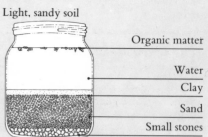

Light, sandy soil

Organic matter
Water
Clay
Sand
Small stones

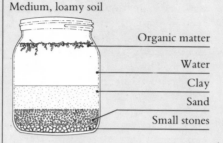

Medium, loamy soil

Organic matter
Water
Clay
Sand
Small stones

Testing your soil You can test your soil by putting a sample into a clean jam-jar with some water. Cover the jar, shake it vigorously, and leave the solution to settle out for an hour or so. Large particles of sand and stones will sink to the bottom; any clay in the soil will form the next layer; and organic material will float to the surface.

widest range of wild flowers you could adjust your soil's acid/alkaline balance so that it has a pH of 6.5–7 (this is also the best balance for organic gardening). This will probably mean adding lime (your soil test kit will advise you how much to add). An excellent alternative to lime is calcified seaweed (usually sold as 'Seagold'), which has a high calcium content, a high level of magnesium, and all the other benefits of seaweed meal, including a small quantity of fertilizer. Although high in calcium, it will not make your soil too alkaline and is very slow-release, so its effect will last for several years.

In order to grow acid-loving plants in alkaline soil, you can make a peat bed on top of the soil retained by a low 'wall' of peat blocks (it is essential the peat never dries out, so a semi-shady position is best). In the same way, if you want to grow true alkaline-lovers in an acid soil, you can make a chalk bank (see p. 137).

Of course, you may prefer to work with the soil you have: the lists below give a selection of plants that will tolerate extreme acidity or alkalinity. The articles on individual plants elsewhere in the book will tell you which other plants will tolerate these soils.

Acid-tolerant plants

Bell heather
Bluebell
Common bird's-foot trefoil
Common dog-violet
Devil's-bit scabious
Dyer's greenweed
Grass-of-Parnassus
Harebell
Heather
Juniper

Mouse-ear hawkweed
Sheep's-bit
Tormentil
Wavy hair-grass
Wild thyme

Alkaline-tolerant plants

Bird's-eye primrose
Bluebell
Burnet saxifrage
Carline thistle
Common bird's-foot trefoil
Common centaury
Common knapweed
Common rock-rose
Common sea lavender
Cowslip
Dog rose
Harebell
Horseshoe vetch
Juniper
Kidney vetch
Lungwort
Pasqueflower
Quaking-grass
Roseroot
Salad burnet
Scentless mayweed
Small scabious
Solomon's-seal
Thrift
Wild strawberry
Wild thyme

Planning a wildflower garden

It's well worth thinking hard about what you want your garden for before you plunge in and start planting. If attracting wildlife is your principal aim, look at **Gardening for wildlife,** p. 148. If you have young children, you will want to think of a site for a swing or sandpit, or a piece of scrubland large enough for a good game of hide-and-seek. Children are always fascinated by ponds, but it is

Soil glossary

Chalk soil a very thin topsoil of only a few inches over chalk or limestone. This soil type is not common in gardens: see p. 137 for how to construct a chalk bank for downland flowers.

Cultivated soil A soil that has been prepared by digging or rotovation for planting or sowing seeds.

Damp soil A soil that contains moisture all year round and may be constantly wet in the rainy season. Marginal and wetland plants would thrive here.

Dry soil A soil that dries out well below the surface layer over the summer period.

Good soil A soil that contains plenty of humus and fertility and is easily worked in all but the wettest weather.

Heavy soil A soil that contains a large proportion of clay: it is unworkable when wet and tends to bake out on the surface in summer. It also takes a long time to warm up in spring.

Light soil A soil containing a large proportion of sand that drains very freely and can be

easily worked in wet weather. It dries out quickly in dry weather, contains little humus and is low in nutrients.

Medium soil A loam soil that is reasonably free-draining in winter and does not dry out completely in summer. Contains plenty of humus and nutrients.

Moist soil A soil that retains at least some moisture all year round, even in summer.

Poor soil Any soil that is devoid of humus and very low in nutrients. Often an exploited soil, impoverished by greedy crops.

Rich soil A loam or clay soil that is rich in humus and fertility. Plants grow abundantly and rich soil produces excellent vegetables.

Well-drained soil Any soil that is either naturally well drained or has been artificially drained. A soil that can be worked at all but the wettest times of year.

Wet soil A soil that retains moisture all year round and where water lies on the surface after heavy rain. It could be very badly drained, or nearly level with the water table. Bog plants would thrive here.

best to site the pond in full view of the house in case all your dire warnings are ignored.

The right wild flowers for each site

Most wild flowers do much better on soils of low fertility (that is, soils that are very low in available nitrogen), so use the rich topsoil in the garden for the vegetable plot and conventional flower borders.

Any areas that are to be short, mown lawn will also require plenty of topsoil to keep them green and looking good during hot summer weather. Meadows will do better on a low-fertility soil that will favour the flowers rather than the grasses. For most wildflowers seedings, 8 cm (3 in) of topsoil is enough to establish a healthy flowering sward from seed.

Planning your grassland

Before turning your whole garden into a single flowering meadow, consider the different kinds of flowering grassland areas that are possible (see pp. 26–29). You will, of course, want to achieve a wild look, but don't forget that you will need to provide access to other parts of the garden (a mown path is ideal), and also perhaps areas for relaxation.

Altering the site

On the whole, your wildflower garden will look better and grow better if you work *with* the natural characteristics of your site rather than against them. Wild flowers are the ideal solution for problem sites such as infertile, sandy soils or waterlogged clay soils. If you want to add variety to your garden, think of adding one

of the major features described on pp. 134–7. Ponds and banks belong naturally together. The soil you excavate to make the pond can be incorporated into the bank or rockery, and a gravel or scree approach to the pond is ideal for access. See pp. 134–7 for details on how to build these features.

Making a plan

Try putting your ideas on paper before you begin planting. Indicate existing areas of sun and shade and fertile/infertile, heavy/well-drained soil. Using tracing paper you could also make an overlay plan showing what the shade and sun areas will be once shrubs, hedges and trees have developed. This kind of plan can be quite an eye-opener: it is just as well to realize before you plant all those

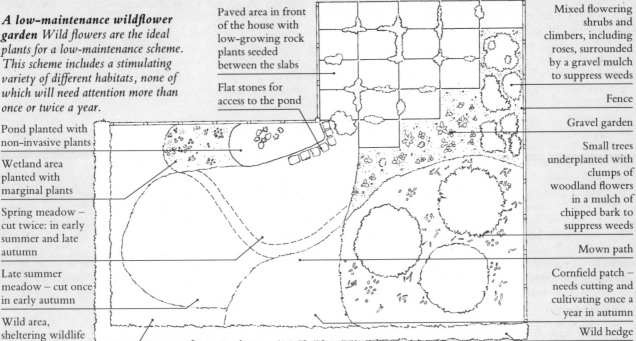

A low-maintenance wildflower garden Wild flowers are the ideal plants for a low-maintenance scheme. This scheme includes a stimulating variety of different habitats, none of which will need attention more than once or twice a year.

Pond planted with non-invasive plants

Wetland area planted with marginal plants

Spring meadow – cut twice: in early summer and late autumn

Late summer meadow – cut once in early autumn

Wild area, sheltering wildlife

Paved area in front of the house with low-growing rock plants seeded between the slabs

Flat stones for access to the pond

Mixed flowering shrubs and climbers, including roses, surrounded by a gravel mulch to suppress weeds

Fence

Gravel garden

Small trees underplanted with clumps of woodland flowers in a mulch of chipped bark to suppress weeds

Mown path

Cornfield patch – needs cutting and cultivating once a year in autumn

Wild hedge

tiny trees that eventually your whole garden will be in deep shade! You can thin them, of course, but make sure you don't have to thin out your favourite specimens.

To make sure your garden will be interesting all year round, you could also make separate overlays showing the main areas of importance in each season. Remember that in the winter, when the weather is too bad to venture outdoors, you will want to be able to see something of interest from inside the house.

Starting from scratch

Acquiring a brand-new garden or taking over a neglected wilderness give the greatest opportunities for planning your wildflower garden exactly as you wish, and building major features such as ponds and banks with the least disruption. The first step is to assess the site as it stands (see pp. 131–132). Get to know it as well as possible – there may be unexpected advantages that are easily overlooked.

A new garden
In a new garden you will either have fresh topsoil brought in by the builder which will possibly yield a small array of annual weeds, or the garden might be a fertile piece of countryside. If you are very lucky, it might even be part of an old meadow or parkland, and contain an interesting range of wild flowers. Therefore, if your new garden looks like old grass, allow a good-sized area to grow up the first year to see what you have. You might be surprised. There must be so many new owners who have moved in and sprayed everything in sight with weedkiller and not realized that they have wiped out cowslips, primroses or even orchids.

Often the new plot will not have any topsoil, or perhaps only in parts. This will give you a chance to plan the garden from scratch and decide where you want fertile topsoil and where areas of low fertility (see p. 133). Now is the time to decide if you wish to create shady woodland areas or to build a pond or rockery. There may even be 'rubbish' on the site that can be put to good use.
Clearing the site If you are faced with a new site it will probably look more like a battlefield or a bomb site than a promising new garden. Before you get the area cleared of the inevitable piles of rubble and sand think about using them to give yourself a head start with your wild garden.

Builders' rubble can be most useful. It can be used to make foundations for paths, or to form the base of a gravel garden (see 'Making paths', p. 137), rock garden or chalk mound (see pp. 136–7). If your pile of builders' rubble happens to be in a convenient, sunny spot, there will not even be any need to move it. If it is in shade or semi-shade but you don't wish to (or can't afford to) move it, distribute some soil over the rubble to fill the gaps, give some fertility and retain moisture; and plant foxgloves, bluebells, red campion, herb-robert, lesser periwinkle, goldenrod, wood sage, wood anemone, greater stitchwort, wood avens and burnet rose.
Planting for quick results In your first year you will want some rapid colour and you will probably not have time to prepare the soil properly. Why not sow a colourful cornfield mixture? This is best sown in autumn but can also be sown in spring. The soil only needs to be roughly prepared and the seed scattered over and rolled in (see p. 130).

An old neglected garden
This, of course, will be a wildlife paradise. Birds will be nesting in every hedge and thicket, and there will be wild flowers and nettles attracting butterflies. Whatever you do, don't rush in and clear everything. My advice would always be, wait a season and take careful stock of what you have in the way of flowers, shrubs, trees and wildlife, and then start to decide what should be cleared, what should be trimmed, and what should be kept.

When we bought our present home we were faced with several acres of blackthorn scrub and nettles; shoulder-high thistles, docks, couch grass and bindweed – and some very long grass struggling for survival in the wilderness.

The blackthorn was cleared with a bulldozer, but we left a quarter of an acre of it, and then discovered that it was a famous haunt of nightingales! I still think that quarter-acre of scrub is worth every bit of the space it takes up just to hear the nightingales for even a few nights a year – and one year they nested and sung right through the day for weeks on end.

The nettles and docks and so on we slashed, scythed, and finally mowed, and I now have a beautiful lawn which flowers every spring. No grass seed was added at all. The remainder of the site I ploughed, harrowed (to make a smooth surface for sowing) and turned into a nursery. Growth soon appeared along the uncultivated paths. Again, I sowed no grass seed, but mowed close, and I now have beautiful green grass from the seed that was stored in the soil. Most tall-growing weeds will disappear with constant mowing.
A programme for rejuvenation You don't need any weedkillers to clear an overgrown site, just hard work from morning till night! You will have the satisfaction of knowing that you haven't destroyed any wildlife or jeopardized your own health.

Mark any good tree seedlings or saplings *before* you go in with the slasher, and do wait until summer or autumn, after the nesting season, before clearing anything.

Overgrown hedges should be cut back to thicken them up and to give yourself a lot more land; they will be just as good for wildlife. Do leave plenty of nettles in a sunny spot for the caterpillars.

Building major features
If you have the space, adding a wetland area, rockery or chalk bank to your wildflower garden will multiply the variety of plants you can grow. If you haven't room for features such as these, you can re-create them on a smaller scale using tubs or other containers (see pp. 97, 98, 110 and 111 for ideas).

Making a pond
It is important to think hard before siting a pond. There should be no pipes, cables or large tree roots near the site; it must be near a water source for filling and topping up the pond; and you will need a ditch or soakaway nearby to take any overflow after heavy rain. Ponds are best sited away from trees and hedges, as autumn leaves can be a big problem. Take advantage of any natural dips in the ground – you will have to move a considerable volume of soil to make the pond so anything that cuts down on this work is a worthwhile bonus.

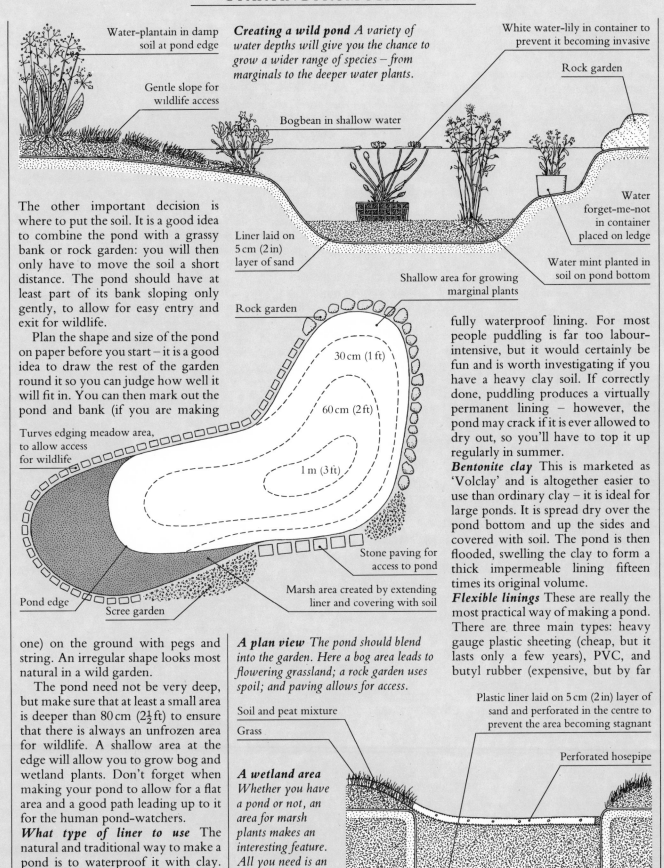

Water-plantain in damp soil at pond edge

Gentle slope for wildlife access

Creating a wild pond *A variety of water depths will give you the chance to grow a wider range of species – from marginals to the deeper water plants.*

Bogbean in shallow water

White water-lily in container to prevent it becoming invasive

Rock garden

Liner laid on 5 cm (2 in) layer of sand

Shallow area for growing marginal plants

Water forget-me-not in container placed on ledge

Water mint planted in soil on pond bottom

Rock garden

30 cm (1 ft)

60 cm (2 ft)

1 m (3 ft)

Turves edging meadow area, to allow access for wildlife

Pond edge

Scree garden

Stone paving for access to pond

Marsh area created by extending liner and covering with soil

The other important decision is where to put the soil. It is a good idea to combine the pond with a grassy bank or rock garden: you will then only have to move the soil a short distance. The pond should have at least part of its bank sloping only gently, to allow for easy entry and exit for wildlife.

Plan the shape and size of the pond on paper before you start – it is a good idea to draw the rest of the garden round it so you can judge how well it will fit in. You can then mark out the pond and bank (if you are making one) on the ground with pegs and string. An irregular shape looks most natural in a wild garden.

The pond need not be very deep, but make sure that at least a small area is deeper than 80 cm (2½ ft) to ensure that there is always an unfrozen area for wildlife. A shallow area at the edge will allow you to grow bog and wetland plants. Don't forget when making your pond to allow for a flat area and a good path leading up to it for the human pond-watchers.

What type of liner to use The natural and traditional way to make a pond is to waterproof it with clay. This is known as 'puddling'. If you have the clay available and lots of time, it will get you and your friends quite fit: the clay needs to be thoroughly trampled down to make a

A plan view *The pond should blend into the garden. Here a bog area leads to flowering grassland; a rock garden uses spoil; and paving allows for access.*

Soil and peat mixture

Grass

A wetland area *Whether you have a pond or not, an area for marsh plants makes an interesting feature. All you need is an old garden hose and a polythene sheet, both of which should be perforated.*

fully waterproof lining. For most people puddling is far too labour-intensive, but it would certainly be fun and is worth investigating if you have a heavy clay soil. If correctly done, puddling produces a virtually permanent lining – however, the pond may crack if it is ever allowed to dry out, so you'll have to top it up regularly in summer.

Bentonite clay This is marketed as 'Volclay' and is altogether easier to use than ordinary clay – it is ideal for large ponds. It is spread dry over the pond bottom and up the sides and covered with soil. The pond is then flooded, swelling the clay to form a thick impermeable lining fifteen times its original volume.

Flexible linings These are really the most practical way of making a pond. There are three main types: heavy gauge plastic sheeting (cheap, but it lasts only a few years), PVC, and butyl rubber (expensive, but by far

Plastic liner laid on 5 cm (2 in) layer of sand and perforated in the centre to prevent the area becoming stagnant

Perforated hosepipe

the strongest, and will last for many years). Flexible liners should be laid over a 5 cm (2 in) layer of sand to eliminate air pockets and ensure no sharp stones pierce them.

Wetland area

A self-contained wetland area can be created very simply by digging out a hollow about 30 cm (1 ft) deep. Line with plastic sheeting and then puncture the lining with a fork to allow seepage into the soil and prevent the water becoming stagnant. Fill the hollow with a rich soil and humus mixture. To prevent the area drying out, lay a 2 cm (¾ in) hose with holes drilled in it down the middle of the area and run water through it.

Making a rock garden

Choose a sunny site for the rock garden and take advantage of any free-draining areas such as slopes or the base of walls, since sharp drainage is vital for growing alpines. The basic construction of a rock garden is the same whatever soil you have, but on a heavy soil it is best to construct it on top of the soil, making a low mound or a raised bed with sloping drystone retaining walls (which should also have drainage and planting holes) to hold it in place (see p. 112). In medium or light soils you can dig out the area for the rock garden so that it ends up more or less level with the surrounding soil – although a slightly raised site may look more natural.

Excavate to a total depth of no more than 30 cm (1 ft) and fill with a 15 cm (6 in) layer of rubble, covered with upturned turves or an 8 cm (3 in) layer of gravel and topped up with 8 cm (3 in) of alpine mix consisting of 3 parts topsoil, 2 parts peat and 1½ parts grit or gritty sharp sand.

The soil will settle after a few weeks, and may need topping up, so it is best to postpone planting for a while. Rocks and large stones will add interest, and will provide a cool, moist root run, although they aren't essential. Buy the largest you can handle, rather than a load of small ones which will be difficult to use in a natural way. The rocks should be placed to give the impression that there is far more rock below the surface than above. This will give the impression of an outcrop of rock exposed by the weather. If the rocks have strata lines, make sure these all

run the same way – the rocks should be roughly parallel, with the occasional vertical fault line for interest. If your rock garden is on a slope, use the rocks to make terraces, with the stone tilted slightly to direct water into the soil. Pack rock garden soil mixture tightly between the rocks once they are in their final position, to keep the rocks stable.

There are ideas for planting rock gardens on pages 110–11. After you have planted the rock garden, cover the remaining soil surface with stone chippings. These will look natural and will also prevent soil splashing on to the leaves.

Making a chalk bank

A chalk bank is ideal for growing many delicate upland flowers (see p. 27), as well as for attracting unusual butterflies and lizards. It should be in full sun, and could be built up against a south-facing wall. The largest mounds should not be higher than 1.2 m (4 ft), and 90 cm (3 ft) is best for a small garden. A higher mound will look odd and out of place in an otherwise level garden. The sides should slope very gently so that there is not excessive water run-off. If the mound is surrounded by grass, this

should be kept short so that seeds from the fertile, flat area don't colonize the mound.

Unless you are close to a plentiful supply of chalk, it is best to use ordinary rubble rather than coarse chalk as the basis for your bank. Choose a sunny site for the mound, covering it with a 45–60 cm (1½–2 ft) layer of medium-sized chalk lumps. Once the required thickness has been reached, tread down the surface to make a seed bed compact enough for planting – you can plant or sow seed straight into the chalk.

Lizards will love a bank such as this, and you can encourage them by building lizard-sized tunnels. This can be done either by laying short lengths of 4–5–cm (1½–2 in) pipe leading to the centre of the mound as you build it (and pulling them out when it is finished), or by ramming a solid iron bar into the rubble area after construction. It helps if the tunnels slope upwards slightly towards the centre of the mound to stop rainwater running in.

The boundaries

Once the site has been cleared and the main features of the garden decided, the best plan of action is to start at the

An area for growing rock plants A wildflower rockery should look as much like a natural rocky outcrop as possible – with large, weathered stones well bedded into the ground, and native rock plants growing in every cranny.

Large rocks arranged naturally and interplanted with wild flowers

8 cm (3 in) layer of rock garden soil mixture

8 cm (3 in) layer of gravel

15 cm (6 in) layer of rubble

Decorative mulch of stone chippings

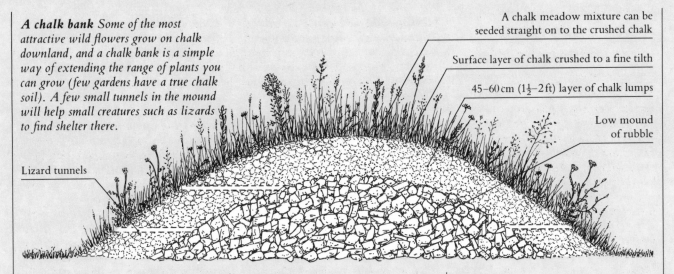

A chalk bank Some of the most attractive wild flowers grow on chalk downland, and a chalk bank is a simple way of extending the range of plants you can grow (few gardens have a true chalk soil). A few small tunnels in the mound will help small creatures such as lizards to find shelter there.

A chalk meadow mixture can be seeded straight on to the crushed chalk

Surface layer of chalk crushed to a fine tilth

45–60 cm (1½–2 ft) layer of chalk lumps

Low mound of rubble

Lizard tunnels

boundary and work in. The first thing you will probably want to achieve is some privacy, shelter from wind, and shade. Stark lines and over-intricate designs will both look out of place in a wildflower garden, so avoid man-made materials such as pre-cast concrete blocks or plastic trellis. There may already be walls and fences around the site; if so, you can soften any hard edges by fixing trellis or wires to the surface and growing an assortment of climbers and wall-trained shrubs up them – try honeysuckle, bittersweet, dog rose, hop, traveller's-joy, hedge bindweed, and sweet briar.

Mixed hedgerows If you have the choice, and a reasonably large garden, there is no doubt at all that the ideal boundary for a wildflower garden is a hedge of mixed species of shrubs and climbing plants (see pp. 59–61 and 142 for how to plant a hedge).

Before planting a hedge, you should be aware of its drawbacks. Hedges take time to establish and use up a lot of space. Their roots spread as far as the hedge is high, creating poor, dry soil conditions, so for the very small garden a hedge is not practical.

Other screens There are plenty of good, sturdy and attractive wooden fencing panels on the market. They should be erected with strong, well-preserved posts, as inadequate supports often give way before the fence itself. The fence should also be treated with a good, long-lasting preservative: remember, once plants are rambling over it you won't be able to apply any further coats.

A sturdy wooden trellis is another solution. Choose one made of rustic poles or solid sawn timber that has

been treated with a preservative stain (a dark one will look more natural). Like the solid fence, trellis should be fixed to stout uprights. It is ideal for climbing plants to ramble through – any of the climbing wild flowers such as honeysuckle, traveller's-joy, hedge bindweed, hops, or the taller vetches will look decorative. In addition, you could try old-fashioned climbing or rambling roses. The trellis *must* be solidly built: a lightweight trellis will not last more than a few years.

Making paths

If you want to lay down permanent paths straight away in a new garden you will have to do some advance planning to ensure they are to be really useful. It is easy either to concentrate entirely on short-cuts – forgetting that you will want to wander all around the garden to enjoy it to the fullest extent – or to introduce fussy paths that lead nowhere at all and are seldom used. The simplest answer is to lay no paths at all for the first year, but to allow your feet to mark them out as you find your way around the garden.

Natural paths Beaten-earth paths in woodland gardens probably need no further surfacing, though if they tend to become wet and muddy you could use a layer of chipped bark. In meadow areas, a mown path will allow you to walk through the long grass and many of the lawn flowers, such as speedwell and daisies, will thrive here. Keep the path regularly mown, but don't cut it too short – 10–15 cm (4–6 in) is short enough – as your path will look very unnatural otherwise, and won't flower either. One mower's width is ideal – don't

make your paths wider than necessary: you will then keep the feeling that you are exploring your garden as you wander through it.

Gravel paths Nearer the house, gravel makes an ideal surface for a garden path. It is not slippery, and you can encourage wild flowers to grow up through it, making it a feature in its own right (see p. 112 for planting ideas). Unwashed gravel from a local supplier is best: buy enough to make a layer at least 5 cm (2 in) thick, laid over an equal layer of sharp sand. On heavy clay, you will need to dig the soil first and make the sand and gravel a total of 15 cm (6 in) deep. This will enable the plants that don't like the wet to root above the wet soil and those that require moisture to root deep into the subsoil. Edge the path with bricks or pieces of timber, which should be wedged into the soil to retain the gravel.

Brick paths Brick is another natural material that looks good in a wildflower garden. Use old or used bricks as these look so much softer in colour than new bricks. They need a sound foundation – a minimum of 7 cm (3 in) consolidated hardcore, covered with 2 cm (1 in) of sand, on to which the bricks are laid. If you want to grow flowers and herbs between the bricks, it's best to plan for them as you are laying the bricks down. Leave 1-brick gaps in the hardcore and sand foundation and fill them with a mixture of soil and sand. If you use sand rather than mortar to grout the bricks, you could also try removing the odd brick or two after the path has been laid and loosening the foundations with a spade to allow the roots to penetrate to the soil beneath.

Converting a conventional garden

The wildflower garden, with its natural, informal planting and flexible boundaries may seem radically different from a conventional garden full of meticulous flowerbeds, showy artificially bred plants, and grass like a bowling green. Rushing in and clearing everything without thought, however, is *not* the best way to alter any garden. Look at the existing layout carefully. There may well be plants and features that are worth keeping. There are no rigid rules when it comes to wildflower gardening, and the odd cultivated plant or fancy dividing screen may well be what gives your garden its unique character in the end.

Planning for change
Make a plan of the garden as it is and then lay tracing paper over it and mark in the features you want to keep, and also existing areas of shade and sun, well-drained or waterlogged soil. Your tracing will now give you an idea of the 'bones' of the garden and you can start filling in what you would like to do with it.

If you have a large garden, or are planning radical changes, it may be helpful to divide your plan into several stages, to be carried out over two or three years.

You can now see what is to be removed and what can be kept till a later stage. This planning is essential otherwise you will tend to work with what is already there and the result will probably be an unsatisfactory compromise.

Changing your approach
One of the most important differences between a conventional and a wildflower garden is how you look after it. For wild flowers to thrive, you must stop using weedkillers and pesticides which destroy the ecological balance necessary to encourage the wildlife that will invade your garden giving added interest to every season. Fertilizers are also unnecessary, indeed harmful, promoting excessive growth. Let your wild flowers grow naturally and find their own balance. Low fertility soils are ideal for growing wild flowers.

Mixing wild and garden plants
Your choice of which garden flowers and shrubs to keep will be very much a matter of personal taste, but it will be fairly obvious which ones look quite out of place with wild flowers. If you want traditional cut-flowers for the house – chrysanthemums, dahlias, asters, and so on – then grow them in a separate flowerbed of their own, and if you want modern hybrid tea roses then choose the more delicate colours and try mixing them with some of the wild plants. There aren't really any rules, and in any case rules are for breaking! Just use your instinct and you will soon decide what is right and what looks inappropriate or out of place.

The plants that always associate best with wild flowers are the old cottage-garden favourites and herbs. Many of these are species plants, in other words wild in some part of the world, or old selected varieties, not far removed from their wild ancestors. Species and old-fashioned roses always make a good background for a wildflower area.

Look around other gardens, not just the grand ones, and pick up ideas for plant associations. There aren't many wildflower gardens at the moment but I'm sure that within the next five years they will be springing up everywhere! Look at road verges as you drive past, and other places where wild flowers grow, and work out what it is that makes these areas so beautiful. It might be simple combinations of colour, sometimes bright but often very subtle. It might be contrasting textures, shapes and heights that are particularly pleasing. It is often a question of scale. A simple example of flower combination is the red field poppy and how it seems to look incredibly beautiful with any other flowers and colours. It is not the colour in itself, but the particular quality of that colour – those very fragile and usually mobile petals that look so delightful amongst bright blue and purple and golden yellow. Most other scarlet flowers would just look gaudy.

From bowling-green to flowering lawn
The simplest option for an uncomfortably neat lawn area is to stop mowing and simply let the lawn grow. Most old lawns are full of flowers including speedwell, daisy, black medick, plantain, cat's-ear, dandelion and clover. Allow the lawn to grow up in the spring and you will have a carpet of colour. In June, start cutting again and return to a normal lawn until the following spring. Extra flowers can be introduced easily by taking out a small piece of turf from a lawn richer in flowers and inserting it into yours. Individual plants may also be planted into the lawn during autumn or winter (see p. 142).

If the lawn has been treated with weedkillers for many years, there may of course be no 'weeds' left to flower. In this case add plenty of plants and allow them to spread.

Don't confuse the flowering lawn with the meadow proper. A flowering meadow needs to be on poor soil, and has far fewer, less vigorous grasses than a lawn. If you want to plant a meadow in an area of existing lush grass, such as a lawn, you will have to take up the turf and sow a meadow mixture (see pp. 129–30).

From patio to flowering path
Patios are ideal sites for growing wild flowers in tubs or stone sinks. Wild flowers will seed themselves happily in the most inhospitable-looking sites, and they will colonize any cracks in the concrete. You may even be able to lift one or two paving stones and loosen the hardcore beneath to make planting holes (see 'Making paths', p. 137).

Choosing trees and shrubs
A high proportion of native trees and shrubs will not only look more appropriate in a wildflower garden, but will attract the maximum variety of wildlife. A few exotic or naturalized species mixed in will look fine in the right setting, but they shouldn't be allowed to dominate – they will distract the eye from the subtler attractions of the native wild flowers around them. Conifers are the worst culprits in this way (in fact, you can't even plant beneath them). Most do not really fit into the wild garden and support very little wildlife, whereas a native birch tree, for example, supports 230 species of insects alone. The only exceptions are native evergreens such as holly, juniper and yew – these offer vital protection for winter. (See page 181 for a list of recommended native trees and shrubs.)

Before *This traditional garden layout is full of straight lines and neat boundaries. Start by drawing a rough plan of the existing layout on a sheet of tracing paper. Think about each feature in turn and how it could be made to look more natural. Then consider the overall plan: decide whether the layout needs to be simpler; think how the features link together – to look natural the transition from one area to another should be gradual, not abrupt.*

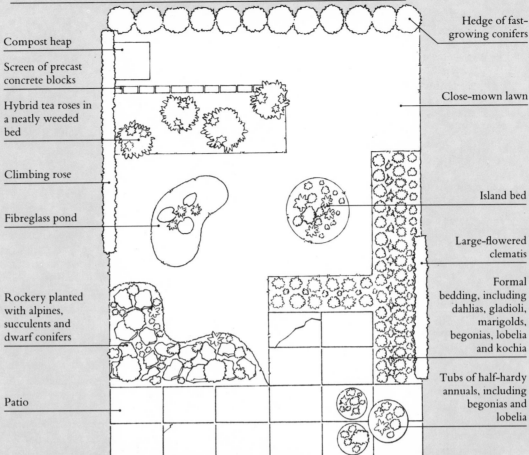

Compost heap

Screen of precast concrete blocks

Hybrid tea roses in a neatly weeded bed

Climbing rose

Fibreglass pond

Rockery planted with alpines, succulents and dwarf conifers

Patio

Hedge of fast-growing conifers

Close-mown lawn

Island bed

Large-flowered clematis

Formal bedding, including dahlias, gladioli, marigolds, begonias, lobelia and kochia

Tubs of half-hardy annuals, including begonias and lobelia

After *One area blends naturally into the next in the new wildflower garden. The curving natural boundaries invite exploration, and a surprising variety of habitats has been accommodated. The pond, rockery, flower border and patio have all been retained but modified to look more natural and the conventional planting replaced with native species. The lawn has been partly replaced by a summer meadow and the greedy, fast-growing conifer hedge changed for one of mixed native species.*

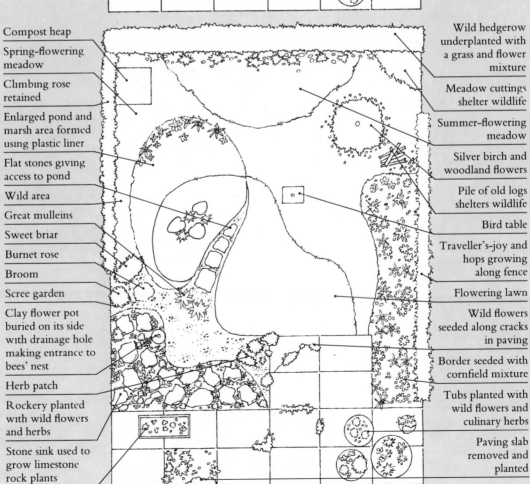

Compost heap

Spring-flowering meadow

Climbing rose retained

Enlarged pond and marsh area formed using plastic liner

Flat stones giving access to pond

Wild area

Great mulleins

Sweet briar

Burnet rose

Broom

Scree garden

Clay flower pot buried on its side with drainage hole making entrance to bees' nest

Herb patch

Rockery planted with wild flowers and herbs

Stone sink used to grow limestone rock plants

Wild hedgerow underplanted with a grass and flower mixture

Meadow cuttings shelter wildlife

Summer-flowering meadow

Silver birch and woodland flowers

Pile of old logs shelters wildlife

Bird table

Traveller's-joy and hops growing along fence

Flowering lawn

Wild flowers seeded along cracks in paving

Border seeded with cornfield mixture

Tubs planted with wild flowers and culinary herbs

Paving slab removed and planted

Looking after a wildflower garden

Our England is a garden, and such
gardens are not made
By singing 'Oh how beautiful!' and
sitting in the shade.
                              Kipling

The idea that the wildflower garden is completely trouble-free is sadly a myth! Nothing worthwhile and productive in this life is free of care. In the wild, the weather beats down old stems, and vegetation rots down into the soil. In the garden this looks too untidy except in the odd corner. Leaving some, less visible, patches of grass and vegetation completely wild will encourage wildlife, but if you let nature have its way entirely in such a small area, only the most vigorous plants will survive. Your carefully chosen selection of wild flowers will be smothered by vigorous grasses, creepers, and a few dominant species of wild flower. One of the objects in having a wildflower garden is to observe nature at work and keep intervention to a minimum; however with this in mind it is important to plan and to maintain the wildflower garden to a regular routine so that it does not get the upper hand. It is a delicate balance to strike and if you turn your back for too long your nature-garden will indeed become an overgrown wilderness.

An annual routine

Having some kind of routine is essential. Details on maintaining the different elements in a wildflower garden are given elsewhere as follows: hedges and scrub, p. 142; woodland, p. 142; lawns and meadows, pp. 144–5; flowerbeds, p. 144. A minimum annual routine would be:

Spring Watch what seedlings are coming up in flowerbeds and weed out those you don't want.

Mow the late-summer flowering meadow areas if growth is vigorous.

Continue seed-sowing.

Summer Mow the flowering lawn and cut spring and early-summer flowering meadow areas.

Cut down some nettles to encourage new growth for the late summer and autumn butterflies.

Autumn Sow annual cornfield and meadow areas.

Cut late-summer flowering meadow areas.

Plant trees, shrubs, and bulbs, and introduce established perennials into flowering meadows and lawns.

Clean out silted-up ponds.

This is the best time to sow most wildflower seeds.

Winter Continue planting as long as the ground is not frozen.

Cut back overgrown hedges and scrub areas.

Shape young trees.

Growing trees and shrubs

Trees and shrubs provide welcome areas of cool and shade in the garden, allowing a wide variety of woodland and hedgerow plants to be grown. There is a huge range of lovely native species to choose from (see list of recommended trees and shrubs on p. 181).

Many gardeners will want to grow their own trees and shrubs from seed, and as seed of many trees can be readily collected in the countryside, this is a very inexpensive method. It also means, if you collect seed nearby, that you will have seed from particular strains of plants that are suited to your soil and local climate. It is amazing how fast trees grow from seed: if they are grown in the right-sized container, they will be ready for planting out in two to three years.

Seeds may also be sown direct into the soil when freshly harvested in summer or autumn. As some may take a year or more to germinate the spot should be well marked and kept weeded. It is advisable to be generous with seed and then transplant the surplus seedlings when they are a few centimetres high.

You will probably find too that self-grown seedlings will introduce themselves into your garden. These are ideal for transplanting, but do be selective. Often the most prolific trees, such as sycamores, are not the most desirable (see 'Recommended trees and shrubs', p. 181).

How to plant trees, shrubs and climbing plants

It is always tempting to buy the tallest tree available, for instant effect. The truth is that small trees need less watering and establish themselves much more quickly than larger specimens. Small trees are also very inexpensive. A silver birch from a specialist tree nursery at 30–45 cm (1–1½ ft) tall, for instance, will cost about a tenth of the price of a 1.8 m (6 ft) specimen. Climbers are sold in containers, but trees and shrubs are also available bare-rooted. (Oaks are best container-grown: if you do buy bare-rooted oaks, choose the smallest available as oaks put down long tap roots as they grow.) Trees, shrubs and climbers are best planted when they are dormant, from October to April.

Preparing the site Think of the ultimate height the trees and shrubs can be expected to reach when deciding where to plant them. Avoid sites too close to buildings, boundaries, or other trees: a distance of at least half their ultimate height is advisable. For a quick effect you can plant trees quite close together – say 1.2 m (4 ft) apart – and then thin out some and coppice others, allowing the best specimens to reach maturity.

When you are ready to plant, prepare the roots. Container-grown plants have their roots in a tight ball and this should be gently loosened so that the roots can be spread out in the planting hole. Bare-rooted plants will

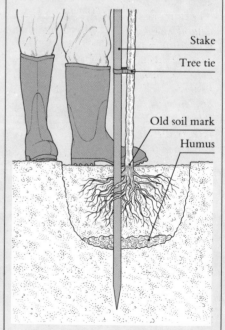

Stake

Tree tie

Old soil mark

Humus

Supporting larger saplings *Before planting, position a stout wooden stake and knock it into the ground at the bottom of the planting hole. Secure the sapling to the stake with a tree tie.*

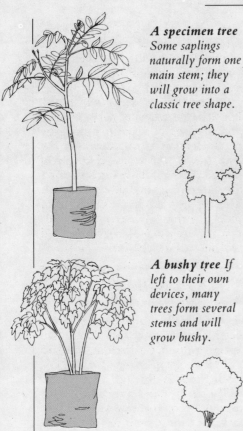

A specimen tree *Some saplings naturally form one main stem; they will grow into a classic tree shape.*

A bushy tree *If left to their own devices, many trees form several stems and will grow bushy.*

come wrapped in a sack to keep them moist. If the roots are at all dry, soak them in a bucket of water for half an hour. Even if they are moist, they should be dipped in water for a few minutes before planting.

Dig out a hole deep and wide enough to allow the roots to be spread over the soil. This makes for quick establishment and good anchorage. Fork the bottom of the hole to loosen the more compact soil and add some home-made compost, special tree-planting compost or bonemeal.

Hold the tree in the hole and place the stake in position (if you put the stake in after filling with earth you may well damage the roots). Stakes are only necessary for trees over 60 cm (2 ft) tall. In fact in a sheltered situation you could dispense with a stake for trees up to 90 cm (3 ft) tall.

Put back the soil making sure no air pockets are left and that the surface is level with the old soil mark (usually visible as a dark stain on the stem). Press the soil down over and around the roots. This firming in of the roots is important as it anchors the plant and ensures that all the roots are in contact with the soil.

If turf has been taken out then put this back upside down on top of the soil to prevent grass growing.

Water the young plants well if the soil is at all dry, using a bucketful of water. If watering is needed during a dry summer then one bucket a week is the best way to water. Watering a little and often when you think of it is not to be recommended. Spread compost, old carpet or roofing-felt around the tree as a mulch to keep weeds down, if you are not able to weed regularly. The mulch will also help to keep moisture in the soil, which means less watering.

Shaping young trees
In a wild situation, or even a very large garden, trees should be allowed to develop completely naturally, but in a smaller garden access is usually required beneath trees, so the lower branches need to be removed. This is best done as the young tree grows, taking off the lowest branches, a few every year, with sharp secateurs until the required stem height is reached.

Prune during the dormant period, from autumn to early spring. You are trying to achieve a good straight stem with branches starting from 1.5 m (5 ft) or so above the ground. If the tree develops two main leading shoots; cut the weakest one off so that the other will grow upright.

Coppicing
Traditionally, this is the practice of cutting back trees every seven to twenty years to within 15–30 cm (6–12 ins) of the ground and allowing vigorous new stems to grow up again. These straight poles would be used for fence posts and firewood. Trees managed in this way can live almost indefinitely.

For the gardener, this method of controlling size has many benefits. Firstly, otherwise tall-growing trees can be kept to a reasonable height. Secondly, a thicket of attractive stems and foliage can be maintained easily

Coppicing *Many trees can be kept small enough to grow in gardens by being cut down every few years in winter to within 30 cm (1 ft) of the ground. New shoots then form.*

and the coppice can be used, according to the kind of wood, for firewood, fence posts, bean poles and pea sticks (see p. 181 for details).

Alder, ash, field maple, hazel, hornbeam, oak, silver birch, small-leaved lime, sweet chestnut and willow can all be coppiced but only some trees will produce poles; others will make much more bushy growth.

Maintaining woodland gardens

The most important rule for the woodland gardener is to do as little as possible. Leave some fallen branches and rotting logs both for wildlife and for the woodland mosses, ferns and flowers that will root themselves there. Don't clear leaves away either – they will rot down to create the leafmould essential to most woodland flowers if they are to self-seed.

If you are creating a woodland garden, with saplings and young trees, it is best not to underplant with bulbs and container-grown perennials until the trees are at least 1.5 m (5 ft) tall, and a woodland-type soil has started to develop. Seeding individual species or a woodland mixture, however, can be done the first spring or autumn after planting.

Planting hedges

Dig out a trench the length of the hedge and a spade's-depth deep. Fork over the bottom of the trench and add some compost. Hedging plants should be planted small – 30–60 cm (1–2 ft) tall is enough and spaced at about 30 cm (1 ft) apart. If you are planting a mixed hedge, it is a good idea to plant some species in blocks rather than alternately. This will give a bolder effect of colour and texture and will look more natural.

Maintaining hedges and scrubland

If you decide to leave your hedges to their own devices that's fine, but don't forget they not only get taller every year but also wider. If not cut they tend also to get thin at the bottom. Once hedges have been let go they are a lot of hard work to bring back again to reasonable proportions. The ladder is suddenly too short and you need a saw, not shears.

Really close-clipped hedges will look out-of-place in a wild garden, however, and will also be inhospitable to wildlife. A good compromise is an annual trim in the winter by hand or power-trimmer. Remove any saplings that have seeded themselves at the same time (you could transplant them to a more suitable site), and cut out any suckers that are causing the hedge to spread too wide by cutting them off below the soil.

Be particularly careful to keep any brambles under control. These advance at an alarming rate, branches rooting as they go, and suddenly you have a thorny problem! Cut brambles back every year over the winter to the boundary you have decided on, and you will get better blackberries and won't lose half your garden.

Grassy hedgebanks are invaluable for wildlife, and so are best not cut. If you want to tidy them, scythe once in late winter/early spring before the flowers start growing.

Growing perennials

Most perennial plants can be grown successfully from seed (see pp. 127–8). This is the most satisfactory and least expensive method of acquiring new plants. Wildflower plants are becoming widely available now, however, from specialist wildflower nurseries, herb nurseries, and even from garden centres. Some are available by mail order (see pp. 183–4 for a list of suppliers). Make sure that the stock is genuinely wild, which means buying plants from a specialist or plants that have a specialist's label in the pot.

Whether you are planting your own young plants or bought-in container-grown perennials, they can be planted into bare soil at any time. (Suitable species can be planted into grassland but this is best done from autumn to spring). In dry weather, however, they will need watering well when you plant them and occasionally thereafter if the soil dries out.

Wild flowers grow naturally in colonies, having spread themselves by self-sown seed or runners. So for a natural look, it is always best to plant in small groups. As your 'colonies' seed themselves they may well move around your garden until they find sites that suit them – invariably they will do best there, even though it may not be what you had planned!

When planting beds of wild flowers, the idea is to have the plants growing thickly so that they support each other and leave no room for unwanted annual weeds. Don't worry about the odd sprawling plant – it will survive quite happily without your intervention.

When flowers are over in the flowerbeds and you have decided which stems to leave for seed, the remainder can be cut down to the base foliage. In many cases plants treated thus will flower again during the autumn, giving an extra bonus. This happens also to grassland cut in June or early July. Any seed-heads that are left will look decorative and will also attract seed-eating birds.

Growing bulbs

As a rule, bulbs should be planted at a depth equal to three times their size. Spring bulbs naturalized in grass are still building up energy for the following season through their leaves well after the flowers are over. Leave the bulb leaves to die down naturally; and don't mow until the foliage has started to go brown. In any case, dying bulb foliage is not very sightly and the long grass hiding it is much more decorative.

If you seed the area with a spring-flowering meadow mixture there will be no temptation to mow until June when the whole display is over and the bulbs are again full of energy for next year.

To plant in grass *Dig out a hole slightly deeper and wider than the rootball of the plant. Remove the plant from its pot – tear or pull off plastic-bag containers – and loosen the rootball. Hold the plant in the hole, so that its soil surface is level with the surrounding turf. At the same time back-fill the hole and firm down the soil around the plant.*

Growing wild flowers in containers

Wild flowers will grow very successfully in containers, allowing you to create a wildflower garden in the smallest space. Containers come in all shapes and sizes but for wild flowers, simple designs and natural materials look best. Wooden tubs, simple terracotta pots or window-boxes are all suitable.

All containers should have drainage holes. Cover the bottom with a layer of broken pot or large pebbles. Upturned turves (in large containers) or a layer of bulky organic matter should go in next. Fill up with a soil-based potting compost, which is best for wild flowers.

Some extra feeding will be necessary in such a restricted area of soil after the first few months. The regular use of a seaweed foliar feed or other organic slow-release fertilizer will be beneficial, as will working some organic compost or manure into the soil each year.

The other important thing to get right is watering. Correct watering makes for healthy plants which are naturally resistant to pests and diseases. Never keep the plants permanently wet; this causes more losses amongst pot plants than too little water. Wait until the surface of the pot is completely dry before re-watering. Watering from the bottom (i.e. into the plant saucer) is best for most plants. If the plant takes up the water quickly, within a few minutes, then you have got it right. If the plant

was already wilting you waited too long! If the water sits there for some time then the plant doesn't require any water. Empty the saucer to prevent the roots drowning. Don't forget that a plant in a large pot although dry on the surface may well be quite wet further down by the roots. Plants in wooden tubs should be watered from the top.

Wild flowers will often behave differently when grown in containers. They may be smaller (in a small container) or larger (if the potting compost is richer than the soil they normally grow in) than usual, and by sowing seed at different times of the year the flowers often come well out of season. Grouping containers of different sizes and planting-times together will ensure a very long flowering season.

Supports for climbing plants

The neatly trained and tied-in climbers of conventional gardens will look out of place in a wildflower garden, and are not much good for wildlife. Plant your climbers a foot apart and let them really ramp. You will need to tie them in and direct them a bit to start with, but after that they will more or less look after themselves, with just a tidy-up in late autumn.

The ideal way to grow climbers in a wildflower garden is to allow them to use trees and shrubs as supports. A natural hedge full of climbers is a marvellous sight in summer and autumn (see pp. 59–61 for planting ideas).

Purpose-made supports should be sturdy and unobtrusive – the best material is rustic poles. Any timber in contact with soil should be particularly well treated with wood preservative. The uprights should

be sunk at least 60 cm (2 ft) into the soil and well firmed in. Metal fence supports make a more reliable foundation, or angle irons sunk 60–90 cm (2–3 ft) into the ground, leaving 60 cm (2 ft) above for fixing the uprights. The posts will then be held clear of the ground and will last many years longer.

If you want to grow climbers on house walls, set the wires or trellis you use to support them at least 10 cm (4 in) away from the wall to allow air to circulate. This helps keep the walls dry and will also encourage wildlife to live in the climber. Ivy will cling to the wall but is no danger to the house structure as long as the brickwork and pointing are good. On an old house, however, you may have to think twice before planting ivy. Ivy will scramble over most surfaces, and is also ideal for areas in deep shade.

A 'wigwam' support for climbing plants can easily be made using five or six rustic wooden poles. A climber such as wild clematis planted at the foot of one pole will quickly cover the whole structure and make a shelter for birds.

A natural screen If you want to separate off an area of your garden, a garden screen made of rustic poles is a good idea. Position and secure the uprights first then nail the cross-pieces and struts using galvanized nails.

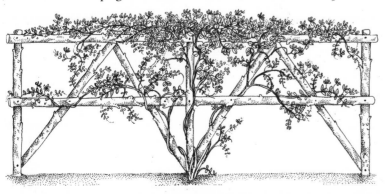

Creative weeding

Controlling self-seeding

The fun of wild plants is that they seed profusely and come true from seed, unlike hybrid and colour-selected flowers. The problem is which ones to allow to seed and how often. As a rule, in grassland you can let everything seed unless you seem to be getting overtaken by one species. In that case, mow before that particular flower sets seed, to stop it spreading any more.

In cultivated soil you have to be much more careful. It is best to stop all windblown seeds setting by removing the seed-heads before they ripen. Other types of seed can be allowed to self-sow, but don't forget that many wild plants produce thousands of seeds which will stay in the soil for years and come up erratically year after year. This applies to annuals as well as perennials. The best answer is to let a few heads self-seed and stop the others.

Seedlings can be thinned at your discretion, but it is not very critical and if the plants are packed tightly together some will simply overcome the others.

Creative weeding

Allowing wild flowers to self-seed will give rise to marvellous combinations of flowers to make your planting more natural. Self-seeding also saves all the work of raising seedlings and planting them out. Even if you only permit controlled self-seeding, as suggested above, you will still have to do some weeding if your flower-beds are not to be unexpectedly dominated by one species, or smothered by unwanted intruders. The difficulty is how to recognize the wildflower seedlings (a) one from another species and (b) from the less-well-loved wild plants that you want to get rid of.

The answer is that you get your eye in amazingly quickly as to what looks interesting (although you might not be able to identify it) and what you quickly recognize as one of those nasty weeds that always take over the whole garden. Many wildflower seedlings (and of course all the weeds) are illustrated in *Weeds* by Roger Phillips (Elm Tree Books, 1986). Most weeds like docks, some thistles and all annual

Some invasive weeds

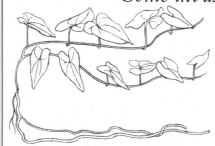

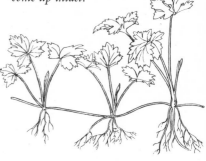

Couch grass
This is extremely invasive in cultivated soil, but easily eradicated with a little care using a fork only. Its white, wiry roots grow near the surface of the soil and do not break very easily, so they should come up intact.

Field bindweed *Try and eradicate it as soon as it starts to grow in the spring, using a weedkiller like sodium chlorate (this is one plant that demands extreme measures!). Otherwise, continually pull up the roots.*

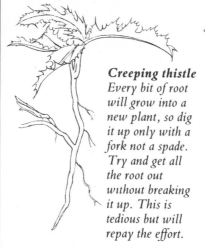

Creeping thistle
Every bit of root will grow into a new plant, so dig it up only with a fork not a spade. Try and get all the root out without breaking it up. This is tedious but will repay the effort.

Creeping buttercup *This is a lovely plant in flower but if the soil is wet it can really get a hold. Each plant rapidly builds up a network of plantlets that will cover the soil. It is easy to eradicate by just digging up with a fork. If you miss any, never let it seed or the cycle will begin again.*

weeds are of some decorative value and often attract wildlife, so a rather laid-back approach to 'weeds' is the best solution! Annual weeds are really designed to fill in blank spaces and as soon as these areas of bare soil are filled (which is the aim in wildflower gardening) the annuals don't get much of a look-in. If you see anything in flower that you think might take over or you just don't like it, take it out *before* it sets seed.

Most of the annual weeds can be classed as wild flowers until they start to overtake the flowers that you are trying to encourage. The plants that really need to be controlled are those perennials with creeping rootstocks like field bindweed, couch grass, creeping thistle and creeping buttercup. Such plants will grow from the smallest piece of root, so take care not to split the roots as you weed. Comfrey is even worse, and trying to move it just increases it, so decide where you want it and let it be!

Of course, all of these problems relate to cultivated soil. In grassland most 'weeds' are controlled by timely cutting and the general competition.

Managing flowering lawns and meadows

Flowering grassy areas, whether lawn or meadow, all need a regular mowing routine during the growing season not only to keep them looking attractive, but also to maintain a good balance of flowers. Leave a rich ancient meadow to its own devices, and within a few years it will just be a mass of grasses and a few, vigorous wild flowers, and of no great interest or beauty at all. Maintenance is the key to growing an interesting mixture of grasses and wild flowers. All the old grasslands are maintained by careful grazing and cutting for hay, and on chalk downland also by rabbit grazing. During the height of the myxomatosis epidemic, great areas of botanical interest that had been grazed by the now decimated rabbit population were lost under grass, scrub and then trees.

Mowing routines

Your mowing routine will dictate exactly which plants will flower in any area.

Spring-flowering lawns (see p. 26) should be left until after they have flowered in spring and early summer; though sometimes if the grass is growing lush and fast an intermediate cut during the spring will be required. Set the blades high at first and reduce the length in easy stages: by July you will have a neat, trim lawn again until next season.

Spring-flowering meadows should be allowed to grow until early July, and then cut and left to grow up to flower again in the autumn. Summer-flowering meadows can be cut in early spring if the grass is too lush and should then be left to grow until early autumn.

Meadows can be cut at various times through the growing season and by cutting them differently every year, it is possible to alter the proportions of the flowers that grow. If you cut only in the autumn it will improve the area if you rake out any dead grass and vegetation as well as raking off the cuttings.

Cutting flowering lawns and meadows

For the flowering lawn all that is required is a wheeled rotary mower (hover and cylinder mowers cut too short). Set at the highest cut this will top the grass and leave the flower foliage alone. It should ideally have a box to collect the mowings.

For the meadow you will need a hand or motor scythe. A motor scythe can be hired quite easily and if you are not experienced at using a hand scythe, and the area is not too small, this is the answer. You could try using a strimmer; but you may find the vegetation too tough for it.

The best way to learn how to hand-scythe properly is to watch someone who knows what they are doing. The main point to remember is that efficient scything requires a blade that is razor-sharp, otherwise it is very hard and unrewarding work.

Your movements should be smooth and economical, resulting in a series of short, rhythmic, quarter-circular swings as you walk down the meadow. Scything is immensely satisfying and once you have established a good rhythm it is a job you can continue all day! The best hand scythe is a short-bladed one like the Turk scythe (see below). Allow long grass to lie for a few days after you have cut it so that the seeds drop out to enrich the meadow.

Grazing the meadow

Sheep are the perfect maintainers of good, flower-rich grassland for the larger meadow. Their grazing will greatly encourage the finer grasses and unless you keep them on the area too long, they will not damage the wild flowers although they will certainly nibble them. Keep them on the meadow for a few weeks at the times you would otherwise cut it.

Keeping the garden healthy

A successful wildflower garden must be a natural garden, where wildlife is encouraged, which means it should be maintained on organic principals. If you start spraying chemicals

around you will completely upset the balance of the whole. Balance is what it is all about and to my mind that applies as much to the whole planet as to a single garden.

Feeding

Wild flowers don't need feeding but the soil may do, preferably with organic fetilizer. Soils with sharp drainage (either good or bad) will benefit in particular from the addition of humus. Light, sandy soil will hold more moisture, and the bacteria that are essential to release soil nutrients will be built up also. Heavy soils will be easier to work in spring and won't bake hard and crack in summer.

The best way to apply organic matter to the soil is in the form of compost. Most of the organic manures that are sold in bags are really too rich for our purposes and release too much nitrogen. Spent mushroom compost is excellent as a top-dressing; it improves clay and sandy soils alike, but it will increase the soil's alkalinity (see p. 132). Incidentally, if you use it on grassland there is a good chance of some mushrooms coming up!

Pest control

In the wildflower garden this is something of a contradiction as pests are always the food of another insect or small mammal and by eliminating

Using a scythe
The best way to learn how to use a scythe is to watch someone experienced at work. Make sure your scythe is very sharp before you start and wear good stout boots to protect your feet and legs. Work systematically across the meadow, swinging the scythe gently and rhythmically as you walk slowly along.

one you starve the other! There are few pests that are worth worrying about in relation to wild flowers, as they hardly ever kill the whole plant. So my advice on pest control is to let the predators do the work.

Town gardens

My comments on pest control so far refer to gardens in green areas. The wildflower gardener in the town will have a much greater problem keeping pests at bay. Their habitual predators may well not be present, and creating what might be an oasis of wild plants in the middle of the city will attract pests like a magnet. The town plot might well be no more than a few tubs of flowers on a small patio or roof garden. The most important thing here for pest control is to make sure plants are potted into suitable compost or soil and fed and watered according to their needs (see p. 143). Peat-based potting composts and chemical feeds are a recipe for aphid

attack: the plants produce too much lush growth. Aphids (greenfly, black-fly and whitefly) are in fact the greatest nuisance in the urban wild-flower garden. Feeding plants regularly with seaweed liquid feed seems to build up resistance to aphid attack.

We recommend two natural pesticides you can use – pyrethrum and derris – but make sure the brand you buy contains no additives. Both should be sprayed in the evening. They won't kill whitefly, but are toxic to bees and ladybirds; derris is particularly toxic to fish.

You can make your own spray against aphids by boiling up rhubarb, elder or wormwood leaves and simmering for half an hour with water (use $\frac{1}{2}$ kg/1 lb leaves to 1 litre/2 pt water) and then straining. Use cold.

There are many country remedies for slugs, the most effective of which is to pick them off at night (when they all come out), by torchlight. For the squeamish, there is one slug-killer

that will not harm anything else (see **Useful Addresses**, p. 183 for suppliers). I have used it successfully for years – the only thing to be careful of is young seedlings. You will find the slugs congregate *underneath* the seed tray, so this is the place to treat.

Bees (left) are valuable pollinators.

Hoverflies (right) eat aphids and other pests.

Ladybirds (left) are also valuable predators of aphids.

Multiplying your plants

Most wildflower plants produce seed in profusion, and this is the best and simplest method of propagating them (see **Collecting seed and raising new plants** pp. 122–30). Some plants – bulbs and shrubs especially – can take rather a long time to mature when grown from seed, however, so there can be advantages to increasing stock by other means.

Bulbs

Most bulbs – for example, bluebells – form large clusters of bulblets that can easily be divided after the bulb has finished flowering and its leaves have died down. The bulblets can then be planted and grown on until they reach flowering size.

Martagon lily bulbs are different: they consist of overlapping fleshy scales. Dig the bulb up in the autumn or after flowering, peel off a few scales and place upright in a seed tray filled with a mixture of 2 parts soil to 1 of leafmould and 1 of sharp sand, with a little charcoal added. Leave room in the tray for more compost to be added as the bulbs swell.

Taking stem cuttings

Stem cuttings should always be taken from firm, healthy stems without flowers or flower buds. Use a sharp knife or scissors, or (for hardwood cuttings) secateurs. There are three types of stem cuttings. Softwood

---

Homemade compost

The basis of a good compost heap is oxygen and moisture. These are both essential to the bacteria that break down the compost materials and turn them into a lovely, dark-brown crumbly textured mixture. The moisture will come off as steam as the heap heats up. Over-watering or treading the heap down and excluding the oxygen just turns it into silage or, usually something a lot worse and smellier!

Starting from the bottom: use straight posts or rows of bricks from front to back to allow air channels under the heap. Then add a layer of woody stems and hedge trimmings that won't rot too fast and will keep the bottom of the heap open for air to get in. Next start putting on a mixture of weeds, old greens, kitchen waste (but not fat and meat which encourage rats), vacuum-cleaner emptyings, lawn mowings, and so on. The key word is *mixture*, as any wet dollops like the kitchen waste or lawn mowings need to be well mixed in with drier stuff. It is best *not* to put seeding plants on the compost heap, as unless the heap becomes very hot, weed seeds will survive. The same also applies to meadow mowings.

Build the heap in 20 cm (8 in) layers. As each layer is complete, apply a proprietary compost activator or a sprinkling of seaweed meal. An alternative is to use a 1 cm ($\frac{1}{2}$ in) layer of manure (chicken or rabbit is ideal) and alternate every 20 cm (8 in) with a generous sprinkling of lime. The best activator of all is urine which should first be diluted and then watered on.

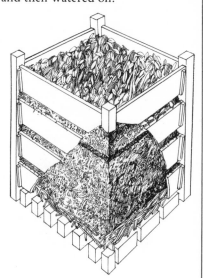

Building a compost heap *Add waste material in 20 cm (8 in) layers, with compost activator in between.*

cuttings are best for increasing woody-stemmed perennials. Cut 5–8 cm (2–3 in) from a growing tip before flower buds have formed. Semi-ripe cuttings are best used for shrubs. Cut an 8–10 cm (3–4 in) length further down the stem as the shoots start to harden in late summer. Hardwood cuttings, for shrubs and trees, come from the woody part of the plant. Cut a 15 cm (6 in) length in autumn. Hardwood cuttings can be planted straight into the soil (add sharp sand before you plant): they will root the following spring. Hormone rooting powder is best used for all cuttings except softwood ones and those of willows and poplars.

Leaf cuttings
Some fleshy leaves will root if placed on the surface of a tray filled with cuttings compost (see below) and kept moist. Cuckooflowers are readily propagated from leaves.

Rooting cuttings
Seed trays or small pots can be used to root cuttings. Fill the container to within $\frac{1}{2}$ cm ($\frac{1}{4}$ in) of the top with a

Many bulbs can be increased by simply separating the clusters of tiny bulblets they produce.

mixture of equal parts peat and perlite (medium grade), or you can use perlite on its own and water well. Trim any leaves from the base of the cutting so that no leaves come into contact with the cutting medium. Insert each cutting into the perlite mixture, making sure that the bottom of the stem is not in contact with the bottom of the seed tray or pot.

Cuttings need light, (but not direct sunlight), warmth and a moist atmosphere. For a few cuttings in a pot this is best achieved by placing the pot inside a plastic bag. Seed trays can be kept in seed propagators, provided there is enough headroom for the cuttings. The bottom heat will speed up rooting considerably.

The developing cuttings
Once the cuttings have produced a good root system the roots will be visible through the drainage holes. If the roots resist a gentle tug on the

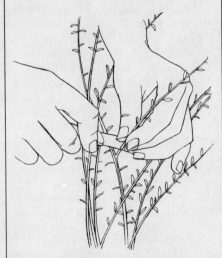

Softwood cuttings 5–8 cm (2–3 in) long can be taken from woody perennials such as broom at any time during the summer months.

stem transfer them into individual pots of compost and place them in a sheltered spot outdoors.

If the cuttings make any weak, spindly growth, cut it back to where there is strong growth in order to ensure that a good, strong, bushy plant develops.

Division
Most herbaceous perennials increase in size at their base year after year. They can be increased by digging up the plant after flowering and splitting it up into smaller sections each with at least one shoot and roots attached and planting them out. Most wild flowers

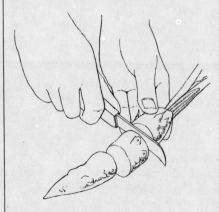

Root cuttings Cut a slice across a thick section of root, making sure you include a bud.

can be divided in this way, including the primrose family (oxlip, cowslip, and so on).

Root cuttings
Plants producing large woody roots can often be propagated in this way. In autumn or spring, cut out a good fat section of root with an eye or bud on it. It should be about 8 cm (3 in) long (length is not at all critical) and plant it out. Elecampane, comfrey and wild cherry are all worth trying.

Runners
Wild strawberries produce a mass of overground runners and a new plant is produced wherever these root. Many other carpeting plants, such as mint, spread by underground root runners. As soon as top growth appears at a distance from the parent plant, the plantlet can be detached for planting elsewhere.

Suckers
Wild roses and some shrubs like blackthorn produce suckers and these can be dug up and planted out as separate plants. Many trees, for example field maple, produce suckers when coppiced.

Division Clump-forming herbaceous plants can be lifted and pulled or cut apart to form new plants in autumn.

Layering
Many woody plants can be layered, but this method is most useful for climbing plants like traveller's-joy. A section of stem is anchored just under the soil – a large stone is ideal for this. Add some sharp sand to the soil where the stem is to root. Once the stem has rooted itself (it will resist a gentle tug, and top growth may be visible), you can detach the new plant by cutting the link to the parent plant.

Gardening for wildlife

The great joy of a wildflower garden is the fantastic range and quantity of wildlife it attracts. This is the one thing that everyone remarks on who comes to my own wildflower garden. I have counted up to forty butterflies on a few square yards of devil's-bit scabious. Not to mention a marvellous range of bees and hoverflies in the summer the garden hums with life. Birds too are easily attracted into such an insect- and seed-rich garden.

In the vegetable garden our attitude to wildlife is coloured by the destruction they can cause. The large white butterfly is a terrible menace, the bullfinch we love to hate, the blackbird does more than its fair share of damage to soft fruit, and pigeons are unmentionable! However in the wild garden, we can enjoy the wildlife without worrying about the damage it might do.

Wild areas

The essential ingredient of the wildlife garden, apart from the multitude of wild flowers, is the wild and unkempt areas. Many gardens, especially small ones, which are easy to keep in order, are far too manicured to provide food and shelter for wildlife. The tidier a garden the less wildlife it will contain, so within reason it is best to save your energy and help the wildlife.

A garden for wildlife doesn't have to be a jungle or particularly untidy, but it must have its wild and natural areas. These can be really very small — for instance, a fallen tree-trunk or a few logs can be a real haven for a terrific range of wildlife and will often make a decorative and sculptural feature. Undergrowth is good: old grass, the occasional heap of woody stems, an ivy-covered wall, a clump of brambles or a tree can be rich in wildlife and provide nesting-places for birds. Birds and insects don't only require live vegetation for survival; dead vegetation is equally important and will complete the balance of wildlife in the garden. Hedges should not be trimmed too neatly but allowed to grow more naturally. Leave a good patch of nettles, other 'weeds' and long grasses, especially in the hedge bottoms. A hedgerow should never be kept completely tidy as the base of a hedge is so valuable as a shelter for wildlife.

The interesting thing about wild and 'untidy' areas in the garden is that they can be easily made to look both intentional and visually acceptable by being bordered by areas that are obviously managed and cared for. For instance, if your whole back garden is wild it can look at some times of the year rather a mess but if you have an area or strip of well mown grass in front of or partially surrounding the longer grass or weed areas then the effect is not only more pleasing but has a managed rather than a derelict look about it. In other words, a definite contrast between areas looks best.

Butterflies

From the first orange tip butterfly in early spring until early autumn when the red admirals are feasting on the fallen apples, the wildflower garden is full of butterflies. Of course if you live in an area rich in butterflies with many woods and wild areas and a minimum of intensive farming, then some of the rarities might well be encouraged into the garden. It is as well to remember, however, when trying to attract butterflies that the only ones which will be drawn to the garden are those which occur locally, or migrant species. Don't expect some rare species like the Adonis blue of old chalk grassland to appear just because you supply its favourite food plant, the horseshoe vetch.

In summer, nectar will be provided in abundance by your wild flowers, but it is worth making a special effort to grow early-flowering food plants such as honesty, dame's-violet and aubretia (all cottage garden favourites) for those butterflies that come out of hibernation very early in the year. Garlic mustard and cuckooflower attract the early-flying orange tip, which will lay its eggs on them.

Late-flowering plants are equally valuable for extending the butterfly season, and the prize amongst these must go to devil's-bit scabious. Red valerian, and the cottage garden iceplants and michaelmas daisies are also beneficial. Moths that fly by day are also attracted to these flowers.

Equally important as providing nectar for the adult butterflies, is to make sure there are food plants for the caterpillars. Chief amongst the food plants are stinging nettles. Don't hide them away in some shady corner, as butterflies normally like to lay their eggs in the sun! They also prefer young nettles, so try to achieve several stages of growth in the nettle patch by cutting a section every three months or so. Red admirals, small tortoiseshells, painted ladies, peacocks and commas all feed on common stinging nettles.

The mustard or cabbage family of plants feeds many butterflies. The lovely orange tips and green-veined

A wild area will provide food and shelter for amphibians and small mammals, birds and insects.

whites prefer cuckooflowers and garlic mustard. The small and large whites, as vegetable gardeners will know, favour cultivated members of this family such as cabbages and cauliflowers, but there is always the chance that a good population of wild species will lure them instead!

Common blues will certainly be attracted by even a small meadow area that contains clovers and common bird's-foot trefoil. Some butterflies feed on shrubs – the beautiful brimstones need buckthorn and holly blues require holly or ivy. Small coppers feed on docks and sorrel, so those docks you have been trying to eradicate are worth keeping after all!

Several meadow and woodland butterflies overwinter as chrysalides on meadow grasses, so do leave an area of grass uncut until the spring. The meadow browns, wall browns, gatekeepers and some of the skippers will appreciate this. Couch grass is particularly liked, so this is a valuable ingredient of a rough grass patch. There are of course many other grasses, mainly the coarse ones, that are food plants, but ryegrass is of no use and all the grass mixtures used for wildlife conservation areas avoid this vigorous species which is in many commercial lawn mixtures.

Bees

Different flowers are designed for different insects to pollinate them. The open flowers like the wild carrot and yarrow can be pollinated by small insects like flies and beetles. Other flowers have their nectar at the base of a tube and rely on bees – those with the longest tubes rely on butterflies and moths with their long tongues. Some flowers can only be entered by a heavy bumble bee and the lighter bees cannot gain entry!

If you grow a selection of wild flowers then they will attract bees as much as they will butterflies. If you keep honey bees then there is no more rewarding sight than to watch them gathering supplies of nectar. Also fascinating to watch is the collecting of pollen by bees. You will notice that every flower has its own particular colour of pollen and the variety of colour and shade is like a beautiful range of natural dye colours. The bees collect the pollen in special 'pollen baskets' on their hind legs and these baskets-full of pollen are easy to see as

the bees go from one flower to the next. Bees are attracted to the flowers by a combination of scent and colour and very often are guided into the flower to the nectar source by 'honey guides' – lines or splashes of colour leading into the flower. These are very noticeable on foxgloves and mallows, but on other flowers you need to use ultra-violet light.

Both bumble and honey bees rely on early spring flowers for food to get them going after a long hard winter and so it is especially important to supply flowers for this end of the season (try snowdrops, cuckooflowers, primroses, willows, buttercups, ground ivy, winter aconites, and garlic mustard. There are as many as 250 species of bees in Great Britain, so you can have a lot of fun trying to identify them.

Hoverflies and ladybirds

There are many different species of hoverfly and to add to the confusion they are great mimics. Their camouflage is an effective method of self-protection, for by looking like a wasp or bee they discourage birds from attacking them. Hoverflies are mostly extremely beneficial; they pollinate flowers and their larvae consume large quantities of aphids, so they are definitely a gardener's friend.

Another colourful friend in the garden is the ladybird: both the adults and larvae are great consumers of aphids. Ladybirds overwinter in sheds and outhouses and around little-used window frames in the house, so try and refrain from too much 'spring cleaning' over the winter – if you need discouragement!

Pollination by bees Many flowers have 'honey guides', often visible only under ultra-violet light. They are designed to lead bees into the flower in search of nectar. As the bee moves about inside the flower, pollen is caught on its furry body, to be brushed off again to pollinate the next flower.

Birds

What with insects, seed-heads, berries and fruits, birds will have a real feast in the wildflower garden. Wild hedges and shrubs or climber-covered walls provide good nesting sites and of course home-made or manufactured nesting-boxes can be used to supplement or, in a small garden, replace the wild hedge.

When the leaves have fallen in the autumn it is great fun to inspect your hedges for old nests and see how many birds have been in residence. In the winter, the waning food supply can be supplemented by putting out extra food and water. You can hope to see blackbirds, thrushes, sparrows, finches, wrens, robins, blue- and great-tits and possibly coal-tits and house-martins or swallows. Bullfinches might not be so welcome (they are voracious seed-eaters) and starlings will arrive of course and push the other birds around in their aggressive way.

Nesting-boxes in the garden In the majority of small gardens there are just not enough suitable nesting sites for the birds you would like to encourage. A variety of nesting-boxes can be readily purchased and the Royal Society for the Protection of Birds (R.S.P.B) sells a good range. Making your own is quite easy and detailed instructions on how to make them are available in various bird books. Michael Chinery's book *The Living Garden* (Dorling Kindersley, 1986; pp. 182–4) has a very informative section on the subject. Nesting-boxes should be fixed firmly to a support out of reach of cats, and away from direct sun. The following birds

A bird-bath A surprising number of birds will be attracted to the smallest puddle of water. Here a shallow depression has been lined with plastic weighed down at the edges with stones, making a permanent puddle.

could be attracted into suitable boxes in the garden: tits, house sparrows, nuthatches, woodpeckers, robins, wrens, and blackbirds.

Bird-baths If you have ever watched birds bathing in a puddle you will know how much they enjoy it. You can provide a permanent puddle for them by making a shallow depression in the ground and lining it with black plastic sheeting weighed down at the edge with pebbles. More elaborate baths on pedestals, often in fibreglass made to look like stone, can be bought from garden centres.

Bird-tables There is no better sight than to watch the birds feeding from your window on a frozen winter's morning. Bird-tables can easily be bought, but they are simple to make, and if you are a handyman a rustic home-made one would look right in the wild garden. Provide a mixture of foods such as fruits, nuts, seeds, bacon rind and any other fats. Hang up a bone for the meat-eaters to peck at. Don't forget in frozen weather that birds need water as well as food.

Wildlife of the pond

Any gardener who wants to attract the maximum amount of wildlife should try to create a pond even if it has to be a very small one. So many ponds and ditches have gone from the countryside that the garden pond is now an important habitat.

Fish and conservation don't go too well together so if you like to keep goldfish and others, think of having a second pond for them, where their carniverous habits cannot damage the other wildlife. You could include sticklebacks in your wildlife pond: they are too small to do any damage to tadpoles.

It is amazing how wildlife arrives when a pond is created and properly planted (see pp. 134–6 and 96–8).

You may well find that a few newts and frogs arrive naturally, but if not then a little spawn or a few tadpoles can usually be obtained from a friend's pond. Never take spawn or tadpoles from the wild as frogs and toads are getting very scarce in the countryside. Frogs will lay their jelly-like mass of spawn in quite shallow water, but toads lay long strings of spawn, like deeper water, and are unlikely to lay in a very small pond.

Tadpoles can be introduced to the pond in spring and will take three months or so to turn into tiny frogs or toads. They will then leave the pond and will not return to breed for three years. Newt eggs are difficult to find as newts lay them individually and hide them by wrapping a leaf around them. They are beautiful little creatures to watch and they will breed in the smallest pond.

Frogs, toads and newts spend most of their time out of the water and need plenty of cover such as old vegetation, log piles or large stones for hibernation – in fact any hiding place that remains nice and moist.

You will probably need to introduce water snails of various sorts from another pond or a water-plant nursery. The ramshorn snail, living on the pond bottom or the giant pond snail just under the water surface, will help to keep the green algae under control, and a few freshwater mussels will filter the water and also help to keep down algae.

Water insects will arrive without any assistance, but if you do want to speed things up, just transport a bucket of water from a friend's well-stocked pond. I could sit for hours watching the hawkers and darters (dragonflies) and damselflies feeding on all the insects that thrive by the pond. If you look into the water you will be amazed by the variety of life. Swallows and martins will love the pond and will spend much time swooping over the water to pick up insects. If you see a heron or king-fisher by your pond the sight will more than compensate for any fish that you might lose! I have seen both by my pond.

Mammals

Wild gardens provide ideal territory for small four-legged creatures. How many moles, field-mice and wood-mice do you see scurrying around your well-mown lawn? But leave the grass and vegetation to grow and, if possible, leave a small area completely uncut with plenty of dead grass and stems and it will soon be colonized.

If you have water or a wet area near then moles will surely appear. In the neat lawn they are certainly too much to bear but in the meadow area they can be tolerated and in fact it is interesting to note the wild flowers that will grow on and around old molehills. Hedgehogs may come into the garden and consume some of your slug population. They are often encouraged by a saucer of bread and milk left out at night!

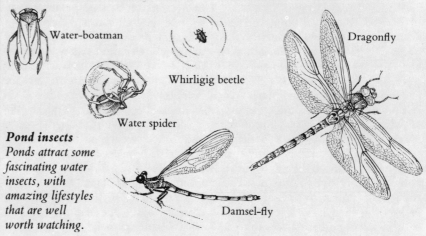

Water-boatman

Whirligig beetle

Water spider

Pond insects
Ponds attract some fascinating water insects, with amazing lifestyles that are well worth watching.

Damsel-fly

Dragonfly

Using wild flowers

Well over 100 wild plants and fruits are not only edible but worth eating: almost all the common hardy vegetables of today have been bred over the centuries from native wild plants. There are at least eighty-five wild plants, trees and shrubs that are used to produce good natural dyes. An enormous number have been used at one time or another for medicinal purposes and there are still over ninety native wild plants and trees actively used in medicine. Whatever wild flowers you choose for your garden you will certainly end up with some plants that have sustained man in some way for hundreds, if not thousands, of years.

Many wild flowers have for long been associated with folklore and magic. Wild plants were once used for strewing on the floor and adding to the filling of mattresses and pillows. Apart from their sweet scent to counteract unsanitary conditions they would also have been valuable as insect and vermin repellants. Indeed many wild plants are still used to deter insect pests.

Wild plants to eat
The lovely dandelion, top of any chemical gardener's hit list and especially hated in lawns, is one of our most nutritious plants. Comparing this common wild flower with the ubiquitous lettuce, dandelion has over three times the vitamin C, six times the vitamin A, over three times the protein value and more than twice the amount of iron, calcium and phosphorus of lettuce. A veritable storehouse of goodness. The young or blanched leaves are an excellent addition to salads and the root makes a most acceptable coffee substitute. In fact, dandelion has been used as a vegetable on and off for centuries and in 1885 there were four or more distinct varieties being sold in France. In Britain we are only just rediscovering the worth of this most persecuted flower. Medicinally, too, dandelions are particularly valuable as a blood cleanser for all liver disorders, especially jaundice. A regular diet of dandelion leaves improves the enamel of the teeth. The white juice of the plant is used to treat warts and blisters and it is a valuable diuretic (hence the French name of *pissenlit*!).

Besides the nutritious dandelion there are many other very common wild plants that are not only tasty but extremely nutritious as well. Many are grown for their thick fleshy roots, for example horse-radish, wild parsnip, white water-lily, marsh-mallow, silverweed, wood avens, sea-holly, chicory and star-of-Bethlehem. Others are used for their leaves served either as salad or cooked – try oxeye daisy, cuckooflower, garlic mustard, wood-sorrel, salad burnet, brooklime, hawthorn, cat's-ear, rough

Refreshing and health-giving teas can be made easily from many wild flowers. Use an infuser or an ordinary teapot and pour freshly-boiled water over the dried flowers or leaves. Wait for a minute before serving.

hawkbit, goat's-beard, hop, common mallow, stinging nettle, ground elder and sorrel.

The mallows are particularly interesting. There are several species that have medicinal properties. The leaves are used in Egypt to make a traditional soup known as *melokhia*. Our own common mallow may be used in a similar way, or, alternatively, the young leaves may be eaten in salads. In fact, every part of the plant can be used in some way; the fruits (called cheeses) can be taken as a tonic, while the root has soothing and healing properties and can be applied as a poultice. Mallow was also cultivated for religious purposes; it is used on the sacred island of Delos in the Cyclades as a symbol of man's first nourishment.

An attractive wetland plant, bistort is still used in Yorkshire as the main ingredient of 'Ledger pudding', which is traditionally eaten during the last two weeks of Lent. Probably the best known of our native spice plants used for their seed are common poppy and fennel.

Our native trees and shrubs yield a marvellous array of fruits – blackberries, raspberries, wild strawberries, rose hips, wild cherries, crab apples, wild plums, gooseberries and red currants.

Sloes, from blackthorns, flavour the delicious liqueur sloe gin as well as making excellent jelly and superb sparkling wine. The sloe is the ancestor of all our cultivated plums. Rowan berries also produce a good jelly. Elderberries are delicious in pies and tarts and make a superb red wine which becomes like port with age. Oil of juniper berries is used both in medicine and for flavouring gin.

Many flowers have great culinary value. The brilliant golden blooms of broom can be sprinkled on a salad as can the lovely flowers of the wild pansy. Elderflowers yield the most delicate wine and are also very good as fritters. Limeflower tea is excellent and has a slight sedative effect. Dogrose flowers can be used fresh in salads and also to make rose wine, rose-petal jelly and crystalized petals. Hawthorn flowers produce an exciting liqueur and heather a good tea.

Wild flowers for medicine
The marvel is that country-dwellers probably have within walking distance, wild plants for treating all the

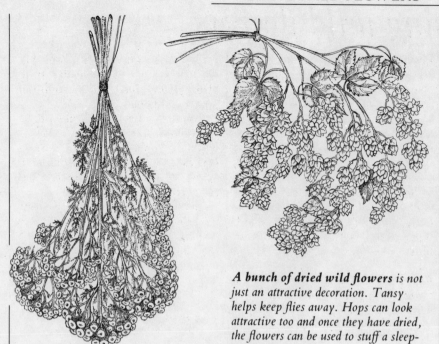

A bunch of dried wild flowers is not just an attractive decoration. Tansy helps keep flies away. Hops can look attractive too and once they have dried, the flowers can be used to stuff a sleep-inducing hop-pillow.

keep moths and other creatures away from clothes or linen; a mixture of wormwood and rosemary dried to a powder and rubbed into dog or cat fur will help repel fleas; and sprigs of penny royal should help deter ants.

Sweet cicely has a myrrh-like perfume. All parts of the plant are used as a flavouring and the large mahogany-coloured seeds were once used ground with wax to rub into furniture. Chamomile gives off a strong scent of apples when crushed, and is still used for fragrant lawns.

Wild flowers for dyeing

Many wild flowers are used to produce dyes, and it is possible to obtain a comprehensive range of colours and shades by using local wild plants.

Red, purple and pink are produced by blackberry (bramble), elderberry (elder), hedge- and lady's bedstraw, hemp-agrimony, tormentil, sloe (blackthorn) and willow. Blues are obtained from blackberry, devil's-bit scabious, elderberry, elecampane, sloe and woad.

Yellow and orange can be obtained from agrimony, St John's-wort, saw-wort, tansy and the common toad-flax. Brown colours can be extracted from buckthorn, burdock, common comfrey, gipsywort, goldenrod, marjoram, sorrel, tansy, weld, wild carrot and yarrow.

Plants yielding greens include agrimony, bramble, common comfrey, fleabane, lily-of-the-valley, marjoram, mullein, sorrel, tansy, weld and yarrow.

The above lists are only a selection of the possible dye plants and of course different colours can be obtained from the same plant by using different mordants.

Further information

It must now be obvious that the subject of useful wild plants would need more than a book to itself. Richard Mabey's *Food for Free* (Fontana Books, 1975) is justly famous; Roy Genders has written a fascinating book on the scented wild flowers of Britain; Jill Goodwin in her superb *Dyer's Manual* describes the wild plants good for making natural dyes; and many herbalists have written of the medicinal value of native wild plants. The full details of these and many other useful books are given in the bibliography on p. 184.

common ailments: bruises, fevers, coughs and colds. Also, it is worth remembering that many of our most despised garden weeds are extremely nutritious as well as being of value as medicines. These include field bindweed, couch grass, cleavers, groundsel, chickweed, horsetail and common nettle.

Bindweed is a blood cleanser and tonic and either the flowers can be eaten raw or the twisting stems made into a tea. Wild carrot (and cultivated carrot) has many very valuable properties and has been used for treatment of cancer, bad eyesight, wounds, tumours, internal ulcers, worms, kidney and bladder troubles, dropsy, varicose veins as well as painful menstruation.

Sea-holly is rich in minerals and is used as a nerve tonic. Common sea-lavender has strong astringent properties and is used to stem bleeding and to treat dysentery. Foxglove (*Digitalis*) is justly famous as a heart remedy. Meadowsweet is a valuable fever herb and is used to treat high blood pressure and diabetes. Yarrow (*Archillea*) is a wound herb named after Achilles the Greek warrior, who used the herb to treat the battle-wounds of his soldiers. It is also a fever herb, used to treat malaria, and other uses include treatment of colds, diarrhoea, pneumonia and falling hair; to treat fever the leaves and flowers are tossed in a hot bath; chewing the leaves relieves toothache.

Although it is safe to treat yourself for minor ailments after consulting a good herbal, you are strongly advised to seek the advice of a qualified herbal or homoepathic practitioner for any ills of a more serious or persistent nature. Some herbs are very strong and should not be used without professional advice. The information given is for general interest only and in no way constitutes medicinal recommendations.

Using fragrant flowers

Many wild flowers are highly scented and can be used to make potpourri, to hang in fragrant bunches in linen cupboards and, in times gone by, for strewing on the floor. Meadowsweet, lady's bedstraw and woodruff were all strewing herbs: they contain coumarin which gives the scent of new-mown hay when the plants are dried. As the name implies, lady's bedstraw was also used for filling mattresses. Meadowsweet can also be used as a complexion tonic; immerse the flowers in shallow rainwater and leave in the sun. The sweet-scented hop is used in pillows to induce sleep.

The wetland flower valerian has strongly smelling roots which are loved by cats and rats. It is said that it was the valerian roots carried by the Pied Piper of Hamelin that attracted the rats, rather than his music. Among the wild flowers whose scent deters pests, tansy will help keep flies away; muslin bags of woodruff help

Wildflower
Catalogue
&
Useful
Information

Wildflower catalogue

This section gives further information on wild plants to grow in gardens. It is divided into three separate sections. On the first two pages there is a directory to all the plants in the book, arranged, like **Creating Wildflower Gardens** (pages 15–120), according to the sites each plant is suited to. So there are lists of plants to grow in each type of garden: sunny, semi-shady, shady, water, rock and seaside. The page number after each plant refers the reader to a full description and growing instructions for the plant. Many plants grow well in more than one situation and these lists provide the necessary cross-references.

The second section – pages 156 to 180 – forms the main part of the plant catalogue. It lists 150 wild plants, additional to those featured in **Creating Wildflower Gardens,** in A to Z order of common name. Each entry contains a description of the plant, suggestions on where to grow it and what other plants to grow it with in the garden, as well as clear and comprehensive growing instructions. These plants have been chosen for their beauty, their adaptability and the comparative ease of growing them. Many appear in the photographs throughout the book. (You can find this out by looking up the plant name in the index on page 185.)

Lastly, on page 181, there is a list of native trees and shrubs recommended as being suitable for growing in a wildflower garden. Each entry contains a brief description of the tree or shrub – its height, shape and colouring – and suggests suitable places to grow it. Some trees and shrubs are more suitable for growing in a large garden – these may have to be coppiced if grown in a small garden. Those trees and shrubs that are particularly attractive to insects and other wildlife are indicated in the relevant entry. Some of these shrubs, particularly climbing shrubs, may be featured in the plant catalogue or in photographs throughout the book. Again, refer to the index for each individual plant.

Plants for sunny gardens

All the plants featured on pages 30 to 47, and in addition:

Agrimony (p. 156)
Alpine lady's-mantle (p. 113)
Autumn hawkbit (p. 156)
Basil thyme (p. 156)
Betony (p. 63)
Bird's-eye primrose (p. 115)
Biting stonecrop (p. 156)
Bittersweet (p. 72)
Black medick (p. 157)
Blackthorn (p. 157)
Bladder campion (p. 157)
Bloody crane's-bill (p. 114)
Bluebell (p. 88)
Bramble (p. 157)
Brooklime (p. 106)
Broom (p. 157)
Buckthorn (p. 157)
Bugle (p. 62)
Burnet rose (p. 158)
Burnet-saxifrage (p. 158)
Bush vetch (p. 158)
Carline thistle (p. 158)
Cat's-ear (p. 158)
Chalk milkwort (p. 158)

Chamomile (p. 159)
Chives (p. 159)
Columbine (p. 86)
Common centaury (p. 159)

Common comfrey (p. 105)
Common fumitory (p. 159)
Common knapweed (p. 159)
Common mallow (p. 159)
Common rock rose (p. 114)
Common sea-lavender (p. 160)

Common sorrel (p. 160)
Common valerian (p. 106)
Common vetch (p. 160)
Common violet (p. 75)
Corn buttercup (p. 160)
Creeping-jenny (p. 160)
Daisy (p. 161)
Dame's-violet (p. 161)
Dandelion (p. 161)
Devil's-bit scabious (p. 73)
Dog rose (p. 161)
Dogwood (p. 161)
Dusky crane's-bill (p. 161)
Dyer's greenweed (p. 162)
Elder (p. 162)
Elecampane (p. 162)
Fennel (p. 162)
Feverfew (p. 162)
Field scabious (p. 162)
Flowering-rush (p. 99)
Foxglove (p. 87)
Germander speedwell (p. 74)
Gipsywort (p. 163)
Globeflower (p. 163)
Goat's-beard (p. 163)
Goldenrod (p. 164)
Grass-of-Parnassus (p. 105)
Greater bird's-foot-trefoil (p. 164)
Greater stitchwort (p. 73)
Great mullein (p. 164)
Ground ivy (p. 164)
Hare's-foot clover (p. 164)
Heather (p. 165)
Hedge-bedstraw (p. 165)
Hedge bindweed (p. 63)
Hedgerow crane's-bill (p. 66)
Hemp-agrimony (p. 100)
Herb-robert (p. 66)
Hoary plantain (p. 165)
Holly (p. 165)
Honesty (p. 165)
Hop (p. 166)
Horseshoe vetch (p. 166)
Hound's-tongue (p. 166)
Ivy-leaved toadflax (p. 166)
Jacob's-ladder (p. 166)
Kidney vetch (p. 167)
Lady's bedstraw (p. 167)
Lady's-mantle (p. 167)
Larkspur (p. 167)
Lesser calamint (p. 167)
Lesser celandine (p. 71)
Lesser periwinkle (p. 75)
Lesser stitchwort (p. 168)
Lords-and-ladies (p. 62)
Maiden pink (p. 168)
Marsh-mallow (p. 168)
Marsh-marigold (p. 99)
Martagon lily (p. 90)
Meadowsweet (p. 100)
Meadow vetchling (p. 168)
Milk thistle (p. 169)
Moschatel (p. 169)
Mountain avens (p. 113)
Mountain pansy (p. 169)
Mouse-ear hawkweed (p. 169)
Musk thistle (p. 169)
Nettle-leaved bellflower (p. 64)
Oxlip (p. 91)
Pasqueflower (p. 115)
Perennial flax (p. 170)
Perforate St John's-wort (p. 67)
Pheasant's-eye (p. 170)
Primrose (p. 70)
Purple loosestrife (p. 102)
Purple saxifrage (p. 170)
Purple toadflax (p. 171)

Red campion (p. 72)
Red dead-nettle (p. 171)
Red valerian (p. 171)
Ribbed melilot (p. 171)
Rough chervil (p. 172)
Sainfoin (p. 172)
Salad burnet (p. 172)
Saw-wort (p. 172)
Scarlet pimpernel (p. 172)
Scented mayweed (p. 173)
Sea campion (p. 173)
Sea holly (p. 173)
Sea wormwood (p. 173)
Sheep's-bit (p. 173)
Silver hair-grass (p. 174)
Silverweed (p. 174)
Slender speedwell (p. 174)
Smooth tare (p. 174)
Snowdrop (p. 65)
Soapwort (p. 174)
Spiny restharrow (p. 175)
Spring squill (p. 175)
Square-stalked St John's-wort (p. 175)
Star-of-Bethlehem (p. 175)
Stinking iris (p. 175)
Summer snowflake (p. 175)
Sweet briar (p. 71)
Sweet cicely (p. 69)
Tansy (p. 176)
Thrift (p. 176)
Tormentil (p. 176)
Traveller's-joy (p. 64)
Tree-mallow (p. 176)

Tufted vetch (p. 74)
Vervain (p. 176)
Wallflower (p. 177)
Wall germander (p. 177)
Water avens (p. 101)
Water mint (p. 103)
Wavy hair-grass (p. 177)
Wayfaring-tree (p. 177)
Weld (p. 178)
Welsh poppy (p. 178)
White bryony (p. 178)
White campion (p. 178)
White clover (p. 178)
White dead-nettle (p. 68)
White horehound (p. 178)
Wild angelica (p. 179)
Wild clary (p. 179)

Wild daffodil (p. 69)
Wild mignonette (p. 179)
Wild parsnip (p. 179)
Wild strawberry (p. 65)
Wood anemone (p. 86)
Wood crane's-bill (p. 89)
Wood sage (p. 180)
Wood vetch (p. 180)
Wormwood (p. 180)
Yellow corydalis (p. 180)
Yellow horned-poppy (p. 180)
Yellow iris (p. 102)
Yellow loosestrife (p. 102)

Plants for semi-shady gardens

All the plants featured on pages 62 to 75, and in addition:
Bell heather (p. 36)
Blackthorn (p. 157)
Bloody crane's-bill (p. 114)
Bluebell (p. 88)
Bramble (p. 157)
Brooklime (p. 106)
Buckthorn (p. 157)
Burnet rose (p. 158)
Burnet-saxifrage (p. 158)
Bush vetch (p. 158)
Columbine (p. 86)
Common centaury (p. 159)
Common comfrey (p. 105)
Common knapweed (p. 159)
Common sorrel (p. 160)
Common valerian (p. 106)
Cowslip (p. 43)
Cuckooflower (p. 32)
Cyclamen (p. 160)
Dame's-violet (p. 161)
Dog rose (p. 161)
Dogwood (p. 161)
Dusky crane's-bill (p. 161)
Elder (p. 162)
Elecampane (p. 162)
Foxglove (p. 87)
Giant bellflower (p. 163)
Gipsywort (p. 163)
Globeflower (p. 163)
Goldenrod (p. 164)
Grass-of-Parnassus (p. 105)
Greater knapweed (p. 33)
Great mullein (p. 164)
Green hellebore (p. 90)
Ground-ivy (p. 164)
Harebell (p. 32)
Hawthorn (p. 164)
Heather (p. 165)
Hedge-bedstraw (p. 165)
Hedge woundwort (p. 165)
Hemp-agrimony (p. 100)
Holly (p. 165)
Honesty (p. 165)
Hop (p. 166)
Ivy (p. 166)
Jacob's-ladder (p. 166)
Lady-fern (p. 167)
Lady's-bedstraw (p. 167)
Lesser stitchwort (p. 168)
Lily-of-the-valley (p. 87)
Lungwort (p. 92)
Maidenhair spleenwort (p. 168)
Marjoram (p. 42)
Marsh-marigold (p. 99)
Martagon lily (p. 90)
Meadow buttercup (p. 44)
Meadow crane's-bill (p. 38)
Meadow saxifrage (p. 45)
Meadowsweet (p. 100)
Mezereon (p. 168)
Monk's-hood (p. 169)
Moschatel (p. 169)

Mouse-ear hawkweed (p. 169)
Musk mallow (p. 41)
Narrow-leaved everlasting pea (p. 170)
Oxeye daisy (p. 39)
Oxlip (p. 91)
Parsley fern (p. 170)
Pasqueflower (p. 115)
Pignut (p. 170)
Purple loosestrife (p. 103)

Quaking-grass (p. 31)
Ragged-robin (p. 40)
Ramsons (p. 171)
Rough chervil (p. 172)
Royal fern (p. 172)
Salad burnet (p. 172)
Saw-wort (p. 172)
Selfheal (p. 44)
Sheep's-bit (p. 173)
Spindle (p. 174)
Square-stalked St John's-wort (p. 175)
Stinking iris (p. 175)
Summer snowflake (p. 175)
Sweet violet (p. 92)
Tansy (p. 176)
Teasel (p. 35)
Thrift (p. 176)
Tutsan (p. 176)
Wall germander (p. 177)
Water avens (p. 101)
Water forget-me-not (p. 177)
Water mint (p. 103)
Wavy hair-grass (p. 177)
Wayfaring-tree (p. 177)
Welsh poppy (p. 178)
White bryony (p. 178)
White clover (p. 178)
Wild angelica (p. 179)
Wild pansy (p. 47)
Wild thyme (p. 116)
Wood anemone (p. 86)
Wood avens (p. 179)
Wood crane's-bill (p. 89)
Wood millet (p. 179)
Woodruff (p. 89)
Wood sage (p. 180)
Wood sorrel (p. 91)
Wood spurge (p. 88)
Wood vetch (p. 180)
Yarrow (p. 30)
Yellow iris (p. 102)
Yellow loosestrife (p. 102)

Plants for shady gardens

All the plants featured on pages 86 to 92, and in addition:
Betony (p. 63)
Bittersweet (p. 72)
Bloody crane's-bill (p. 114)
Bramble (p. 157)
Bugle (p. 62)
Bush vetch (p. 158)
Common violet (p. 75)
Common valerian (p. 106)

Cyclamen (p. 160)
Dogwood (p. 161)
Giant bellflower (p. 163)
Gipsywort (p. 163)
Goldenrod (p. 164)
Greater stitchwort (p. 73)
Ground-ivy (p. 164)
Hedge woundwort (p. 165)
Hemp-agrimony (p. 100)
Herb-robert (p. 66)
Holly (p. 165)
Honeysuckle (p. 68)
Hop (p. 166)
Ivy (p. 166)
Lady-fern (p. 167)
Lesser celandine (p. 71)
Lesser periwinkle (p. 75)
Lords-and-ladies (p. 62)
Marsh-marigold (p. 99)
Mezereon (p. 168)
Monk's-hood (p. 169)
Moschatel (p. 169)
Narrow-leaved everlasting pea (p. 170)
Nettle-leaved bellflower (p. 64)
Pignut (p. 170)
Primrose (p. 70)
Ramsons (p. 171)

Red campion (p. 72)
Royal fern (p. 172)
Snowdrop (p. 65)
Solomon's-seal (p. 70)
Spindle (p. 174)
Stinking iris (p. 175)
Summer snowflake (p. 175)
Tutsan (p. 176)
Water avens (p. 101)
Wild angelica (p. 179)
Wood avens (p. 179)
Wood millet (p. 179)
Wood vetch (p. 180)
Yellow archangel (p. 67)

Plants for water gardens

All the plants featured on pages 99 to 106, and in addition:
Amphibious bistort (p. 156)
Arrowhead (p. 156)
Bugle (p. 62)
Cuckooflower (p. 32)
Fringed water-lily (p. 163)
Fritillary (p. 37)
Frogbit (p. 163)
Gipsywort (p. 163)
Greater bird's-foot-trefoil (p. 164)
Ragged-robin (p. 40)
Royal fern (p. 172)
Square-stalked St John's-wort (p. 175)
Water forget-me-not (p. 177)
Water plantain (p. 177)
Wild angelica (p. 179)
Yellow water-lily (p. 180)

Plants for rock gardens

All the plants featured on pages 113 to 116, and in addition:
Basil thyme (p. 156)
Biting stonecrop (p. 156)
Bladder campion (p. 157)
Chalk milkwort (p. 158)
Chives (p. 159)
Common bird's-foot-trefoil (p. 40)
Common centaury (p. 159)
Common fumitory (p. 159)
Creeping-jenny (p. 160)
Dyer's greenweed (p. 162)
Harebell (p. 32)
Herb-robert (p. 66)
Horseshoe vetch (p. 166)
Ivy-leaved toadflax (p. 166)
Jacob's-ladder (p. 166)
Maidenhair spleenwort (p. 168)
Maiden pink (p. 168)
Mountain pansy (p. 169)
Parsley fern (p. 170)
Perennial flax (p. 170)
Purple saxifrage (p. 170)
Red valerian (p. 171)
Rock cinquefoil (p. 171)
Sea campion (p. 173)
Sheep's-bit (p. 173)
Silver hair-grass (p. 174)
Snowdrop (p. 65)
Spring squill (p. 175)
Thrift (p. 176)
Wallflower (p. 177)
Wall germander (p. 177)
Welsh poppy (p. 178)
Wild carrot (p. 35)
Yellow corydalis (p. 180)

Plants for seaside gardens

Biting stonecrop (p. 156)
Broom (p. 157)
Burnet rose (p. 158)
Carline thistle (p. 158)
Cat's-ear (p. 158)
Common bird's-foot-trefoil (p. 40)
Common centaury (p. 159)
Common restharrow (p. 41)
Common sea-lavender (p. 160)
Common valerian (p. 106)
Corn marigold (p. 34)
Dyer's greenweed (p. 162)
Fennel (p. 162)
Goat's-beard (p. 163)
Greater knapweed (p. 33)
Harebell (p. 32)
Hare's-foot clover (p. 164)
Herb-robert (p. 66)
Hound's-tongue (p. 166)
Kidney vetch (p. 167)
Lady's bedstraw (p. 167)
Maiden pink (p. 168)
Marsh-mallow (p. 168)
Milk thistle (p. 169)
Scentless mayweed (p. 173)
Sea campion (p. 173)
Sea holly (p. 173)
Sea wormwood (p. 173)
Sheep's-bit (p. 173)
Silverweed (p. 174)
Spring squill (p. 175)
Thrift (p. 176)
Tree-mallow (p. 176)
Wild carrot (p. 35)
Wormwood (p. 180)
Yarrow (p. 30)
Yellow horned-poppy (p. 180)

Agrimony
Agrimonia eupatoria

Site: Sun
Soil: Well-drained
Season: June–September
Height: 15–60 cm (6 in–2 ft)
Perennial; needs care

Agrimony, or church-steeples, is a pretty plant to include in a sunny border. It has slender, tapering spikes of pale yellow, star-shaped flowers and finely cut, decorative leaves that grow in alternate large and small pairs. Agrimony also has a pleasant scent, rather like apricots, which attracts bees and other insects. It is a herb that has long been used for medicinal purposes and, more recently, for dyeing cloth.

How to grow
Plant seed ½ cm (¼ in) deep from February to May, or from August to November, the late season sowing being better. Seeds are large with burr-like hairs. Agrimony establishes well in grass.

Amphibious bistort
Polygonum amphibium

Site: Water garden
Soil: Wet
Season: July–September
Height: to 50 cm (20 in) on land to 1 m (3 ft) in water
Perennial; easy to grow

Amphibious bistort is a tall plant with long-stalked leaves and pinkish spires of flowers. Grow a mass of amphibious bistort for a stunning effect. There is also a form of this plant that grows on land.

How to grow
Seeds of amphibious bistort are not readily available and it is more satisfactory to buy plants from a specialist water-plant nursery. Amphibious bistort can easily be propagated by taking off a small piece of the plant and dropping it into the pond.

Arrowhead
Sagittaria sagittifolia

Site: Water garden
Soil: Free-floating in water
Season: July–August
Height: 30–90 cm (1–3 ft)
Perennial; easy to grow

A stately plant for the garden pond is arrowhead, named after its very ornamental, arrowhead-shaped leaves that grow above the water. The plant has attractive white flowers, splashed with purple, that grow in small clusters on flowering stems. To prevent arrowhead from becoming invasive, remove the seed-heads before they ripen.

How to grow
If fresh seed can be obtained, sow it in moist soil in spring. Seeds of arrowhead are not readily available and it is better to buy plants from a specialist water-plant nursery. Arrowhead can easily be propagated by taking off a small piece of the plant and dropping it into the pond.

Autumn hawkbit
Leontodon autumnalis

Site: Sun; seaside garden
Soil: Fertile
Season: June–October
Height: 15–50 cm (6–20 in)
Perennial; easy to grow

Autumn hawkbit has dandelion-like yellow flowers and long, toothed leaves that grow from the base of the stem. It looks pretty growing with daisies on a lawn or in meadow grass.

How to grow
Sow seed where it is to flower, during spring or early autumn. Press the seeds into the soil surface; do not cover with soil. Seed may be sown in a seed tray in spring. Plant the seedlings into grass in the following spring or autumn.

Basil thyme
Acinos arvensis

Site: Sun; rock garden
Soil: Well-drained
Season: May–September
Height: 10–20 cm (4–8 in)
Annual; easy to grow

Basil thyme is a delightful creeping and sprawling plant with small, fragrant leaves and bright violet two-lipped flowers with white blotches on the lower lip. It was used as a herbal remedy for the treatment of toothache and to soothe nerves. Its flowering tops can be used as a seasoning in place of thyme.

How to grow
Sow the seed thinly in spring where the plants are to flower and cover only very lightly with soil. Thin seedlings to 15 cm (6 in) apart. Basil thyme self-seeds readily.

Biting stonecrop
Sedum acre

Site: Sun; rock garden; seaside garden
Soil: Poor and dry
Season: June–July
Height: 2–10 cm (1–4 in)
Perennial; easy to grow

Biting stonecrop is a fast-spreading little plant that forms a carpet of golden-yellow flowers in the summer and makes excellent ground cover in a sunny spot. The tiny flowers are star-shaped and, when in bloom, they hide the numerous spreading branches covered with fleshy, stubby leaves.

Biting stonecrop grows on walls, roofs, in the rock garden and in gravel.

How to grow
Container-grown plants can be purchased and planted at any time in fair weather. Soil should be well-drained and gritty. Divide plants in late summer. Take stem cuttings in May–June and root in gritty, sandy compost. Pieces, with roots attached, may also be pulled off the parent plant.

Seed should be sown on the surface of a gritty, sandy compost in autumn.

Black medick
Medicago lupulina

Site: Sun
Soil: Well-drained
Season: April–July
Height: 5–50 cm (2–20 in)
**Short-lived perennial; easy
to grow**

Black medick is a low-growing plant that looks pretty growing in rough grassland. It has small heads of clear, yellow flowers and tiny, rounded leaflets covered in fine, downy hairs. The plant has distinctive kidney-shaped seeds that go black when ripe.

How to grow
Black medick is a basic ingredient of most meadow mixtures, so its seed is not normally sown alone. To sow seed into existing grass, first cut the grass short and rake out any debris to reveal the bare soil. Scatter the seed and then roll or tread it in. This is best done in late summer.

Blackthorn
Prunus spinosa

Site: Sun; semi-shade
Soil: Most soil types
Season: March–May (flowers)
August–October (fruit)
Height: to 4 m (12 ft)
Perennial shrub; easy to grow

Blackthorn is a very good hedging shrub and will grow in most soils. Its beautiful covering of white blossom welcomes each new spring; in late summer and early autumn, luscious-looking blue berries, called sloes, cover its branches. These are acid to taste, but make a very pleasant jelly. Sloe gin can be made by soaking blackthorn berries and sugar in gin, which then turns a rich purple-pink.

How to grow
Small plants can be obtained from tree nurseries and may be bought by the hundred for hedging. Plant from autumn to spring. **WARNING:** *Blackthorn spreads rapidly by vigorous suckers. To prevent this, grow grass in front of it; this can then be mowed or grazed.*

Bladder campion
Silene vulgaris

Site: Sun; rock garden
Soil: Well-drained
Season: May–August
Height: 25–90 cm (10 in–3 ft)
Perennial; easy to grow

Bladder campion has small, white flowers that grow from inflated bladder-like calyces, which is how the plant got its name. The flowers emit a pleasant, clove-like aroma at night. The waxy, greyish-green foliage can be eaten raw in salads, or boiled, and tastes rather like green peas.

Bladder campion will grow well in a rock garden and also establishes well in meadow gardens. It looks especially good growing on a grassy bank. It is a nectar plant for butterflies.

How to grow
Sow the seed in spring or late summer where it is to flower and cover very lightly with soil. Seed may also be sown in trays in spring and early summer. It may be planted successfully into grassland.

Bramble
Rubus fruticosus

Site: Sun; semi-shade; shade
Soil: Most soil types including acid
Season: May–September (flowers)
August (fruit)
Height: to 90 cm (3 ft)
Perennial; easy to grow

Bramble is a lovely scrambling shrub to naturalize in a hedge as it roots and spreads very quickly. Its beautiful flowers vary in colour from white to cerise and they are a good source of pollen for bees and butterflies. From August onwards, great clusters of blackberries decorate its branches, while the leaves take on lovely autumn colours.

How to grow
Extract the seed by crushing the ripe berries. Sow in sandy soil in a seed tray and cover lightly with soil. Leave outside over winter with a glass covering and plant out in the spring. Or peg a young shoot to the soil and roots will quickly form. The new growth can then be cut off and planted out.

Broom
Sarothamnus scoparius (syn. *Cytisus scoparius*)

Site: Sun; seaside garden
Soil: Well-drained; prefers some acidity
Season: May–June
Height: to 2½ m (8 ft)
Perennial; needs care

Broom is a deciduous shrub with long, straight branches covered, in early summer, with a mass of golden-yellow flowers, followed by black seed pods. It looks spectacular in a sunny border if you have the room. It is a good bee plant and also has medicinal properties. The shrub was once used for making brooms, hence its common name.

How to grow
Rub the seed between sheets of sandpaper to speed germination. Sow the seed where it is to flower in the autumn and cover lightly with soil. Thin plants to 120 cm (4 ft) apart.

Buckthorn
Rhamnus catharticus

Site: Sun; semi-shade
Soil: Fertile and alkaline
Season: May–June (flowers)
September–October (fruit)
Height: to 6 m (18 ft)
Perennial shrub; easy to grow

Buckthorn is a deciduous shrub that can be grown as part of a hedge or on its own. It has tiny greenish-yellow flowers, followed by red and then black berries. The berries were once used as a purgative, boiled and sweetened with sugar. They yield a yellow dye when unripe and a green dye when ripe.

How to grow
Sow seeds in autumn 1–2 cm (1 in) deep in a nursery bed. Plant out into permanent positions when they are about 15 cm (6 in) tall. Plants may be obtained from tree nurseries; plant bare-rooted plants from autumn to spring. Make sure you get the right species as there are two others both called buckthorn.

Burnet rose
Rosa pimpinellifolia

Site: Sun; semi-shade; seaside garden
Soil: Well-drained
Season: May–July (flowers)
August–September (fruit)
Height: 15–60 cm (6 in–2 ft)
Perennial shrub; needs care

Burnet rose is a low-growing, thicket-forming shrub that gives a beautiful display of sweetly scented, creamy-white flowers, sometimes splashed with pink, in the summer. These are followed in the autumn by purplish-black hips.

Plant burnet rose with purple heather and dyer's greenweed for a colourful display.

How to grow
Seed can take a year or two to germinate. Stratify the seed (see p. 126) over winter in moist peat; sow in spring. You can also buy plants from specialist nurseries.

Burnet-saxifrage
Pimpinella saxifraga

Site: Sun; semi-shade
Soil: Poor and dry
Season: July–September
Height: 30–90 cm (1–3 ft)
Perennial; needs care

Burnet-saxifrage is a tall, slender plant with umbrella-shaped flower-heads covered in white flowers. This plant looks at home growing in a summer meadow and will establish well on light soil, especially if it is slightly chalky. It can also be planted in a mixed border of wild flowers, where its delicate flowers will form a lovely foil for brighter blooms. The leaves are also decorative and the basal leaves look similar to those of salad burnet. Burnet-saxifrage has a distinct, sweetish smell.

How to grow
Scatter the seed where it is to flower in autumn and cover with a fine sprinkling of soil. Seedlings will emerge in the spring. Burnet-saxifrage naturalizes well in poor grassland. It self-seeds readily.

Bush vetch
Vicia sepium

Site: Sun; semi-shade; shade
Soil: Well-drained and fertile
Season: April–September
Height: 30 cm–1 m (1–3 ft)
Perennial; easy to grow

Bush vetch is a pretty, sprawling plant to grow in the hedgerow or rough grassland. It flowers normally from spring to early summer. Each rounded flower-head holds up to six bluish-purple blooms which are very attractive to bumblebees.

Bush vetch spreads very quickly by way of clinging tendrils at the end of each leaf, so leave it plenty of space!

How to grow
Rub the seed between two sheets of sandpaper to speed germination before sowing in a seed tray in autumn. Cover with soil. Plant out in spring or autumn. Bush vetch may be planted into grass. It will self-seed once established.

Carline thistle
Carlina vulgaris

Site: Sun; seaside garden
Soil: Well-drained
Season: July–October
Height: 10–60 cm (4 in–2 ft)
Biennial; easy to grow

This attractive thistle is a biennial plant, growing only a prickly rosette of leaves in the first year, and producing decorative, straw-coloured flower-heads and prickly stem leaves in the second. The flowers expand to look like sun-rays in dry weather and close up when it is damp. It is a favourite plant of bees and butterflies. Carline thistles are also very decorative when dried.

How to grow
Sow the seeds in spring where they are to flower and cover lightly with soil. Thin seedlings to 20 cm (9 in) apart in good soil or less in poor soil.

Cat's-ear
Hypochoeris radicata

Site: Sun; seaside garden
Soil: Well-drained
Season: May–September
Height: 20–60 cm (8 in–2 ft)
Perennial; easy to grow

Cat's-ears are delightful flowers, similar to dandelions, and if allowed to spread in your summer meadow garden, they form a sheet of glowing yellow flowers. They have wiry stems and roughly hairy leaves which can be eaten in salads. The bright flowers are very attractive to bees and other insects.

How to grow
Sow seed in a sunny position in spring or autumn; barely cover with soil. Cat's-ears increase rapidly from seed and are best confined to grassland.

Chalk milkwort
Polygala calcarea

Site: Sun; rock garden
Soil: Well-drained and alkaline
Season: May–July
Height: 5–20 cm (2–8 in)
Perennial; needs care

Chalk milkwort is a lovely spreading plant for the rock garden or sunny bed. It forms a mat of distinctive grey-green leaves above which grow short, stiff spikes of ice-blue flowers, visible from quite a distance.

How to grow
Seed might be difficult to obtain; small plants can be purchased from specialist alpine nurseries. These can be planted at any time during the growing season.

Chamomile
Chamaemelum nobile

Site: Sun
Soil: Well-drained soils with low fertility
Season: June–August
Height: 10–30 cm (4–12 in)
Perennial; easy to grow

Chamomile is a vigorous, spreading plant with daisy-like white flower-heads with yellow centres and pretty, feathery foliage. Plants can be used to make a fragrant lawn if they are kept cut closely with shears or a mower. Plants should not be allowed to flower the first year.

Chamomile leaves have a pleasant scent of apples. The flower-heads are used to make a herbal tea that can aid digestion and calm nerves.

How to grow
Sow seed in trays in spring for flowers the same year. Press into the soil; do not cover. Mature plants can be split up in spring.

Chives
Allium schoenoprasum

Site: Sun; rock garden
Soil: Moist with poor to average fertility
Season: June–July
Height: 15–40 cm (6–16 in)
Perennial; easy to grow

Wild chives is a rare native plant, similar to the cultivated varieties grown in many gardens. They have purple, pompom-like flower-heads on narrow stems and narrow cylindrical leaves all growing from the base of the plant. Clumps of chives growing *en masse* can look quite stunning and they make decorative edging plants.

Chives is a member of the onion family and is used as a flavouring for soups, sauces, salads and potatoes.

How to grow
Sow fresh seed in April or May (it will not keep more than two years) where it is to grow and cover very lightly with soil. Chives self-seeds and mature plants may easily be split in early spring.

Common centaury
Centaurium erythraea

Site: Sun; semi-shade; rock garden; seaside garden
Soil: Most soils, including dry ones
Season: June–September
Height: 3–30 cm (1–12 in)
Annual; germination can be slow

Common centaury is a charming, delicate plant, varying in size according to where it is planted, from a few centimetres high to a 30 cm (1 ft) tall, graceful plant with several stems. It produces small, soft-pink tubular flowers with yellow centres, and greyish-green foliage. Allow it to self-seed in a rockery, on grassland or in a mixed wildflower bed, where it will look very pretty.

How to grow
Sow seed from February to May, barely covering with soil. It will self-seed in bare ground or thin grass.

Common fumitory
Fumaria officinalis

Site: Sun; rock garden
Soil: Well-drained
Season: May–September
Height: 30–50 cm (12–20 in)
Annual; easy to grow

Common fumitory is an unusual plant that makes an attractive addition to a cornfield garden or a filler for any bare patches of ground. It has slender, feathery leaves which have a bluish-green tinge, and spikes of small, tubular pink flowers. From a distance, a group of these plants can look like a haze of blue smoke, hence the name.

How to grow
Sow the seed in spring where it is to flower and cover lightly with soil. Germination takes a week or two.

Common knapweed
Centaurea nigra

Site: Sun; semi-shade
Soil: Moderately fertile
Season: June–September
Height: 30–60 cm (1–2 ft)
Perennial; easy to grow

Common knapweed, or hardheads, is a colourful, thistle-type plant. It has reddish-purple flowers packed on to globular flower-heads, and lance-shaped leaves. This plant grows quite tall and would look lovely as part of a summer meadow garden or on a hedgebank or border.

Common knapweed is a favourite plant of bees and butterflies – on the continent it is the foodplant of the knapweed fritillary. It also looks quite beautiful when dried.

How to grow
Sow the seed either where it is to flower or in trays in spring, and cover very lightly with soil. Germination takes only a few weeks. Common knapweed is best planted in grass from autumn to early spring.

Common mallow
Malva sylvestris

Site: Sun
Soil: Well-drained
Season: June–September
Height: 30–90 cm (1–3 ft)
Perennial; easy to grow

Common mallow is a bushy plant with large, ivy-shaped leaves and big, rose-purple flowers. It looks spectacular at the back of a wildflower border or growing against a wall.

Common mallow has long been valued for its medicinal properties; it acts as a soothing agent for sore and inflamed skin and is good for rubbing on bee stings.

How to grow
Sow the seed in spring or autumn where it is to flower and lightly cover with soil. Thin out the seedlings to 60 cm (2 ft) apart.

Common sea-lavender
Limonium vulgare

Site: Sun; seaside garden
Soil: Damp and fertile
Season: July–October
Height: 10–40 cm (4–16 in)
Perennial; needs care

Common sea-lavender is one of the loveliest seaside plants. It has tiny, bluish-purple flowers densely packed on branching stems and large, greyish leaves. For a pleasant effect plant a large group of common sea-lavender in an area that can be kept moist.

Common sea-lavender flowers also look pretty when dried.

How to grow
Sow seed in the autumn in a seed tray and cover very lightly with soil. Leave the tray outside over winter covered with a piece of glass and germination will take place in spring. Plant out 10 cm (4 in) apart.

Common sorrel
Rumex acetosa

Site: Sun; semi-shade
Soil: Moist and fertile
Season: May–June
Height: 30–80 cm (1–2½ ft)
Perennial; easy to grow

In late summer, common sorrel will add a bright splash of red to any garden. The colour comes from the plant's glossy, arrow-shaped leaves which turn crimson, and its tiny, greenish-red, papery flowers. Grow common sorrel in a summer meadow or hedgerow garden for the best effect. The leaves of common sorrel add a sharp taste to salads. However, cultivated sorrel, grown for salad crops and sold as a herb, has larger leaves and is more palatable.

How to grow
Seed is normally sown in a meadow mixture, but if plants are required to naturalize in grassland, sow the seed in a seed tray in spring and cover lightly with soil. Germination is rapid. Plant out in spring or autumn.

Common vetch
Vicia sativa

Site: Sun
Soil: Fertile
Season: May–September
Height: 15–120 cm (6 in–4 ft)
Annual; easy to grow

Despite its name, this plant is not the most common of the vetches. It is a pretty plant to let scramble along your sunny hedgerow or to establish in grassland. It has short-stalked, mauve flowers that grow in pairs on its stems at the base of each leaf, and slightly hairy, long seed pods. Common vetch can climb up other plants to as high as 120 cm (4 ft).

How to grow
Common vetch seed is usually sown with a seed mixture for naturalizing in grassland. Scatter the seed in grassland and roll or tread it into the soil. If the plants become too rampant, cut them down before the seed ripens.

Corn buttercup
Ranunculus arvensis

Site: Sun
Soil: Well-drained
Season: May–July
Height: 15–50 cm (6–20 in)
Annual; easy to grow

Corn buttercups were once plentiful in cornfields but have now been weeded out by modern farming methods. Their flowers are a bright, cheerful yellow and are attractive to butterflies. This is a flower to grow along with other cornfield flowers like wild pansy, mayweed, cornflower and corncockle. The ripe seeds are especially beautiful – their ball-like, spiny shape is perfectly made for distribution by passing animals.

Corn buttercups are poisonous and can cause illness if eaten by humans.

How to grow
Sow the seed in spring and cover lightly with soil. Corn buttercups will self-seed readily.

Creeping-jenny
Lysimachia nummularia

Site: Sun; rock garden
Soil: Damp and fertile
Season: May–August
Height: Low and creeping
Perennial; easy to grow

Creeping-jenny, or moneywort, is a sprawling plant that spreads along the ground to produce a dense mat of shining, bright green leaves and vivid yellow, cup-shaped flowers. It is a useful groundcover plant for a shady woodland or a moist meadow garden.

How to grow
Sow the seed in spring or autumn where it is to flower and lightly cover with soil. Seedlings may be thinned to 15 cm (6 in) apart. Young plants may be planted into short grass from autumn to spring.

Cyclamen
Cyclamen hederifolium

Site: Semi-shade; shade
Soil: Rich and moist
Season: August–October
Height: 10–30 cm (4–12 in)
Perennial; needs care

Cyclamen, or sow-bread, is a delightful autumn-flowering plant for a semi-shady woodland garden, with its delicate pink or white flowers. It looks most effective planted in a drift, under the partial shade of deciduous trees or shrubs. Plants require reasonably bare soil to grow well.

Cyclamen is not a native plant but has become well established.

How to grow
Plant corms from July onwards, 2–4 cm (1–2 in) deep, and 15 cm (6 in) apart in rich, well-drained soil in a semi-shady position, sheltered from cold winds. Plants may be obtained from specialist wildflower nurseries.

Daisy
Bellis perennis

Site: Sun
Soil: Fertile
Season: March–October
Height: 7–15 cm (3–6 in)
Perennial; easy to grow

Daisies are delightful flowers, loved by children yet destroyed by lawn enthusiasts. Their pretty yellow flower-heads are surrounded by a ring of white rays, sometimes tinged pink. The leaves are spoon-shaped and form a rosette at the base of the plant. The daisy is a good nectar plant for butterflies.

Daisies are an essential ingredient of the flowering lawn and look beautiful growing with speedwell. They also grow quite large and make a good edging for a border.

How to grow
Sow the seed in a well-raked lawn in spring or late summer. Scatter the seed very thinly and press in or water in if dry. Keep soil from drying out until the plants are established.

Dame's-violet
Hesperis matronalis

Site: Sun; semi-shade
Soil: Good cultivated soil
Season: May–July
Height: 40–90 cm (15 in–3 ft)
Short-lived perennial; easy to grow

Dame's-violet, or sweet rocket, is a widely naturalized plant that has charming white or violet flowers which become fragrant towards evening. The plant grows quite tall and can look lovely in a border, or planted in drifts in a damp, sunny spot for a mass of flowers. Dame's-violet is a butterfly nectar plant and a food plant of the orange-tip butterfly.

How to grow
Sow the seeds $\frac{1}{2}$ cm ($\frac{1}{4}$ in) deep in early summer where they are to flower. Small plants should be thinned to 30–45 cm (12–18 in) apart. Plants will readily self-seed.

Dandelion
Taraxacum officinale

Site: Sun
Soil: Most soils
Season: March–October
Height: 5–30 cm (2–12 in)
Perennial; easy to grow

Golden-flowered dandelions are familiar and cheerful plants, yet are a constant source of annoyance to most gardeners! Their sun-like flower-heads grow on single stalks above a flat rosette of toothed leaves, and can look quite beautiful growing in a lawn with daisies and speedwell. The flowers are followed in June by 'clocks' – ribbed fruit bearing tiny parachutes of white hairs, giving the plant a fluffy appearance.

Dandelions are very nutritious and their young leaves taste delicious in salads. Bees are attracted to them.

How to grow
Sow seed from spring to early autumn and barely cover with soil. Plants will self-seed most freely.

Dog rose
Rosa canina

Site: Sun; semi-shade
Soil: Any good cultivated soil
Season: June–July (flowers)
August–November (fruits)
Height: to 3 m (9 ft)
Perennial shrub; needs care

With its large, fragrant flowers of pale pink or white, the dog rose is a familiar and welcome sight. The flowers are followed in autumn by a profusion of flask-shaped, scarlet hips which are very decorative and also medicinal; rosehip syrup is made from them. Dog rose grows vigorously and its long season of interest makes it an ideal plant to grow up trees or in hedges in the garden.

How to grow
Seed can take a year or two to germinate. Stratify the seed (see p. 126) over winter; sow in spring in a seed tray or in open ground. You can also buy plants from specialist nurseries; plant bare-rooted plants in spring and container-grown plants at any time of the year.

Dogwood
Swida sanguinea (syn. Cornus sanguinea)

Site: Sun; semi-shade; shade
Soil: Well-drained and fertile
Season: June–July (flowers)
September (fruit and stems)
Height: to 4 m (12 ft)
Perennial deciduous shrub; easy to grow

Dogwood is a hedging shrub bearing hawthorn-scented, white flowers in summer and clusters of small, black berries in September. The leaves and stems of dogwood can turn a beautiful red colour in autumn and are highly decorative. Its berries are inedible; they have a high oil content and were once used for lighting lamps.

How to grow
Young plants may be obtained from specialist tree nurseries. Plant from autumn to spring.

Dusky crane's-bill
Geranium phaeum

Site: Sun; semi-shade
Soil: Fertile
Season: May–June
Height: 60–90 cm (2–3 ft)
Perennial; needs care

Dusky crane's-bill is remarkable for its unusual, deep-purple, almost black flowers. It is a good plant for sunny or semi-shady gardens: plant it in informal groups for the unusual flower colour to be shown off to its best advantage. It will also provide excellent ground cover.

Dusky crane's-bill is a plant from southern Europe that has become naturalized in some places.

How to grow
If seed can be obtained, sow in a seed tray in spring and lightly cover with soil. Plant out when the seedlings are large enough to handle, in spring or autumn. Dusky crane's-bill plants can be purchased from nurseries specializing in unusual plants.

Dyer's greenweed
Genista tinctoria

Site: Sun; rock garden; seaside garden
Soil: Well-drained
Season: July–September
Height: 30–70 cm (1–2½ ft)
Perennial shrub; needs care

Dyer's greenweed is a hardy shrub that thrives in poor soil. It is a dwarf form of broom, with small, glossy leaves and spires of golden-yellow pea flowers. It is a good plant for the rock garden, and to grow as a specimen shrub.

A yellow dye can be made from its flowers; when mixed with the blue dye from woad this produces a green dye, hence the plant's name.

How to grow
Rub the seeds between sheets of sandpaper to speed germination; sow in autumn. Germination is usually in spring. Plants may be obtained from specialist nurseries and planted during spring or autumn.

Elder
Sambucus nigra

Site: Sun; semi-shade
Soil: Fertile
Season: May–June (flowers)
August–November (fruit)
Height: to 7 m (22 ft)
Perennial deciduous shrub; easy to grow

Elder is a very decorative shrub. Its small, creamy-white flowers growing in flat-topped masses are frequently visited by insects in early summer, and make a delicious wine. In autumn it produces heavy clusters of black elderberries, which are eaten by birds, or can be made into wine or jam.

How to grow
Sow the ripe berries 2 cm (1 in) deep in a pot and leave outside over winter. Plant out when the young plants are large enough to handle. Elder can also be obtained from specialist nurseries. If bushes grow too large, they can be cut down or trimmed to size.

Elecampane
Inula helenium

Site: Sun; semi-shade
Soil: Any moist soil
Season: July–August
Height: 60–150 cm (2–5 ft)
Perennial; easy to grow

Elecampane is a plant of ancient introduction. It is a tall, handsome plant for the back of a border. It has large, daisy-shaped flower-heads, rich golden-yellow in colour, carried at the ends of branching stems. The plant's lower leaves can grow up to 30 cm (1 ft) long.

The flowers of elecampane can be used to dye cloth.

How to grow
Sow the seed in a seed tray, barely covering with compost, during spring or autumn. Plant out 1 m (3 ft) apart between spring and autumn. Elecampane self-seeds profusely if its seed-heads are not removed.

Fennel
Foeniculum vulgare

Site: Sun; seaside garden
Soil: Rich and well-drained
Season: July–October
Height: 1½–2 m (4–6 ft)
Perennial; easy to grow

Fennel is a plant of ancient introduction, and is very decorative with green, lace-like foliage and masses of tiny yellow flowers. There is also a bronze variety. Fennel has a distinctive aniseed aroma and its leaves are used to flavour fish and egg dishes. It grows particularly well against a wall.

Fennel is a good nectar plant for bees and can also be used to dye cloth.

How to grow
Plant seeds from February to May ½ cm (¼ in) deep in well-drained soil in a sunny position. Thin seedlings to 45–60 cm (1½–2 ft) apart. Cut all the stems back to 7 cm (3 in) above the soil after the flowers have faded in autumn or winter.

Feverfew
Tanacetum parthenium

Site: Sun
Soil: Most soils
Season: July–August
Height: 25–60 cm (10 in–2 ft)
Perennial; easy to grow

Feverfew produces a lovely show of flowers year after year. The flower-heads are daisy-like and grow in clusters above intricate, light green foliage. Feverfew looks pretty growing between paving or bricks or bordering a path in a herb garden. It also mixes well with wild flowers in a bed or border. It has a strong, pungent smell when crushed, and bitter leaves. It is a good bee plant.

How to grow
Scatter the tiny seeds thinly on the soil surface and water them in. The best times to sow seed are early spring and late summer. Feverfew self-seeds profusely.

Field scabious
Knautia arvensis

Site: Sun
Soil: Well-drained and fertile
Season: July–September
Height: 25 cm–1 m (10 in–3 ft)
Perennial; needs care

Up to fifty mauve flowers make up the lovely pin-cushion flower-heads of field scabious. It is a large, attractive plant and looks most effective in a sunny meadow garden growing amongst grasses.

Field scabious provides nectar for butterflies and bees.

How to grow
Field scabious seed is erratic and difficult to germinate. Sow the seed in a seed tray in spring or autumn and lightly cover with soil. Plant out into meadow grass during the following spring or autumn.

Fringed water-lily
Nymphoides peltata

Site: Water garden
Soil: Rich
Season: June–September
Height: Floating stems to 1.5 m (5 ft)
Perennial; easy to grow

Fringed water-lily is like a miniature water-lily in that its round, glossy leaves float on the water surface. It has delightful, funnel-shaped, yellow flowers with distinctive fringed petals, which stand just above the water surface. Fringed water-lily roots on the pond bottom and can grow through 1.5 m (5 ft) of water.

How to grow
Plants may be obtained from specialist water-plant nurseries. Plant into the pond bed at any time during the growing season; anchor the roots down with a piece of turf. Sow seeds when ripe into a shallow tray of water. When they sprout, plant them into small pots. Keep the compost moist at all times.

Frogbit
Hydrocharis morsus-ranae

Site: Water garden
Soil: Wet
Season: July–August
Height: to 10 cm (4 in) above water
Perennial; easy to grow

Frogbit is a pretty perennial plant for the garden pond. It has circular leaves that form a rosette around small, white flowers, which are blotched yellow in the centre. Both leaves and flowers float on the water surface. The plant spreads rapidly by its horizontal underwater stems that produce new plants at regular intervals.

How to grow
Plants can be purchased from suppliers of pond and water plants. To plant frogbit, simply throw the plants in the water, preferably during spring. The fleshy roots can be divided with a sharp knife during the growing season.

Giant bellflower
Campanula latifolia

Site: Semi-shade; shade
Soil: Damp and fertile
Season: July–August
Height: 60–120 cm (2–4 ft)
Perennial; needs care

Giant bellflower is a most spectacular plant. It has beautiful pale blue, or sometimes white, bell-shaped flowers adorning tall stems, above a mass of oval-shaped foliage. Giant bellflowers are most impressive grouped against a wall, or at the back of a border in a shady garden.

How to grow
Sow the seed in autumn either where it is to flower or in trays and cover lightly with soil. Trays should be left outside over winter covered in glass; germination will occur in spring.

Gipsywort
Lycopus europaeus

Site: Sun; semi-shade; shade; water garden
Soil: Moist
Season: June–September
Height: 30 cm–1 m (1–3 ft)
Perennial; needs care

Tiny white or pinkish, bell-shaped flowers grow in clusters at the base of each pair of leaves on the stems of gipsywort. The leaves are deeply toothed. This plant forms clumps and will grow well on the banks of a garden pond. But keep it under control or it can become invasive.

Gipsywort can be used to produce a strong black dye.

How to grow
Sow the seed in a seed tray in the autumn. Cover lightly with soil and leave the tray outside covered with glass. Plant the seedlings out 30 cm (1 ft) apart when they are large enough to handle.

Globeflower
Trollius europaeus

Site: Sun; semi-shade
Soil: Wet and rich
Season: June–August
Height: 10–50 cm (4–20 in)
Perennial; needs care

Globeflower is a most decorative plant to grow in a moist situation. It grows wild mainly in the north of England and Scotland. It has big, soft-yellow, spherical flower-heads above decorative foliage, similar to that of a buttercup, but distinctly larger and more glossy. Globeflowers look attractive growing with water forget-me-not, wood crane's-bill and ferns, beside a garden pond.

How to grow
Sow the seed (as fresh as possible) during late summer/early autumn where it is to flower and cover lightly with soil. Germination can be erratic. Once plants are established, the roots can be divided in spring and planted out in a moisture-retentive soil.

Goat's-beard
Tragopogon pratensis

Site: Sun; seaside garden
Soil: Well-drained
Season: June–July
Height: 30–70 cm (1–2 ft)
Biennial; easy to grow

Goat's-beard, or Jack-go-to-bed-at-noon, is a colourful flower to grow in the meadow or rough grass area. It has yellow, dandelion-like flowers that open early in the day and close at noon, and long, grass-like leaves. Attractive, round balls of fruits develop after flowering. These are covered in tufts of long, silky hairs and are similar to the dandelion 'clock' but last longer. Another name for goat's-beard is field salsify as its roots are edible, like parsnips, and the leaves are eaten in salads.

How to grow
Sow the large seeds in spring or autumn where they are to flower and cover with soil. Seed sown in autumn will flower the following year. Goat's-beard self-seeds readily.

Goldenrod
Solidago virgaurea

Site: Sun; semi-shade; shade
Soil: Well-drained
Season: July–September
Height: 30–60 cm (1–2 ft)
Perennial; easy to grow

Goldenrod is an ideal plant for the herbaceous border, as it spreads rapidly to form clumps. In late summer sprays of bright yellow flowers crowd its branched stems amongst sharply-pointed, hoary leaves. It was once used as a herbal remedy to treat internal and external wounds.

How to grow
Sow the seed in spring or autumn where it is to flower and cover lightly with soil. You can also sow in trays in spring or early summer. Goldenrod can be naturalized into poor grassland on well-drained soil.

Greater bird's-foot-trefoil
Lotus uliginosus

Site: Sun; water garden
Soil: Wet and fertile
Season: July–September
Height: 30–60 cm (1–2 ft)
Perennial; needs care

Greater bird's-foot-trefoil is taller and more luxuriant than common bird's-foot-trefoil. It has larger, deep yellow flowers, without the touch of red that is characteristic of other bird's-foot-trefoils, and broad, dark green leaves. This plant grows in marshy ground and would thrive on the banks of a garden pond, scrambling between some of the taller wetland plants.

How to grow
Rub the seed between sheets of sandpaper to speed germination. Sow the seed in spring or autumn and lightly cover with soil. Thin the seedlings to 15 cm (6 in) apart.

Great mullein
Verbascum thapsus

Site: Sun; semi-shade
Soil: Well-drained and fertile
Season: June–August
Height: 30 cm–2 m (1–6 ft)
Biennial; easy to grow

Great mullein is an impressive plant for the back of a sunny border. It produces tall spikes of densely-packed yellow flowers above large, downy leaves and is a very good bee plant. The leaves attract the caterpillars of the mullein moth.

Great mullein was once used as a herbal remedy to treat bronchial troubles; a yellow hair dye can also be made from its flowers.

How to grow
Sow the tiny seed in autumn where the plants are to flower and press or water the seed into the soil. Seed can be rather erratic in germination. In the first year of growth, the plant will develop a large rosette of woolly leaves and the long flower stem will be produced the following season. Great mullein self-seeds readily.

Ground-ivy
Glechoma hederacea

Site: Sun; semi-shade; shade
Soil: Rich and fairly moist
Season: March–May
Height: 10–30 cm (4–12 in)
Perennial; easy to grow

Ground-ivy will provide good ground cover in a semi-shady garden. Its evergreen leaves are dainty and kidney-shaped and it has small, mauve, lavender-like flowers.

Ground-ivy leaves have a pungent, minty scent and have been used in making ale. A tea made from the plant is supposed to cure coughs.

How to grow
Sow seed in a seed tray in spring or autumn, and cover lightly with soil. Plant out the seedlings when they are large enough to handle.

Hare's-foot clover
Trifolium arvense

Site: Sun; seaside garden
Soil: Light and well-drained with some fertility; likes acid soil
Season: June–September
Height: 10–20 cm (4–8 in)
Annual; easy to grow

Hare's-foot clover's neat and pretty flower-heads are soft and downy. They are creamy coloured, with a pinkish tinge, and stand erect above small, trefoil leaves. Hare's-foot clover is mat-forming and grows well in poor, dry soil. It can be naturalized in a sandy, gravelly path where it will self-seed year after year.

Bees and butterflies are very attracted to hare's-foot clover.

How to grow
Rub the seed between sandpaper to trigger growth before sowing in spring. Press the seed into the soil; do not cover. Seed can also be sown in late summer.

Hawthorn
Crataegus monogyna

Site: Semi-shade
Soil: Tolerant of most soils
Season: May–June (flowers)
August–November (fruit)
Height: to 5 m (15 ft)
Perennial shrub; easy to grow

Hawthorn is well worth growing for its beautiful display of white blossom in early summer and decorative red berries in autumn. The flowers have a strong, sweet scent and the shrub is very tough and thorny. It grows very rapidly once established and would make a good specimen shrub or thick hedge in the garden.

How to grow
Young plants are readily obtained at tree nurseries and are often sold by the hundred for hedging. Plant the young shrubs from autumn until early spring; protect them from rabbits and hares by using tree sleeves.

Heather
Calluna vulgaris

Site: Sun; semi-shade
Soil: Acidic and poor
Season: July–September
Height: to 60 cm (2 ft)
Perennial under-shrub; needs care

Heather is an attractive evergreen plant. It has small, pinky-purple flowers that form loose spikes at the tops of the stems, and tiny leaves that clothe the numerous stems all year. Heathers look best grouped *en masse* or grown as background shrubs.

Heather provides food for different forms of wildlife, including bees, butterflies and caterpillars.

How to grow
Take cuttings in August 2 cm (1 in) long and insert around the inside edge of a pot containing a peat/sand mixture. Store in a shaded frame. Or sow seed in autumn in a peaty soil and cover with sand. It might take up to two years to germinate. Plants can be propagated by layering in the spring. Small plants can also be obtained from specialist nurseries.

Hedge-bedstraw
Galium mollugo

Site: Sun; semi-shade
Soil: Prefers well-drained soil
Season: June–September
Height: 45 cm–1 m (1½–3 ft)
Perennial; easy to grow

Hedge-bedstraw is a scrambling plant with fine, pointed leaves and small white flowers, and will grow well in a summer hedgerow garden. It was once used in cheese-making, and a red dye can be obtained from its roots.

How to grow
Sow the seed in spring or autumn in a seed tray and lightly cover with soil. Autumn-sown seed will germinate in early spring. Plant the seedlings out in the following spring or autumn when they are large enough to handle.

Hedge woundwort
Stachys sylvatica

Site: Semi-shade; shade
Soil: Rich and moist
Season: July–August
Height: 30 cm–1 m (1–3 ft)
Perennial; easy to grow

Hedge woundwort is a tall, hairy plant carrying loose spikes of purple-brown flowers above heart-shaped leaves. It can look attractive growing with black horehound, betony and wood dock along a hedgerow.

Hedge woundwort is a good bee plant and has long been used as a herbal remedy to treat wounds and stem bleeding. Its leaves contain volatile oil with antiseptic properties.

How to grow
Sow the seed in late summer or autumn where the plants are to flower, and cover lightly with soil. Seed may also be sown in spring or autumn in a seed tray. Plant out the seedlings when they are large enough to handle. Hedge woundwort self-seeds readily.

Hoary plantain
Plantago media

Site: Sun
Soil: Most soils
Season: May–August
Height: 15–30 cm (6–12 in)
Perennial; easy to grow

Hoary plantain is a rather unusual plant with pale pink or white fluffy flowers growing on oval flower-heads topping long stalks. It is a very decorative version of the more common ribwort plantain, which has dark brown flower-heads and a cream 'halo'. The plant has a flat rosette of leaves, covered in white hairs, growing at its base. It has a delicate scent and is very attractive to bees and caterpillars.

Hoary plantain looks very pretty at the front of a wild border, dotted among low-growing plants, or growing in clumps in rough grass.

How to grow
Sow seed from February to May or from August to November and cover very lightly with soil. Plants will self-seed readily once established.

Holly
Ilex aquifolium

Site: Sun; semi-shade; shade
Soil: Well-drained
Season: May–August (flowers)
September–March (fruit)
Height: 3–12 m (10–36 ft)
Perennial shrub or tree; easy to grow

Holly is a superb formal or hedging shrub providing year-round interest. The spiny, evergreen leaves almost hide the clusters of small, white flowers in summer; in winter, scarlet berries adorn the bush, providing Christmas decoration and winter food for birds. It is slow-growing.

Holly is a food plant of the holly blue butterfly.

How to grow
Holly is best grown from a containerized plant; plant from autumn to spring. Seed, when gathered in autumn, should be stratified (see p. 126) for eighteen months and sown in spring. Semi-ripened wood cuttings may be taken in late summer and rooted in a coldframe.

Honesty
Lunaria annua

Site: Sun; semi-shade
Soil: Light and well-drained
Season: April–June
Height: to 1 m (3 ft)
Biennial; easy to grow

Clumps of honesty can add welcome colour to a lightly shaded corner of the garden, or will happily colonize cracks in paving slabs, and will appear in lots of unlikely places! Its flowers form loose, fragrant clusters of brilliant purple or white and are succeeded by fruits that split to reveal almost transparent, disc-shaped membranes, which also provide pretty decoration in the winter garden or when dried.

Butterflies love honesty, and the plant also supplies food for caterpillars of the orange-tip butterfly.

How to grow
Scatter the seeds in summer where they are to flower. Plants will flower the following spring. Honesty self-seeds readily.

Hop
Humulus lupulus

Site: Sun; semi-shade; shade
WARNING: *Wild hops should not be grown in commercial hop-growing areas.*
Soil: Rich and moist
Season: July–August (flowers)
September–October (fruit)
Height: to 6 m (18 ft)
Perennial climber; needs care

Hops are climbing plants that look attractive growing through a hedge. There are separate male and female plants: the male plant has yellowish flowers growing in branched clusters; the female plant has tiny, green, scented flowers and, in the autumn, globular greenish fruits.

Wild hops should not be grown in a commercial hop-growing area since they might contaminate the crop.

How to grow
Sow seeds in summer or autumn, in trays, and cover with soil. Cover with a sheet of glass and leave in a cool spot. Germination may be erratic.

Horseshoe vetch
Hippocrepis comosa

Site: Sun; rock garden
Soil: Well-drained
Season: May–August
Height: 10–40 cm (4–16 in)
Perennial; easy to grow

Horseshoe vetch is a trailing, low-growing plant with pretty, golden-yellow pea flowers, occasionally striped with red. It looks rather like bird's-foot-trefoil except that its leaves are composed of rows of leaflets, and the seed pods are a distinctive horseshoe shape. It makes a colourful rockery plant and is also ideal for growing in the chalk meadow.

Horseshoe vetch is a nectar plant for bees and provides food for the caterpillars of the adonis blue butterfly.

How to grow
Rub the seed between sheets of sandpaper to speed germination. Sow the seed ½ cm (¼ in) deep in spring or late summer where it is to flower. Thin the seedlings to 30 cm (1 ft) apart. Small plants may easily be transplanted into a chalk meadow.

Hound's-tongue
Cynoglossum officinale

Site: Sun; seaside garden
Soil: Light and well-drained
Season: June–August
Height: 30–90 cm (1–3 ft)
Biennial; needs care

Hound's-tongue is a tall plant that will grow well in a sunny garden. It has small, funnel-shaped, crimson flowers above soft, downy, grey leaves. The plant has a distinctive odour and is an important nectar plant for bees and butterflies.

Hound's-tongue was once used as a poultice herb to treat burns, scalds and scabies.

How to grow
Sow the seed in late summer where the plants are to flower and cover lightly with soil. The seed cases are extremely hard (they look like miniature hedgehogs!) and will need time and the winter frosts to break them down. Flowering occurs the season after the seedlings emerge. Hound's-tongue self-seeds readily.

Ivy
Hedera helix

Site: Semi-shade; shade
Soil: Rich and well-drained
Season: September–November (flowers)
November–December (fruit)
Height: to 30 m (100 ft)
Perennial climber; easy to grow

Ivy is an evergreen climbing plant that grows up walls, trees and hedges, or forms a dense carpet along the ground. Ivy leaves are dark green and glossy and provide the perfect background for the yellowish-green flowers on globular flower-heads. There are also decorative black berries in winter.

How to grow
Ivy may be grown from seed but might take a long time to germinate. Seed should be stratified (see p. 126) before sowing. Or obtain a plant from a specialist nursery or pinch a length of stem with aerial roots growing from it from a hedgerow. Peg this cutting on the soil and a new plant will quickly grow.

Ivy-leaved toadflax
Cymbalaria muralis

Site: Sun; rock garden
Soil: Well-drained
Season: May–September
Height: 10–75 cm (4 in–3½ ft)
Perennial; easy to grow

Ivy-leaved toadflax is a creeping plant which grows on walls and over rocks. It has a tangle of glossy, ivy-shaped leaves and lilac, snapdragon-like flowers with a yellow centre; a white form is also quite common. Once established, it will spread rapidly and seed in the cracks of a wall or the crevices of a rock garden.

Ivy-leaved toadflax is a good nectar plant for bees.

How to grow
Sow the seed in spring where the plants are to flower and cover lightly with soil. Germination will take place within a few weeks.

Jacob's-ladder
Polemonium caeruleum

Site: Sun; semi-shade; rock garden
Soil: Fertile and well-drained
Season: June–July
Height: 30–90 cm (1–3 ft)
Perennial; easy to grow

Jacob's-ladder is now very rare in the wild, being confined to rocky woodlands and meadows in the north of England. Its beautiful cobalt-blue flowers and decorative, bright green foliage, which look like the steps of a ladder, have made this flower an old cottage-garden favourite. A form with white flowers is also common.

Jacob's-ladder is an accommodating plant that will thrive in a sunny border and in a semi-shady situation. It makes a fine feature in the rock garden and can also be naturalized in short grassland.

How to grow
Sow the seeds in spring or autumn where they are to flower and cover lightly with soil. Jacob's-ladder self-seeds readily around the parent plant.

Kidney vetch
Anthyllis vulneraria

Site: Sun; seaside garden
Soil: Well-drained; tolerates poor fertility
Season: June–September
Height: 25–30 cm (9–12 in)
Perennial; easy to grow

Kidney vetch is a lovely plant. Its large, rounded flower-heads are crowded with downy yellow flowers; although on plants growing near the sea, the flowers can vary from cream to crimson. The leaves are pale green and silky.

Kidney vetch is very attractive to wildlife. It is a rich source of nectar, bringing bees to its flower-heads; and butterflies lay their eggs on the plant, making it the main source of food for caterpillars of the small blue.

How to grow
Rub the seed between sheets of sandpaper to speed germination. Sow in spring or early autumn either where it is to flower or in trays. It will establish well in dry grassland.

Lady-fern
Athyrium filix-femina

Site: Semi-shade; shade
Soil: Damp
Season: Spring, summer and autumn
Height: Fronds – 20 cm–1 m (8 in–3 ft)
Perennial; easy to grow

Lady-ferns have a very delicate texture and a graceful, feathery appearance. Their fresh green fronds look quite beautiful growing with violets and columbines in a shady border or woodland garden. Lady-ferns form clumps, which can be divided, and they spread quite quickly.

How to grow
Lady-fern may be grown from spores (see p. 127) which are ripe in July–August. Small plants may easily be purchased from a specialist fern nursery and planted out in a suitable site shaded from the midday sun.

Lady's bedstraw
Galium verum

Site: Sun; semi-shade; seaside garden
Soil: Well-drained
Season: July–August
Height: 15 cm–1 m (6 in–3 ft)
Perennial; germination tricky

Lady's bedstraw is a pretty yellow-flowered plant to grow *en masse* in a sunny meadow or seaside garden. It has thread-like leaves and golden-yellow flowers growing in dense panicles. The plant spreads by underground runners.

Lady's bedstraw has many practical uses, including producing yellow or red dye; and curdling and colouring milk for cheese-making.

How to grow
Sow seeds in spring or autumn in a seed tray and cover very lightly with soil. Seed can take many weeks to germinate: a November sowing will germinate in February. Plant out in spring 45 cm (18 in) apart.

Lady's-mantle
Alchemilla vulgaris

Site: Sun
Soil: Moist and fertile
Season: June–September
Height: 15–45 cm (6–18 in)
Perennial; needs care

Lady's-mantle, or lion's foot, is a low-growing herb which provides attractive ground cover in a garden. It has large, distinctive leaves of pale green and loose clusters of tiny, yellowish-green flowers which look attractive for many weeks.

Lady's-mantle was believed, by medieval alchemists, to have celestial powers; the dew from its leaves was used in their experiments to turn metal into gold!

How to grow
Sow the seed in a seed tray in early summer. Do not cover it, but make sure that it does not dry out. Plant out when the seedlings are large enough to handle. Young plants can also be obtained from wildflower suppliers. Divide mature plants in spring. Lady's-mantle self-seeds easily.

Larkspur
Delphinium ambiguum (syn. *Consolida ambigua*)

Site: Sun
Soil: Well-drained
Season: June–July
Height: 30–60 cm (1–2 ft)
Annual; easy to grow

Naturalized larkspurs, which are smaller than the cultivated varieties, are elegant plants with loose spikes of intense purplish-blue flowers above feathery, fern-like leaves. They will grow well in a cornfield garden, or can be added to a mixed wildflower border for a dramatic effect.

Larkspurs are very attractive to butterflies and other insects.

How to grow
Sow seeds in early autumn or early spring in well-drained soil in a sunny position. Cover lightly with soil. Thin seedlings to 30 cm (1 ft) apart.

Lesser calamint
Calamintha nepeta

Site: Sun
Soil: Well-drained and alkaline; tolerates poor fertility
Season: July–September
Height: 30–60 cm (1–2 ft)
Perennial; germination tricky

Lesser calamint makes a lovely show growing in a group on a bank. It has tiny, delicate, pale mauve flowers, and its stems and leaves are pale grey and covered in fine, downy hairs. Its most remarkable feature is its wonderful aromatic scent, which attracts butterflies, making another bonus to growing the plant. It is also a nectar plant for bees.

How to grow
Sow the seed in spring or autumn either where the plants are to flower or in trays and cover lightly with soil. If sown in autumn in trays, leave the trays outside over winter covered with a sheet of glass.

Lesser stitchwort
Stellaria graminea

Site: Sun; semi-shade
Soil: Most soils retaining some moisture; grows well on acid soils
Season: May–July
Height: 15–60 cm (6 in–2 ft)
Perennial; easy to grow

Lesser stitchwort is a plant of rough grassland and hedgerows. It is most attractive, having tiny white flowers with yellow centres sprinkled among its foliage. It differs from greater stitchwort in that it has smooth-edged leaves and much smaller flowers. Lesser stitchwort is a straggly plant and often uses other plants for support. It looks particularly effective scrambling over large-leaved plants that show off the tiny white flowers.

How to grow
Sow the seed in spring or autumn in a seed tray and cover very lightly with compost. Or scatter seed, where it is to flower, in spring or autumn and press or water it into the soil. Lesser stitchwort will self-seed.

Maidenhair spleenwort
Asplenium trichomanes

Site: Semi-shade; rock garden
Soil: Well-drained; will tolerate dry conditions
Season: All year
Height: 5–35 cm (2–14 in)
Perennial evergreen; needs special care

This is one of the most decorative ferns; it has a lovely feathery appearance. Neat pairs of leaflets grow along the length of the black, hair-like stems.
 Maidenhair spleenwort will grow in crevices in walls, rockeries or paving and, once established, may reproduce itself to form an attractive natural grouping.

How to grow
Ferns grow from dust-like spores (see the detailed cultivation instructions on p. 127). It is best to buy mature plants from a specialist supplier. Plant in well-drained soil during spring or early autumn.

Maiden pink
Dianthus deltoides

Site: Sun; rock garden; seaside garden
Soil: Well-drained; likes acid soil
Season: June–September
Height: 15–45 cm (6 in–1½ ft)
Perennial; easy to grow

Maiden pink is a lovely spreading plant for rock gardens or gravel paths. It forms a low spreading mat of grey-green foliage and, in summer, a mass of rose-red flowers, delicately freckled with pale spots. The flowers have no scent but attract insects by their brilliant colouring. In dull weather the flowers close.

How to grow
Sow the seed where it is to flower in spring and lightly cover with soil. When the seedlings are large enough, thin to 30 cm (1 ft) apart. Maiden pink spreads readily by self-seeding.

Marsh-mallow
Althaea officinalis

Site: Sun; seaside garden
Soil: Moist or wet
Season: July–September
Height: 60–120 cm (2–4 ft)
Perennial; needs care

Marsh-mallow is a tall, stately plant. Its large, pale-pink flowers grow in clusters from the upper part of the stem, and its velvety leaves appear slightly folded, like a fan. It is a most beautiful plant to grow as a feature, or in a clump at the back of a border.
 The roots of the marsh-mallow have been used as a remedy for various pains and swellings, as well as for making the sweets known as marshmallows. Butterflies are attracted to the flowers.

How to grow
Sow the seed where it is to flower or in trays in autumn and cover lightly with soil. Trays should be left outside over winter covered with sheets of glass. Germination is erratic but should take place in spring. The plants will take two seasons to flower.

Meadow vetchling
Lathyrus pratensis

Site: Sun
Soil: Fertile
Season: May–August
Height: 30–120 cm (1–4 ft)
Perennial; easy to grow

Meadow vetchling is a slender, leafy plant with small, yellow pea flowers, frequently visited by bumblebees and butterflies. It is a scrambling plant which will form large clumps in time. For the best effect, grow a mass of meadow vetchling in a summer meadow garden or rough grass area.

How to grow
Rub the seed between sheets of sandpaper to speed germination. Sow in spring where the plants are to flower and cover with soil to the depth of the seed. Plants may be transplanted into grass during spring.

Mezereon
Daphne mezereum

Site: Semi-shade; shade
Soil: Rich and moist
Season: February–March (flowers) July–September (fruit)
Height: 50 cm–1 m (1½–3 ft)
Perennial; needs care

Mezereon is a slow-growing upright bush well worth growing for its lovely early season flowers and pleasant scent; it looks best in a woodland-type setting. This is a rare native plant which is specially protected in the wild. Its flowers are tiny, rosy pink and tubular-shaped and they grow in clusters up the stems before the leaves appear and when little else is in flower. Bright scarlet berries are produced in late summer, which are poisonous but highly attractive and are eaten by birds.

How to grow
Seeds are difficult to obtain but plants are widely available from nurseries and garden centres. Plant during early autumn or spring in well-drained soil in light or deep shade.

Milk thistle
Silybum marianum

Site: Sun; seaside garden
Soil: Well-drained
Height: 1–1½ m (3–5 ft)
Biennial; easy to grow

Milk thistle is a spectacular, architectural plant with large, purple flower-heads and decorative, white-veined, spiky leaves. It makes an arresting feature in any border, or it can be naturalized in a more informal setting. The first season of its two-year cycle produces a very decorative low rosette of white-veined leaves, and in the second year bees and butterflies will be attracted to its colourful flower-heads. It is a naturalized plant from southern Europe.

How to grow
Sow the seed 1 cm (½ in) deep in late spring or early summer where it is to flower. Milk thistles do not transplant very well. Plants self-seed readily.

Monk's-hood
Aconitum napellus

Site: Sun; semi-shade; shade
Soil: Moist and fertile
Season: May–September
Height: 1–1½ m (3–5 ft)
Perennial; easy to grow

Monk's-hood, or aconite, is a striking plant which grows over 1 m (3 ft) high. It has tall, purple-blue spires of hood-shaped flowers above attractive, finger-shaped foliage. This plant will look stunning grouped against a shady wall at the back of a border or in a woodland setting. It is very attractive to bumblebees.

Monk's-hood has medicinal properties and is still important in homoeopathic medicine. However, it is very poisonous and can cause serious illness if eaten.

How to grow
Sow seed under cover in March or outside in April where it is to flower. Monk's-hood self-seeds, and the roots can be divided in autumn after the stem has died. **WARNING:** *Wear gloves while handling the roots.*

Moschatel
Adoxa moschatellina

Site: Sun; semi-shade; shade
Soil: Fertile and damp or moist
Season: April–May
Height: 5–15 cm (2–6 in)
Perennial; needs care

Moschatel is a small, spreading plant with delicate, yellowish-green flowers and pale green leaves. The small flowers are arranged on the stem in an unusual cube-like shape, which gives this plant its alternative common name of 'townhall clock'.

Moschatel will provide attractive ground cover in a shady woodland garden, and should be grown in a large group for the best effect.

The most pleasing characteristic of moschatel is its lovely musk-like scent which becomes stronger at dusk and in damp weather, and attracts insects.

How to grow
Sow the seed in autumn in a seed tray and cover lightly with soil. Leave outside, covered with glass, over winter.

Mountain pansy
Viola lutea

Site: Sun; rock garden
Soil: Poor and well-drained
Season: May–August
Height: low and creeping
Perennial; easy to grow

Mountain pansy is a lovely plant for the rock garden. It produces delightful, large flowers of bright yellow and sometimes purple-violet, and it also forms mats of foliage along the ground, quickly nestling in any available crevice. It looks pretty growing in stone walls and gravel paths.

How to grow
Scatter seed in spring or late summer where it is to flower and water it into the soil. Mountain pansy can easily be divided when it is established and it self-seeds readily.

Mouse-ear hawkweed
Hieracium pilosella

Site: Sun; semi-shade
Soil: Most soil
Season: May–September
Height: 5–30 cm (2 in–1 ft)
Perennial; easy to grow

Mouse-ear hawkweed is a small, spreading plant, ideal for rough grass or hedgerows. It spreads rapidly by means of runners and seeds to form cheerful splashes of colour. It has bright lemon-yellow flower-heads, similar to those of the dandelion, but streaked with red underneath, growing on single flowering stems above a rosette of lobe-shaped leaves. The plant is covered with white hairs.

Mouse-ear hawkweed was once used as a remedy to treat jaundice.

How to grow
Sow the seed in spring where it is to flower and press into the soil; do not cover with soil. If plants are required for grassland, first sow seeds in a seed tray in spring or autumn and then plant out when the seedlings are large enough to handle.

Musk thistle
Carduus nutans

Site: Sun
Soil: Fertile, cultivated soil
Season: May–August
Height: 20 cm–1 m (9 in–3 ft)
Biennial; easy to grow

This handsome thistle, also known as nodding thistle, is distinguished by its big, drooping, reddish-purple flowers above long, spiky stems and leaves. The flower-heads are cup-shaped and backed by small spines.

Musk thistle has a strong, musky odour; butterflies are attracted to the plant, as are some seed-eating birds.

How to grow
Sow the seed where it is to flower 1 cm (½ in) deep in late summer. The leaf rosette should establish during the autumn and winter and send up a flowering stem the following spring. Musk thistle will self-seed.

Narrow-leaved everlasting-pea
Lathyrus sylvestris

Site: Sun; semi-shade; shade
Soil: Fertile and well-drained
Season: June–August
Height: 1–3 m (3–9 ft)
Perennial climber; easy to grow

Narrow-leaved everlasting-peas are closely related to sweet peas and look rather similar. They have small, buff-yellow flowers flushed pink and long, narrow leaves. The plant looks attractive climbing through a hedge or shrub in a semi-shady spot.

How to grow
Rub the seed between sheets of sandpaper to speed germination. Sow seed in spring 1½ cm (¾ in) deep, where it is to flower. Further seed may be collected from the large numbers of seed pods produced by the mature plant.

Parsley fern
Cryptogramma crispa

Site: Sun; semi-shade; rock garden
Soil: Poor, moist and acid
Season: Spring–autumn
Height: 15–20 cm (6–8 in)
Perennial; needs care

Parsley fern is a pretty fern with very decorative, feathery fronds which resemble the herb parsley, hence its name. It is an extremely hardy plant, thriving in barren, rocky outcrops, and will grow well in a rock garden in light shade or full sun, perhaps serving as a backdrop to more colourful rock plants. However, parsley fern will not grow in alkaline soil, so test your soil first.

How to grow
Plants may be obtained from a specialist fern nursery. This fern needs acid conditions so a large pocket of peat mixed with granite chips would be ideal. This must not be allowed to dry out. Parsley ferns may also be grown from spores (see page 127).

Perennial flax
Linum anglicum (syn. L. perenne)

Site: Sun; rock garden
Soil: Well-drained
Season: May–August
Height: 30–60 cm (1–2 ft)
Perennial; easy to grow

Perennial flax is a tufted plant with numerous small leaves and pretty, sky-blue flowers on thin, waving stems. It looks best planted in large, informal clumps, perhaps to soften the edge of a border or path, and allowed to spread by self-seeding.

How to grow
Sow the seed where it is to flower, or in a seed tray, in spring, and lightly cover with soil. Thin seedlings to 15 cm (6 in) apart. Seedlings may be transplanted into grass; they will establish in chalk or sandy soils.

Pheasant's-eye
Adonis annua

Site: Sun
Soil: Cultivated soil that is well-drained, fertile and alkaline
Season: May–July
Height: 10–40 cm (4 in–1½ ft)
Annual; needs care

Pheasant's-eye has lovely scarlet flowers with dark centres, like red buttercups, and decorative, feathery leaves. It will add bright splashes of red to a sunny cornfield garden, and its brilliant colour also attracts butterflies. Pheasant's-eye is a plant from southern Europe, where it is regarded as a weed and is destroyed, and has naturalized in cornfields. It is now a rare and declining species.

How to grow
Sow the seed where it is to flower in autumn by broadcasting and raking in. It can also be sown in spring, but this is not so reliable. It will not establish in grass. Pheasant's-eye self-seeds readily.

Pignut
Conopodium majus

Site: Semi-shade; shade
Soil: Fertile and not too dry
Season: May–June
Height: 25–50 cm (10–20 in)
Perennial; needs care

Pignut has delicate umbels of pretty white flowers growing in clusters on branched flower-heads, and distinctive, finely divided leaves, similar to, but darker than, those of the wild carrot. In fact, pignuts are related to the carrot family and their brown, tuberous roots are edible and especially liked by pigs. Pignuts are perennial plants that look attractive growing in a woodland setting or in the shade of a hedgerow.

How to grow
Sow the seed in autumn where the plants are to flower and cover lightly with soil. They will germinate either in autumn or in the following spring. Divide mature plants in spring.

Purple saxifrage
Saxifraga oppositifolia

Site: Sun; rock garden
Soil: Poor, not too dry and slightly acid
Season: March–May
Height: creeping and mat-forming
Perennial; easy to grow

Purple saxifrage is a delightful, sprawling plant that flowers in brilliant profusion in early spring. Small starry flowers, from pink to deep purple, grow from trailing, wiry stems, almost hiding its tiny leaves. Grow a mass of purple saxifrage in a rock garden for a beautiful carpet of colour.

How to grow
Sow the tiny seed in spring in a seed tray of gritty, sandy compost; do not cover. Plants may easily be divided in spring. Cuttings of non-flowering stems may be taken from mature plants in May–June and inserted into gritty, sandy compost. They will require minimum moisture to root.

Purple toadflax
Linaria purpurea

Site: Sun
Soil: Well-drained
Season: June–August
Height: 60 cm–1 m (2–3 ft)
Perennial; easy to grow

Purple toadflax is a very decorative plant to grow in a mixed border. It grows up to 1 m (3 ft) tall and produces slender spikes of bright violet, snapdragon-like flowers and short narrow leaves.

Purple toadflax is a naturalized plant from Italy.

How to grow
Scatter seed in spring or autumn where it is to flower. Cover with a sprinkling of soil.

Ramsons
Allium ursinum

Site: Semi-shade; shade
Soil: Moist and fertile
Season: April–June
Height: 30–45 cm (1–1½ ft)
Perennial; needs care

Ramsons, or wild garlic, is an extremely pretty plant for the shady woodland garden. Clusters of snow-white flowers grow on long stalks above broad, bright-green leaves. Ramsons looks especially effective growing in large drifts alongside bluebells and columbines. It has, however, a distinctive, onion-like smell that makes it for some a plant best viewed at a distance!

How to grow
Sow the seed in autumn where the plants are to grow and cover lightly with soil. Germination will take place in early spring. The small bulbs may be divided once the plant has died down in early summer. Ramsons self-seeds easily and in a wet area it can be invasive.

Red dead-nettle
Lamium purpureum

Site: Sun
Soil: Any fertile soil
Season: March–October
Height: 10–45 cm (4–18 in)
Annual; easy to grow

Red dead-nettle is a very adaptable plant that is tolerant of most sites and soils. It is often regarded as a weed which is a pity since it is an attractive plant, flowering for a long period. Its flowers are pinkish-purple and slightly hooded and grow in small clusters amongst the heart-shaped, purplish leaves. The leaves emit a pungent smell when crushed. This is an important early-season bee and butterfly nectar plant.

How to grow
Sow the seed where it is to flower in spring and barely cover with soil. The plants will self-seed readily and maintain themselves year after year in cultivated soil.

Red valerian
Centranthus ruber

Site: Sun; rock garden
Soil: Well-drained; low fertility
Season: June–August
Height: 30–90 cm (1–3 ft)
Perennial; needs care

The deep-red flowers of red valerian make warm splashes of colour in a rock garden, or growing in the cracks between paving stones. It is often grown on or against a wall. Red valerian is a bushy, greyish-green plant with large, branched flower-heads clustered with elegant, fragrant flowers. It is very attractive to butterflies. The flowers can also appear in all shades of pink and white.

Red valerian was introduced from central and southern Europe.

How to grow
Sow the seed in trays in late summer or early autumn. Cover lightly with soil and leave outside over winter covered with glass. Plant out in the following autumn 30 cm (1 ft) apart. Cut the plants back each year to prevent them self-seeding.

Ribbed melilot
Melilotus officinalis

Site: Sun
Soil: Fertile
Season: June–September
Height: 30–120 cm (1–4 ft)
Biennial; easy to grow

Ribbed melilot is a tall plant bearing long spikes of small, yellow flowers. It grows very quickly and looks attractive growing in a summer meadow garden or wildflower bed, where it will attract bees and caterpillars. It is a naturalized plant.

Ribbed melilot was once used medicinally for making poultices. It gives off a lovely smell of new-mown hay when it dries.

How to grow
Sow the seed in late spring or early summer either where it is to flower or in trays. Cover lightly with soil.

Rock cinquefoil
Potentilla rupestris

Site: Rock garden
Soil: Well-drained
Season: May–June
Height: 20–50 cm (8–20 in)
Perennial; easy to grow

Rock cinquefoil is a beautiful and rare native plant well worth growing for its large, white strawberry-like flowers which grow in loose clusters on branching stems 30 cm (1 ft) or more high. This flower provides a pleasing contrast to the low-growing and carpeting alpines.

How to grow
Sow the seed on the surface of the soil or seed tray in spring or autumn. The seed tray should be made up with a gritty or sandy compost. Mature plants may be divided in March or April. Plants can be obtained from specialist alpine nurseries.

Rough chervil
Chaerophyllum temulentum

Site: Sun; semi-shade
Soil: Fertile and well-drained
Season: June–July
Height: 30–90 cm (1–3 ft)
Biennial; easy to grow

Rough chervil is a hedgerow plant that thrives in dappled sunlight. It is similar to but more delicate looking than cow parsley, with its big, umbrella-shaped flower-heads of tiny, white flowers and attractive foliage. It can be distinguished by its purple spotted stems and later flowering.

Rough chervil is a poisonous plant.

How to grow
Sow the seed in late spring or early summer where the plants are to flower and cover lightly with soil. Flowers and seeds will be produced the year after sowing. Rough chervil self-seeds readily.

Royal fern
Osmunda regalis

Site: Semi-shade; shade; water garden
Soil: Rich and moist
Season: March–September
Height: 1–2 m (3–6 ft)
Perennial; easy to grow

The royal fern is the most noble of all the ferns. Planted near the water's edge it will grow into a fine specimen plant. Its elegant fronds are buff-pink in colour with cream streaks, when they begin to unfurl in spring. When mature, they are a perfect clear green colour and look quite beautiful; in autumn they turn a lovely gold and red-brown. Royal ferns grow into dense bushy clumps which can be divided and replanted.

How to grow
Royal ferns may be grown from spores (see p. 127). Young plants can be obtained from specialist fern nurseries and should be planted during March–April or September–October.

Sainfoin
Onobrychis viciifolia

Site: Sun
Soil: Well-drained
Season: May–August
Height: 10–80 cm (4 in–2½ ft)
Perennial; easy to grow

Sainfoin is a bushy plant with cone-shaped spikes, pretty, bright pink flowers streaked with red, and vetch-like leaves. It makes a colourful splash of pink in a summer meadow garden and is very attractive to bees. It is a flower of chalk grassland. The seeds of sainfoin are beautiful, and worth examining under a magnifying glass.

How to grow
Before planting, rub the large seeds between sandpaper to trigger germination. Sow the seed where it is to flower 1 cm (½ in) deep in spring or early autumn.

Salad burnet
Poterium sanguisorba (syn. Sanguisorba minor)

Site: Sun; semi-shade
Soil: Any well-drained soil
Season: May–August
Height: 20–45 cm (9 in–1½ ft)
Perennial; easy to grow

Salad burnet is a delightful plant of the chalk grassland. It is extremely attractive with its greenish-red, pom-pom-like flower-heads and intricate, evergreen foliage. When the leaves are bruised, they emit a pleasant, perfume; they taste of cucumber and can be used in salads and sauces.

Plant salad burnet with thyme and chamomile in your herb garden, like the Elizabethan gardeners used to, for a pleasing range of colours and scents. The herb is deep-rooting and very drought-resistant. It also grows well in grassland.

How to grow
Sow seed in spring or early autumn and cover lightly with soil. Plants should be spaced 20 cm (8 in) apart. Salad burnet self-seeds readily.

Saw-wort
Serratula tinctoria

Site: Sun; semi-shade
Soil: Moist to dry and fertile
Season: July–September
Height: 20–80 cm (8 in–2½ ft)
Perennial; easy to grow

Saw-wort looks like a small knapweed, with purplish-pink, fluffy flower-heads on branching stems. It looks pretty growing in a hedgerow, providing bright splashes of colour amongst the greenery. Saw-wort grows in a range of soils from fenland to dry, gravelly soils; it is now becoming scarce in the wild.

The plant was once used as a herbal remedy to treat wounds. A yellow-green dye can be obtained from its leaves, when mixed with alum.

How to grow
Sow the seed in a seed tray in spring or autumn and cover lightly with soil. Plant out the seedlings when they are large enough to handle.

Scarlet pimpernel
Anagallis arvensis

Site: Sun; seaside garden
Soil: Any good cultivated soil
Season: May–August
Height: Low and spreading
Annual; easy to grow

Scarlet pimpernel is a small and delicate, sprawling plant with bright, starry flowers, usually red, but there are also rare blue or pink forms that are very pretty. It does best on rather bare ground between other, more upright, plants. Its leaves are shiny and oval-shaped, with a pointed tip, and grow in pairs. Scarlet pimpernels have no nectar or scent and so are not visited by many insects.

How to grow
Sow the seeds in spring or autumn where they are to grow and cover lightly with soil. Scarlet pimpernel self-seeds readily.

Scented mayweed
Matricaria recutita (syn. Chamomilla recutita)

Site: Sun
Soil: Dry
Season: May–August
Height: 10–50 cm (4–20 in)
Annual; easy to grow

Scented mayweed, or German chamomile, is usually the first of the mayweeds to flower. The plants are much finer than other mayweeds and the white, daisy-like flowers smaller. The flowers have a very strong, sweet scent. Grow scented mayweed in the cornfield garden as it looks lovely alongside red poppies. It can also be liberally scattered amongst wild flowers in the bed or border.

Scented mayweed flowers are used medicinally, being especially good for soothing children's teething pains.

How to grow
Scatter the tiny seed in spring or early summer where it is to flower; do not cover with soil.

Scentless mayweed
Tripleurospermum inodorum
(syn. Matricaria perforata)

Site: Sun; seaside garden
Soil: Fertile
Season: July–September
Height: 15–60 cm (6 in–2 ft)
Annual; easy to grow

Scentless mayweed's large, cheerful, daisy-like flower-heads and thread-like leaves can brighten up any dull patch of your garden, and look especially decorative in a cornfield garden. It is a very adaptable plant and will grow in most soils; for this reason it has long been regarded as a common weed. The plant has virtually no scent, hence its name. In arable fields where it is abundant, it has almost finished flowering by the end of July.

How to grow
Scentless mayweed is a standard constituent of a cornfield mixture. Scatter the seed where it is to flower in late summer or early spring and water it into the soil. The plant self-seeds readily but will not establish in grass.

Sea campion
Silene maritima

Site: Sun; rock garden; seaside garden
Soil: Well-drained; alkaline to slightly acid
Season: May–July
Height: 15–20 cm (6–8 in)
Perennial; easy to grow

Sea campion forms neat, spreading cushions of small, glaucous, waxy leaves above which stand short stalks bearing large, white flowers. The flowers have cylindrical inflated calyces, smaller than the great balloons that characterize bladder campion to which it is related. Grow sea campion with a mass of thrift for an attractive blend of colours. Or grow it in a rock garden where it can be set off beautifully by a carpet of wild thyme.

How to grow
Sow the seed in spring or autumn where the plants are to flower and cover lightly with soil. Seed may also be sown in a seed tray if plants are required for planting out later.

Sea-holly
Eryngium maritimum

Site: Sun; seaside garden
Soil: Tolerates poor soils
Season: July–August
Height: 30–90 cm (1–3 ft)
Perennial; needs care

Sea-holly is an unusual and lovely plant. Its thistle-like flower-head is crowded with tiny, metallic-blue flowers, and its spiny leaves are a bluish-green colour, edged with white. It is a very decorative plant for the seaside garden.

The roots of sea-holly used to be candied with sugar and sold as an aphrodisiac!

How to grow
Plant seeds ½ cm (¼ in) deep in autumn in a sandy soil in full sun. Germination will take place in spring. Sea-holly plants may be obtained from specialist nurseries.

Sea wormwood
Artemisia maritima

Site: Sun; seaside garden
Soil: Well-drained
Season: July–September
Height: 20–50 cm (8–20 in)
Perennial; needs care

Sea wormwood is a delicate, finely textured, spreading plant that makes an attractive silver bush in a flower border or seaside meadow garden. Its small, dark-gold flowers are carried in graceful sprays above the intricate foliage and the plant is very aromatic.

How to grow
Sow the dust-like seed in a seed tray; water in lightly but do not cover with soil. Cover the tray with glass until germination takes place. Plant out 1 m (3 ft) apart in spring or autumn. Plants can easily be divided in spring.

Sheep's-bit
Jasione montana

Site: Sun; semi-shade; rock garden; seaside garden
Soil: Well-drained
Season: May–August
Height: 5–50 cm (2–20 in)
Biennial; easy to grow

This is a small, sometimes sprawling, plant which enjoys an acid soil. It is suitable for a rock or gravel garden and also looks pretty growing in clumps amongst heathers in a border. It has dense flower-heads that look like powder-blue pincushions, and small leaves that emit a strong smell when bruised.

How to grow
Sow the seed where it is to flower, in spring or autumn, and press it into the soil or sand. Sheep's-bit self-seeds readily in a suitable soil.

Silver hair-grass
Aira caryophyllea

Site: Sun; rock garden
Soil: Well-drained
Season: May–July
Height: 5–30 cm (2–12 in)
Annual; easy to grow

Silver hair-grass is one of our most attractive native grasses, with a lovely light and delicate appearance. When growing in a mass the tiny heads give a marvellous misty impression. Grow silver hair-grass in a large rock garden or on any dry, gravelly or waste piece of ground where it will produce a lovely effect.

How to grow
Scatter the seed in spring where the plants are to grow. Cover lightly with soil or just rake in and firm the soil. Silver hair-grass self-seeds readily.

Silverweed
Potentilla anserina

Site: Sun; seaside garden
Soil: Most soil types
Season: May–July
Height: low and creeping
Perennial; easy to grow

Silverweed is a low, spreading plant which makes attractive ground cover in a sunny site. It has glossy, silvery leaves with hairs underneath and pretty, rose-like yellow flowers. It thrives in moist soils but also grows in dry situations.

The roots of silverweed used to be eaten; they were sometimes roasted and even made into bread. The leaves have also been eaten and are loved by geese. Herbalists used the roots to treat sore throats and mouth ulcers.

How to grow
Sow the seed in spring or autumn where it is to flower and cover lightly with soil. Seed may also be sown in a seed tray if plants are required for planting out. Silverweed spreads rapidly from runners and may easily be divided in summer and autumn.

Slender speedwell
Veronica filiformis

Site: Sun
Soil: Fertile
Season: March–July
Height: creeping and mat-forming
Perennial; easy to grow

Slender speedwell is a creeping, mat-forming plant which spreads rapidly. It has pretty blue flowers with a white lower lip, similar to but smaller than germander speedwell, and small, kidney-shaped leaves, and looks lovely growing on a lawn, or in rough grass which is kept reasonably short.

How to grow
Seed is not easily available so small plants should be obtained (perhaps from a neighbour's lawn). A small piece of turf with some plants in it can be planted out in spring or autumn. The plants will gradually spread through the grass.

Smooth tare
Vicia tetrasperma

Site: Sun
Soil: Most soils including acid
Season: May–August
Height: 20–30 cm (8–12 in)
Annual; easy to grow

Smooth tare is essentially a very attractive foliage plant with 3–6 pairs of bright green, slender leaves growing like the steps of a ladder. The flowers are a rich lilac colour but are very small. The seed pods always contain four seeds; this distinguishes it from the hairy tare which is normally two-seeded.

A few tares sown among other wild flowers in a border look most attractive and they are easily pulled out if they get out of hand. It is also a good constituent of a flowering meadow mixture.

How to grow
Seed is normally sold in a flowering grass mixture. Rub the seed between sheets of sandpaper to speed germination and then press it into the soil in spring or autumn.

Soapwort
Saponaria officinalis

Site: Sun
Soil: Fertile
Season: July–September
Height: 30–60 cm (1–2 ft)
Perennial; needs care

Soapwort is so called because its leaves and roots, when boiled in water, yield a soapy lather that was once used to wash wool. It is quite a tall plant although without support it often sprawls, with showy flesh-pink flowers growing in compact clusters, and handsome, pale green leaves. This plant is an ancient introduction.

A mass of soapwort can look lovely growing in a border or amongst grass and other flowers in a bank and will spread quickly.

How to grow
Sow the seed in early autumn, either where it is to flower or in a seed tray. Cover lightly with soil. Leave the tray outside over winter covered with glass. Germination usually takes place in spring but can be erratic.

Spindle
Euonymus europaeus

Site: Sun; semi-shade; shade
Soil: Fertile
Season: May–June (flowers)
September–December (fruit)
Height: to 6 m (18 ft)
Perennial shrub; easy to grow

The deciduous spindle bush is unobtrusive for most of the year, with small green flowers in loose clusters, and simple pointed leaves. But in the autumn, its leaves turn bronze and deep pink fruits are produced. These then split to reveal brilliant orange berries which are highly poisonous to humans. Grow spindle in a hedgerow for striking winter interest.

How to grow
Spindle plants are easily obtained from forest tree nurseries; plant during winter or early spring. Seed may take two years to germinate. Stratify the seed (see p. 126) over winter and sow in a seed tray in spring. Cuttings of the ripened branch tips can be taken in early autumn.

Spiny restharrow
Ononis spinosa

Site: Sun
Soil: Medium to heavy
Season: June–September
Height: 30–40 cm (12–16 in)
Perennial; needs care

Spiny restharrow is a shrubby plant bearing pretty, purple-pink flowers throughout the summer. It has spiny stems and small, green leaves and looks attractive either planted as low hedging or growing naturally in a sunny meadow garden. It is very similar to common restharrow (see p. 41). Spiny restharrow is a food plant for caterpillars.

How to grow
Before planting, rub the seed between sandpaper to trigger germination. Sow in spring or autumn and cover with a fine sprinkling of soil. Seed is erratic in germination but will germinate when conditions are right. Spiny restharrow self-seeds readily.

Spring squill
Scilla verna

Site: Sun; seaside garden
Soil: Well-drained
Season: April–May
Height: 5–15 cm (2–6 in)
Perennial bulb; needs care

Spring squill is a lovely, dainty plant bearing clusters of star-shaped, bluish-violet flowers and green, grass-like leaves. Plant a drift of spring squill in short grass, perhaps beneath a deciduous tree, for a lovely, misty-blue haze. The flowers are followed by black, globular seed pods, which also look quite distinctive among the leaves.

How to grow
Spring squill will take several years to flower from seed. Sow the seed in autumn in a seed tray and cover with soil. Leave the tray outside over winter covered with glass; germination will take place in spring. Bulbs will take a further season to develop. Bulbs can be obtained from bulb specialists; plant these in the autumn and barely cover with soil.

Square-stalked St John's-wort
Hypericum tetrapterum

Site: Sun; semi-shade; water garden
Soil: Fertile
Season: June–September
Height: 30–70 cm (1–2½ ft)
Perennial; easy to grow

Square-stalked St John's-wort is similar in appearance to perforate St John's-wort (see p. 67) except that its flowers have an orange centre and it has a square, not round, stem. Another characteristic of this plant is that it will grow happily at the edge of a garden pond as it likes marshy ground. It looks attractive growing alongside other wetland plants such as valerian and loosestrife and grows well in wet grassland.

How to grow
Sow the seed in a seed tray, with the lightest covering of compost, during spring or autumn. Plant out when the seedlings are large enough to handle from autumn to spring.

Star-of-Bethlehem
Ornithogalum umbellatum

Site: Sun
Soil: Fertile and well-drained
Season: April–June
Height: 10–30 cm (4–12 in)
Perennial bulb; easy to grow

Star-of-Bethlehem is so called because of its star-shaped flowers which are white with a green stripe down the back of each petal. The flowers are sensitive to light and only open in sunny weather. Plant a mass of Star-of-Bethlehem in rough grass or on a lawn, or around small shrubs, to give a dazzling display of early summer blooms. Its bulbs are edible.

How to grow
Plants will take several years to flower from seed. Sow seed as soon as it is ripe in a seed tray and cover lightly with compost. Plant out the seedlings 4 cm (2 in) apart in another tray and leave for a further season for the bulbs to swell. Bulbs may be obtained from specialist nurseries and planted where they are to flower a bulb's depth deep.

Stinking iris
Iris foetidissima

Site: Sun; semi-shade; shade
Soil: Well-drained and fertile
Season: May–July (flowers) September–March (fruit)
Height: 30–80 cm (1–2½ ft)
Perennial; easy to grow

Stinking iris, or gladdon, makes a splendid, ornamental addition to a shady garden. Their small, purple flowers, tinged with yellow, look pretty above the fan of evergreen, sword-like leaves. The special feature of the stinking iris is its glowing reddish-orange seeds which are vividly displayed through the winter.

The plant's unflattering name comes from the smell of its leaves when they are crushed or bruised, which is rather like raw beef.

How to grow
Sow the seeds 1 cm (½ in) deep where the plants are to flower during autumn. Germination will take place in early spring. Thin the seedlings to 15 cm (6 in) apart.

Summer snowflake
Leucojum aestivum

Site: Sun; semi-shade; shade; water garden
Soil: Rich and damp
Season: April–May
Height: 30–60 cm (1–2 ft)
Perennial bulb; easy to grow

Summer snowflakes, with their graceful, bell-shaped flowers, pure white tinged with green, and spiky, narrow leaves, are ideal for growing at the edge of a garden pond. Plant alongside marsh marigolds and let the clumps increase each year.

How to grow
Plant in late summer or early autumn 10 cm (4 in) deep and 15–20 cm (6–8 in) apart in moist soil, in sun or partial shade. Divide the clumps when they become crowded.

Tansy
Tanacetum vulgare

Site: Sun; semi-shade
Soil: Moist
Season: July–September
Height: 30–120 cm (1–4 ft)
Perennial; needs care

Tansy is an impressive and decorative plant for the wildflower border or herb garden. It has disc-shaped flower-heads crowded with golden-yellow flowers, and dark green, lacy foliage which is very aromatic. However, it can be very invasive and should not be allowed to self-seed.

Tansy was once a popular herb; its leaves were used to flavour egg dishes and tansy buns. Tansy is very attractive to bees, and a yellow dye can be made from the flowers. There is a most decorative garden variety that is shorter with crisper leaves.

How to grow
Sow the seed where it is to flower in spring or early autumn, or in trays in spring. Seeds might be slow germinating. Tansy may be divided in spring or autumn.

Thrift
Armeria maritima

Site: Sun; semi-shade; rock garden; seaside garden
Soil: Tolerant of most soils
Season: April–May
Height: 10–20 cm (4–8 in)
Perennial; easy to grow

Thrift is a charming, little flower best grown *en masse*, when it forms a great carpet of rose-pink or white flowers. The beautiful, starry flowers are grouped on dense, rounded flower-heads above rosettes of narrow, fleshy leaves which form very dense clumps.

Thrift has a scent of honey and is a good nectar plant for butterflies. It will grow in wet or dry situations.

How to grow
Sow seed in a seed tray in autumn or spring and cover lightly with soil. Plant out when the seedlings are large enough to handle. Germination in spring is usually quite rapid. Or, take basal cuttings 4 cm (2 in) long in July–August; put them in a sand or peat compost and keep them in a shaded frame until they are rooted.

Tormentil
Potentilla erecta

Site: Sun
Soil: Most fertile soils; likes acid soils
Season: May–October
Height: 5–50 cm (2–20 in)
Perennial; easy to grow

Tormentil has pretty, buttercup-like, golden-yellow flowers that grow on branching stems. It looks particularly attractive growing amongst short grasses and heath, and will grow especially well on peat. It is pollinated by insects in warm weather, but when it is wet, or at night, it pollinates itself.

A red dye can be extracted from its roots and the plant also has medicinal properties, being highly astringent. It is also used for tanning leather.

How to grow
Sow the seed in spring or autumn where the plants are to flower and cover lightly with soil.

Tree-mallow
Lavatera arborea

Site: Sun; seaside garden
Soil: Poor and very well-drained
Season: July–October
Height: 60 cm–3 m (2–9 ft)
Perennial; easy to grow

The tree-mallow is a bushy plant closely covered with crinkled, downy leaves and, in summer, large, pinkish-purple mallow flowers with dark centres. The stems become very woody like a small tree. It has an old-fashioned cottage-garden appearance and looks attractive growing with pinks, roses and herbaceous plants that flower from midsummer onwards. An ideal situation is up against a wall where it will get the drainage and shelter it requires.

How to grow
Sow the seed where it is to flower in spring and cover lightly with soil. When the young plants are a few centimetres high, thin to 1 m (3 ft) apart. Plants can be obtained from specialist wildflower nurseries.

Tutsan
Hypericum androsaemum

Site: Semi-shade; shade
Soil: Well-drained and fertile
Season: June–August (flowers)
August–September (fruits)
Height: 40 cm–1 m (16 in–3 ft)
Perennial; easy to grow

This shrubby, semi-evergreen plant, with its long season of interest, makes an attractive addition to any shady border. It grows well on sandy soil. In early summer small, rich yellow flowers cluster at the ends of every branch. These are followed in the autumn by fleshy, red fruits, which turn black as they ripen. The foliage also provides a handsome background in its autumn colours.

How to grow
Sow the seed in a seed tray, with the lightest covering of compost, during spring or autumn. Plant out when the seedlings are large enough to handle.

Vervain
Verbena officinalis

Site: Sun
Soil: Well-drained
Season: July–September
Height: 30–90 cm (1–3 ft)
Perennial; easy to grow

Vervain is a bushy plant with rough stalks bearing tiny, lilac-coloured flowers on long, slender spikes, and grey-green leaves. Grow vervain in a clump to obtain the best effect. It looks particularly good growing with some of the small-flowered vetches, with tares growing into it; smooth tare would be especially suitable. Vervain also grows well in pots.

Vervain is said to possess medicinal and magical powers, to cure and protect against infection.

How to grow
Sow the seed during spring or autumn where it is to flower and press or water it into the soil. Seedlings may be thinned to 30 cm (1 ft) apart. Vervain grows easily in a seed tray if container plants are required.

Wallflower
Cheiranthus cheiri

Site: Sun; rock garden
Soil: Well-drained
Season: April and intermittently to September
Height: 20–60 cm (8 in–2 ft)
Short-lived perennial; easy to grow

Wild wallflowers make a vivid addition to any garden. They have dense spikes of rich yellow flowers above strap-shaped leaves. Plant them in a large mass to produce a blaze of colour, or grow them in small, informal patches near the house, where you will get the maximum benefit from the heady fragrance! Wallflowers look lovely naturalized in cracks in old walls, in the rock garden or in shingle paths.

Wallflowers are short-lived but they self-sow profusely producing new plants throughout the summer.

How to grow
Sow the seed where it is to flower, in late spring or early summer. Cover the seed lightly with soil.

Water-plantain
Alisma plantago-aquatica

Site: Water garden
Soil: Wet
Season: July–August
Height: 30 cm–1 m (1–3 ft)
Perennial; easy to grow

This is a plant for the edges of ponds and streams. Its handsome, broad green leaves provide lush foliage all year round, with tall flower-spikes of tiny white flowers an added attraction in the summer. The flowers are very sensitive to light, opening for only a few hours each afternoon.

To prevent water-plantain from seeding itself and dominating your pond or stream, remove the flower stalks as soon as the flowers are over.

How to grow
Sow the seed where the plants are to flower in spring or autumn in moist soil and lightly cover with soil. Water-plantain requires moisture all year round, but especially in the summer when most soils are dry on top.

Wall germander
Teucrium chamaedrys

Site: Sun; semi-shade; rock garden
Soil: Well-drained and fertile
Season: July–September
Height: 10–20 cm (4–8 in)
Perennial; needs care

Wall germander is a small, bushy plant with shiny, dark-green leaves and rosy-pink flowers on short spikes. It has a creeping rootstock. Its evergreen leaves and late flowering season make it an ideal plant for the rock garden. It is also a most decorative plant for establishing in a wall. The leaves of wall germander have a pungent, aromatic scent, especially when crushed. Wall germander is an alien herb from southern Europe which has naturalized on old walls.

How to grow
Wall germander is difficult to grow from seed. Sow seed in a seed tray in spring and give it some heat. Or sow in a seed tray outside in early summer and cover lightly with soil. To establish wall germander in a wall, plant seedlings rather than plants.

Wavy hair-grass
Deschampsia flexuosa

Site: Sun; semi-shade
Soil: Well-drained; will grow in acid soil
Season: June–July
Height: 50 cm–2 m (2–6 ft)
Perennial; easy to grow

Wavy hair-grass is a tuft-forming grass which spreads by rhizomes. It has delicate rose-pink flower-heads on wavy branches, and looks best growing *en masse* in a summer meadow or in a shady clearing. From a distance it will look like a pink mist when in flower.

How to grow
Sow the seed in spring in well-drained sand or peat and firm in. Seed may also be sown in early autumn. It is unnecessary to thin the seedlings.

Water forget-me-not
Myosotis scorpioides

Site: Semi-shade; water garden
Soil: Wet
Season: May–September
Height: 15–30 cm (6–12 in)
Perennial; easy to grow

Water forget-me-not is a pretty plant to grow beside a garden pond, with its clear blue flowers with yellow centres and long, pointed leaves. The plant spreads quite rapidly to produce a showy display of flowers. Its roots should always be kept moist.

How to grow
Seeds of water forget-me-not are not easily available but young plants may be purchased from specialist water plant nurseries. Plant at any time during the growing season.

Wayfaring-tree
Viburnum lantana

Site: Sun; semi-shade
Soil: Well-drained and reasonably fertile
Season: May–June (flowers) July–September (fruit)
Height: 2–6 m (6–18 ft)
Perennial; easy to grow

The wayfaring-tree can be grown as an ornamental shrub, or as part of a hedge. Its creamy flowers are massed together in rounded clusters amongst felted, grey-green foliage. These are followed by bunches of green berries which turn red and finally glossy black when they are ripe.

How to grow
To grow wayfaring-trees from seed takes two seasons, so it is best to buy a container-grown plant, which can be obtained from a specialist tree nursery. Plant from autumn to spring.

Weld

Reseda luteola

Site: Sun
Soil: Well-drained and fertile
Season: June–August
Height: 50 cm–1½ m (2–5 ft)
Biennial; needs care

Weld is an impressive plant, growing to 1½ m (5 ft) high. In the first year it produces a rosette of leaves from which grows the flower-spike in the second year. Small, yellow flowers cover the tall flower-spikes, and its leaves are long and narrow. Weld makes an impressive feature or architectural plant and looks particularly stunning against the skyline.

A bright yellow dye can be obtained from weld flowers; in fact, the plant used to be cultivated solely for this purpose.

How to grow
Sow the seed in late summer where it is to flower and cover lightly with soil. Germination should take place in the spring.

Welsh poppy

Meconopsis cambrica

Site: Sun; semi-shade; rock garden
Soil: Fertile and moist
Season: June–July
Height: 30–60 cm (1–2 ft)
Perennial; needs care

The Welsh poppy is a delicate bushy plant producing a mass of bright yellow, papery flowers and attractive light green foliage. It grows easily on walls and looks pretty in a rock garden. It will also look attractive growing in an informal group amongst ferns and Solomon's-seal.

How to grow
Sow the seed in autumn where it is to flower, pressing the seed into the soil but not covering it. Seed may also be sown in a seed tray in spring or autumn. Germination can be slow. Welsh poppy self-seeds readily.

White bryony

Bryonia dioica

Site: Sun; semi-shade
Soil: Well-drained
Season: May–September (flowers)
August–October (fruit)
Height: up to 3 m (10 ft)
Perennial climber; needs care

White bryony is a climbing plant that can grow rapidly through shrubs, trees and hedges, clinging with its spiral tendrils. In the summer it produces small clusters of greenish-white flowers, which are frequently visited by bees; these are followed in the autumn by strings of orange, yellow and red berries. However, be careful: the berries are highly poisonous to animals and humans.

How to grow
The berries should be stratified over winter (see page 126) and then sown in spring into a seed tray and covered lightly with soil.

White campion

Silene alba

Site: Sun
Soil: Most fertile soils
Season: May–August
Height: 30 cm–1 m (1–3 ft)
Short-lived perennial; easy to grow

White campion has delicate white flowers that give off a faint scent after dusk. It is related to red campion and, if grown together, the two will often interbreed to produce flowers in varying shades of pink.

For a good effect, white campion should be grown in a large clump, perhaps as a background to smaller, more colourful plants. The flowers also look marvellous when grown amongst other flowers and grasses in a meadow mixture.

How to grow
Sow the seed in early autumn or spring where it is to flower and cover lightly with soil. White campion self-seeds readily.

White clover

Trifolium repens

Site: Sun; semi-shade
Soil: Well-drained
Season: June–September
Height: 5–20 cm (2–8 in)
Perennial; easy to grow

White clover is a pretty flower that is too often regarded as a garden weed. It has white or rosy flowers growing in a loose cluster above trefoil leaves and is a constituent of many flowering meadow and pasture mixtures. It spreads quickly by its creeping stems, which root as they go.

White clover provides an abundant supply of nectar for bees.

How to grow
Sow seed in late summer or spring where the plants are to flower and cover lightly with soil. Clover can be seeded into grass provided the grass is thin and the soil has been well raked before sowing.

White horehound

Marrubium vulgare

Site: Sun
Soil: Well-drained and fertile
Season: June–October
Height: 30–60 cm (1–2 ft)
Perennial; needs care

White horehound is an unusual and decorative, bushy plant. Clusters of small, white flowers grow up the stems amongst silvery-green, wrinkled foliage, which gives the appearance of being frosted. The whole plant has a musky, spicy smell and is very attractive to bees. White horehound fits naturally into the herb garden and makes a nice contrast to green-leaved flowers and herbs.

White horehound has been used in the treatment of coughs and other chest ailments.

How to grow
Sow the seed in spring in a seed tray and cover lightly with soil. Seed is very erratic in germination and seedlings will appear in ones and twos over many months. Plants are easily obtained from herb nurseries.

Wild angelica
Angelica sylvestris

Site: Sun; semi-shade; shade; water garden
Soil: Damp and fertile
Season: July–August
Height: 30 cm–1½ m (1–5 ft)
Perennial; easy to grow

This is a dramatic, stately plant for the back of a border or the edge of a stream. The tall flower stalks rise from a clump of attractive, divided leaves. The umbrella-shaped flower-heads are made up of balls of tiny white or pale pink flowers; they are also attractive as dried flowers.

How to grow
Sow seed as soon as it is ripe (in July–August) where it is to flower and cover with a light sprinkling of soil. Dried (or packeted) seed can also be sown in the autumn. The seeds will germinate in spring after the winter cold has activated them. Space young plants 60–90 cm (2–3 ft) apart. Wild angelica self-seeds profusely.

Wild clary
Salvia horminoides

Site: Sun
Soil: Well-drained and fertile
Season: May–September
Height: 30–90 cm (1–3 ft)
Perennial; needs care

Wild clary is a slightly aromatic plant with wrinkled, toothed leaves that always look grey and dusty, and small, blue-violet flowers carried on tall stems. It looks attractive growing with other lightland flowers like bird's-foot-trefoil and kidney vetch. This is a plant that establishes easily in grass on a light soil and looks good growing in this situation.

How to grow
Sow the large seed ½ cm (¼ in) deep where it is to flower in spring or early autumn. Germination may be slow.

Wild mignonette
Reseda lutea

Site: Sun
Soil: Well-drained
Season: May–August
Height: 30–75 cm (1–2½ ft)
Biennial/perennial; easy to grow

Wild mignonette looks a little like weld with its tall, floppy flower-spikes massed with creamy-yellow, fragrant flowers. It is a shorter plant, however, and its leaves are more divided and crinkly. It is a constituent of many flowering meadow mixtures for light soils.

Wild mignonette is very attractive to bees and butterflies.

How to grow
Sow the seeds in autumn or spring where the plants are to flower and cover lightly with soil. This plant does very well in sandy soils.

Wild parsnip
Pastinaca sativa

Site: Sun
Soil: Fertile and well-drained
Season: June–August
Height: 30–120 cm (1–4 ft)
Biennial; easy to grow

Wild parsnip is a tall, branching plant for the sunny hedgerow or meadow garden. It has large, umbrella-shaped flower-heads packed with tiny, greenish-yellow flowers, and felted leaves. Wild parsnip looks attractive growing in rough grass with hog-weed and willowherb.

Although it is a poor substitute for the cultivated parsnip, which has been bred from this species, wild parsnip has been used as a vegetable in times of shortage.

How to grow
Sow the seed in autumn where it is to flower and cover lightly with soil. If plants are required for naturalizing, the seed may be sown in a seed tray in autumn. Plant out when the seedlings are large enough to handle.

Wood avens
Geum urbanum

Site: Semi-shade; shade
Soil: Fertile
Season: June–August
Height: 30–60 cm (1–2 ft)
Perennial; easy to grow

The dainty, bright yellow flowers of wood avens, or herb bennet, are best seen in a shady part of the garden, where its dark green leaves can also provide useful ground cover.

The roots of wood avens have a delicate, clove-like aroma, and have medicinal properties.

How to grow
Sow the seed where it is to flower in spring or autumn and cover lightly with soil. Plants may be thinned to 15 cm (6 in) apart.

Wood millet
Milium effusum

Site: Semi-shade; shade
Soil: Damp and heavy
Season: May–July
Height: 45–180 cm (1½–6 ft)
Perennial; easy to grow

Wood millet is one of our attractive woodland grasses, often now sown to provide food for game birds and as an ornamental grass, but an indicator of ancient woodlands where growing naturally. It grows in loose tufts, producing small spikes of green flowers. It can look very decorative in a shady spot and should be sown in a woodland grass and flower mixture.

How to grow
Sow the seed where it is to flower in early autumn or spring. Scatter the seed and then rake it into the soil, and roll or firm it in.

Wood sage
Teucrium scorodonia

Site: Sun; semi-shade
Soil: Well-drained; neutral to acid
Season: July–September
Height: 15–60 cm (6 in–2 ft)
Perennial; easy to grow

Wood sage has decorative foliage and bears pale, greenish-white flowers on one-sided flower-spikes. Its leaves are heart-shaped and smell of garlic when crushed, giving the plant its country name of garlic sage. This plant grows well in a semi-shady situation but also thrives in full sun on sandy and gravelly soils.

Wood sage tastes of hops and has been used as a substitute in some areas. It also has many medicinal properties and has been used to treat blood disorders, colds and fever.

How to grow
Sow the seed in spring or autumn in a seed tray and cover lightly with soil. Plant the seedlings out in spring or autumn when they are large enough to handle.

Wood vetch
Vicia sylvatica

Site: Sun; semi-shade; shade
Soil: Most soils of reasonable fertility
Season: June–August
Height: 60 cm–2 m (2–6 ft)
Perennial; easy to grow

Wood vetch is one of our loveliest vetches with large, white flowers with marked bluish-purple veins. It is a vigorous climbing plant and can look superb scrambling through a bush or hedgerow. Wood vetch can be used all over the garden to great decorative effect. It is also a valuable fodder plant for livestock.

How to grow
Rub seeds between two sheets of sandpaper to speed germination. Sow seeds in spring or autumn where they are to flower. Cover with soil or press into the soil.

Wormwood
Artemisia absinthium

Site: Sun; seaside garden
Soil: Well-drained and fertile; enjoys an acid soil
Season: July–August
Height: 60–120 cm (2–4 ft)
Perennial; needs care

Wormwood is an attractive, bushy, silvery-grey foliage plant. It has a silky texture and tiny yellow flowers that give it a warm look in summer. Wormwood makes an excellent background plant and its form and colour are unique in the wild garden. The whole plant is aromatic and it is an effective insect repellant, particularly of ants. Wormwood is an ingredient of absinthe, a drink so potent that it was banned throughout medieval Europe.

How to grow
Sow the dust-like seed in a seed tray; water in lightly but do not cover with soil. Cover the tray with glass until germination takes place. Plant out from autumn to spring.

Yellow corydalis
Corydalis lutea

Site: Semi-shade; rock garden
Soil: Well-drained and fertile
Season: May–September
Height: 15–30 cm (6–12 in)
Perennial; easy to grow

Yellow corydalis is a delicate, sprawling plant with bright yellow, tubular flowers and pretty, fern-like foliage. Its flower stalks are twisted so that the flowers all face the same way.

Yellow corydalis is an ideal plant for sunny corners of the garden; it will soon colonize any available space, including paving cracks, and looks especially good growing out of a wall. It is an introduced plant.

How to grow
Sow seeds in spring where the plants are to grow and cover lightly with soil. Cut the plants back in the autumn after flowering if you do not want the plant to self-seed.

Yellow horned-poppy
Glaucium flavum

Site: Sun; seaside garden
Soil: Well-drained
Season: June–October
Height: 30–90 cm (1–3 ft)
Perennial; needs care

The yellow horned-poppy is an extremely attractive plant. It has large, floppy, bright yellow flowers, and fleshy, greyish-green leaves. Its curved, slender seed pods can sometimes reach 30 cm (1 ft) in length. An ideal spot to grow this plant is an area of deep shingle.

Yellow horned-poppy is a poisonous plant that should not be eaten.

How to grow
Sow the seed in a seed tray during autumn and leave outside or in a cool place, covered with glass over winter. Germination should take place in spring. Plant out during summer when the seedlings are large enough to handle. The plants should flower in the second year.

Yellow water-lily
Nuphar lutea

Site: Sun; water garden
Soil: Rich
Season: June–August
Height: to 15 cm (6 in) above water
Perennial; easy to grow

The yellow water-lily is a must for the garden pond, if the pond is big enough. The dark-green, leathery leaves of yellow water-lily can measure as much as 40 cm (16 in) across. They float on the water surface surrounding the simple yellow flowers. Following the flowers are unusual, bottle-shaped fruits, which gave the alternative name of 'brandy bottle' to the plant.

How to grow
Plants can be purchased from specialist water-plant nurseries. Plant them into the soil of a natural pond and weigh them down with a piece of turf or a stone. If restricted growth is required, submerge the plant in a suitable container.

Trees for large gardens

Alder (*Alnus glutinosa*)
Likes a moist situation. Grows to 19 m (65 ft); may be coppiced to produce straight poles – the wood is durable under water.

Ash (*Fraxinus excelsior*)
Grows into a full tree 30–42 m (100–140 ft), or can be coppiced for furniture-making or firewood.

Beech (*Fagus sylvatica*)
Grows to 30 m (100 ft), but will also make an excellent, dense hedge. Keeps its bronze leaves through winter and bursts into delicate pale green leaf in spring. Good for furniture and wood turning.

Bird cherry (*Prunus padus*)
A handsome small tree, growing to 15 m (50 ft), with drooping spikes of fragrant white flowers in spring.

Field maple (*Acer campestre*)
A small tree or shrub; its leaves provide lovely autumn colour. Grows to 4.5–9 m (15–30 ft). Excellent for hedges. Makes lots of bushy growth when coppiced.

Hornbeam (*Carpinus betulus*)
Grows to 19 m (65 ft); can be coppiced (for firewood) and is good for hedging. Good autumn colour.

Pedunculate oak (*Quercus robur*)
Grows to more than 30 m (100 ft), but may be coppiced. Supports a record number of insects.

Rowan (*Sorbus aucuparia*)
Small (approximately 15 m/50 ft) and ornamental. Masses of white flowers in spring; red berries and good autumn colour. Gives light shade and may be planted near buildings.

Scots pine (*Pinus sylvestris*)
Very decorative when young but grows large, to 36 m (120 ft), and is more suited to windswept Scotland.

Silver birch (*Betula pendula*)
Fast-growing with attractive bark and catkins, and casts only light shade. Grows to 12–18 m (40–60 ft). Can be coppiced and makes good firewood.

Small-leaved lime (*Tilia cordata*)
Grows to approximately 30 m (100 ft); may be coppiced to produce straight poles. Its flowers attract bees.

Wild cherry (*Prunus avium*)
Makes a handsome, medium-sized tree, growing to 18 m (60 ft) or more. It is covered with white blossom in spring and has an attractive bark and superb autumn colour.

Willow (*Salix species*)
There are many very tall willows: they can grow up to 25 m (80 ft). All are valuable to wildlife, and support many insects. May be coppiced for colourful shoots and straight poles.

Trees and shrubs for small gardens

Blackthorn, see p. 157.

Beech (for hedges), see above.

Bird cherry, see above.

Broom, see p. 157.

Buckthorn, see p. 157.

Cherry plum (*Prunus cerasifera*)
Rather similar to blackthorn, but flowers earlier and has larger white flowers. Glossy leaves and twigs, and green-yellow, cherry-sized fruits. Makes a spreading tree 3 m (10 ft) tall.

Crab apple (*Malus sylvestris*)
Attractive spring flowers and autumn fruits for jelly. Grows to 9 m (30 ft). Lovely autumn colour and makes good firewood.

Dog rose, see p. 161.

Dogwood, see p. 161.

Elder, see p. 162.

Field maple, see above.

Field rose (*Rosa arvensis*)
A shrubby, trailing rose with reddish stems. It has white flowers and small red hips. Grows to 2 m (6 ft) and is good in hedgerows.

Goat willow (*Salix caprea*)
Needs a damp soil. It has showy catkins and grows to 10 m (33 ft), or can be kept coppiced to provide bushy growth. Loved by bees.

Guelder-rose (*Viburnum opulus*)
Red berries loved by birds and white flowers which attract hoverflies. Grows to 5 m (15 ft).

Hawthorn, see p. 164.

Hazel (*Corylus avellana*)
Produces edible nuts; a good hedgerow shrub. Grows to 4–6 m (13–20 ft) and is good for coppicing. Supports 70 insect species.

Holly, see p. 165.

Hornbeam (for hedges), see above.

Juniper (*Juniperus communis*)
An evergreen tree with silvery-green, spiny needles. Grows to 2 m (6½ ft) but there are prostrate forms. The female trees have berries that are green the first year, turning purple in the second year when ripe. (You will need to grow both male and female plants to get berries.)

Mezereon, see p. 168.

Purple willow (*Salix purpurea*)
Needs a damp soil. Attractive catkins and reddish twigs. Grows to 3 m (10 ft). Keep coppiced for the colourful new growth.

Rowan, see above.

Silver birch, see above.

Spindle, see p. 174.

Sweet briar, see p. 71.

Yew (*Taxus baccata*)
An evergreen tree with spreading horizontal branches that can live for over 1,000 years. It has needle-like, dark green leaves and red fruit containing poisonous seed. The leaves are particularly poisonous to livestock when withered and dry. Grows to 25 m (80 ft) or can be used to make a dense, but slow-growing hedge.

Wayfaring-tree, see p. 177.

Wild privet (*Ligustrum vulgare*)
Grows to 5 m (15 ft). Food plant of the spectacular privet hawk moth.

Bibliography

Anderson, E. B. *Rock Gardens* RHS/Penguin Books, London, 1959

Baines, Chris *How to Make a Wildlife Garden* Elm Tree Books, London, 1985

Book of British Birds Readers' Digest, London, 1969

Bowen, Ursula *How to Make a Small Pond* Berks Books and Oxon Naturalists' Trust, Oxford

Carter and Hargreaves *A Field Guide to Caterpillars of Butterflies and Moths* Collins, London, 1986

Chinery, Michael *A Field Guide to the Insects of Britain and Northern Europe* Collins, London, 1973

Chinery, Michael *The Living Garden* Dorling Kindersley, London, 1986

Clapham, Tutin and Warburg *Flora of the British Isles* (2nd edn) Cambridge University Press, London, 1962

Dony, J., Perring, F. and Rob, C. M. *English Names of Wild Flowers* BSBI, London, 1980

Duncan and Robson *Pennine Flowers* Dalesman Books, Clapham, North Yorkshire, 1977

Elliott, Joe *Alpines in Sinks and Troughs* The Alpine Garden Society, Woking, 1981

Evans, Alfred *The Peat Garden* Wisley Handbook 41, RHS, London, 1981

Fitter, Alistair *An Atlas of the Wild Flowers of Britain and Northern Europe* Collins, London, 1978

Fitter and Richardson *Collins Pocket Guide to British Birds* Collins, London, 1966

Gardening with Wildlife RSPB, Sandy, Bedfordshire

Genders, Roy *The Scented Wild Flowers of Britain* Collins, London, 1971

Goodwin, Jill *A Dyer's Manual* Pelham Books, London, 1982

Grieve, M. *A Modern Herbal* Jonathan Cape, London, 1975

Grigson, Geoffrey *The Englishman's Flora* Paladin, St Albans, 1975

Halliday and Malloch *Wild Flowers and their Habitats in Britain and Northern Europe* Eurobook Ltd, 1981

Hartmann and Kester *Plant Propagation* Prentice-Hall Inc, Englewood Cliffs, New Jersey, USA, 1968

Hoskins, W. G. *English Landscapes* BBC Publications, London, 1974

Howes, F. N. *Plants and Beekeeping* Faber & Faber, London, 1979

Kaye, Reginald *Ferns* Wisley Handbook 32, RHS, London, 1980

Killingbeck, John *Creating and Maintaining a Garden to Attract Butterflies* National Association for Environmental Education, Walsall, 1985

Mabey, Richard *Food for Free* Collins, London, 1973

Mabey, Richard *The Flowering of Britain* Arrow Books, London, 1982

Mabey, Richard *The Common Ground* Arrow Books, London, 1981

McEwan, Helen *Seed Growers Guide to Herbs and Wildflowers* Suffolk Herbs, Suffolk, 1982

McHoy, Peter *Rock Gardening* Blandford Press, Poole, 1986

McHoy, Peter *Water Gardening* Blandford Press, Poole, 1986

Martin, W. Keble *The Concise British Flora in Colour* Ebury Press/Michael Joseph, London, 1965

Perring and Farrell *British Red Data Book 1* (2nd edn) RSNC, Nettleham, 1983

Phillips, Roger *Grasses, Ferns, Mosses & Lichens* Ward Lock, London, 1980

Phillips, Roger *Wild Flowers of Britain* Pan Books, London, 1980

Phillips, Roger *Native and Common Trees* Elm Tree Books, London, 1986

Phillips, Roger *Woodland Wild Flowers* Elm Tree Books, London, 1986

Pownin, Oleg *Trees and Bushes of Britain & Europe* Paladin, St Albans, 1977

Pratt, Anne *The Flowering Plants and Ferns of Great Britain* SPCK, London

Rix, Martin and Phillips, Roger *The Bulb Book* Pan Books, London, 1983

Rose, Francis *The Wildflower Key* Frederick Warne, London, 1981

Rothschild, Miriam and Farrell, Clive *The Butterfly Gardener* Michael Joseph/Rainbird, London, 1983

Shoard, Marion *The Theft of the Countryside* Maurice Temple Smith, London, 1980

Simpson, Francis W. *Flora of Suffolk* Suffolk Naturalists' Society, Ipswich, 1982

Stuart, Malcolm *The Encyclopaedia of Herbs and Herbalism* Orbis, London, 1979

Thomas, J. A. *Butterflies of the British Isles* Country Life Books, Twickenham, 1986

Wells, Bell and Frost *Creating Attractive Grassland Using Native Plant Species* NCC, Shrewsbury, 1981

Index

Acknowledgments

Author's acknowledgments
My special thanks must go to my wife Caroline for helping in so
many ways, especially with proof reading and editing and for
keeping Suffolk Herbs going whilst I was writing.

My thanks to Mike King of the British Trust of Conservation
Volunteers London for research and ideas for the water garden
section; and to the many people who gave technical advice and
information, especially Alec Bull, Patrick Hughes, Rosie Lean and
Francie Mount; to Geoff Oxburrow for allowing us to photograph
his wildflower garden; and to Robin Ford, Warden of Cornard
Mere, for providing plant specimens to photograph.

Many people have helped me over the years with advice on
producing wild flowers and seed, especially Terry Wells and Alan
Frost of the Institute of Terrestrial Ecology, Monks Wood, Edgar
Milne Redhead and John Chambers. My special thanks go to the
late Luther Howard who helped, encouraged and advised us over
many years.

My grateful thanks to Pat Bunch, Sylvia Cassell and Donna
Minns of Suffolk Herbs and Angelika Stevens for their help with
typing, proof reading and research.

Finally my thanks to photographers Geoff Dann and Jerry
Harpur for their superb photographs, and at Dorling Kindersley,
Art Director, Roger Bristow, Art Editor, Jane Warring, Editors,
Jane Birdsell and Heather Dewhurst, and Editorial Director, Jackie
Douglas for their work in producing this book.

Dorling Kindersley would like to thank Arthur Brown for help
with the design and Suzanna Longley for help with the editing, and
the following for their help in producing this book: Sandra Archer,
Lynn Bresler, Jenny Engelmann, Jane Heller, Fiona Macmillan,
Tessa Richardson-Jones, and Patrizio Semproni.

Also the following people for their help in providing plants and
props for photography: John M. Birdsell, Joy George, George and
Sylvia Innes, Joy and Philip Knox, J. K. Marston (fern specialist),
Christopher Passmore, Peter Hall, Sue Middleton and Aaron
Dutton of Lavender Road Pond, and Ray Busfield and Joe Kelly of
Gillespie Park, London Borough of Islington Recreation Services
Department.

Photographic credits:
All photography by Geoff Dann except for:
A-Z Collection: 69R
Jane Birdsell: 12C
Roger Bristow: 13BR, 14BL
Eric Crichton: 65L, 71L, 87L, 89, 99R, 102L, 104L, 113R
Andrew N. Gagg: 36R, 38L, 62R, 66L, 75L, 90L, 92R, 101R, 105L,
115L
John Glover: 35R, 43L, 68R, 75R, 91L
Jerry Harpur: 31R, 32L, 34R, 37R, 41L, 42L, 45R, 46L, 47L, 64, 70,
71R, 87R, 90R, 103L, 106L, 113L, 114R, 115R, 116
David Lamb: 9TR, 120B
John Stevens: 11CB, 85B
Jane Warring: 8BR, endpapers

T = top, B = bottom, L = left, R = right, C = centre

Illustrators
David Ashby
Ray Brown
Ray Burrows
Vana Haggerty
Ron Hayward
Vanessa Luff
John Woodcock